KNOWLEDGE ENCYCLOPEDIA
DINOSAUR!

SECOND EDITION

Senior Editor Ann Baggaley
Editor Jessica Cawthra
Jacket Designer Surabhi Wadhwa, Tanya Mehrotra
Jacket Editor Emma Dawson
DTP Designer Rakesh Kumar
Jackets Editorial Coordinator Priyanka Sharma
Managing Jackets Editor Saloni Singh
Jacket Design Development Manager Sophia MTT
Producer, Pre-production Gillian Reid
Senior Producer Jude Crozier
Managing Editor Francesca Baines
Managing Art Editor Philip Letsu
Publisher Andrew Macintyre
Associate Publishing Director Liz Wheeler
Art Director Karen Self
Publishing Director Jonathan Metcalf

FIRST EDITION

DK UK:
Senior Art Editor Stefan Podhorodecki
Senior Editors Francesca Baines, Jenny Sich
Project Editor Steven Carton
Art Editor Paul Drislane
Managing Art Editor Michael Duffy
Managing Editor Linda Esposito
Publisher Andrew Macintyre
Jacket Design Development Manager Sophia MTT
Jacket Designer Laura Brim
Jacket Editor Maud Whatley
Producer (Pre-Production) Luca Frassinetti
Producer Gemma Sharpe
DK Picture Library Romaine Werblow
Art Director Phil Ormerod
Associate Publishing Director Liz Wheeler
Publishing Director Jonathan Metcalf

DK India:
Senior Art Editor Anis Sayyed
Editorial team Priyanka Kharbanda, Deeksha Saikia, Rupa Rao
Project Art Editor Mahipal Singh
Art Editors Vikas Chauhan, Vidit Vashisht
Jacket Designer Suhita Dharamjit
DTP Designer Vishal Bhatia
Picture Researcher Surya Sarangi
Managing Editor Kingshuk Ghoshal
Managing Art Editor Govind Mittal
Managing Jacket Editor Saloni Singh
Pre-Production Manager Balwant Singh
Production Manager Pankaj Sharma

This edition published in 2019
First published in Great Britain in 2014 by
Dorling Kindersley Limited,
80 Strand, London WC2R 0RL

Copyright © 2014, 2019 Dorling Kindersley Limited
A Penguin Random House Company
19 20 21 22 10 9 8 7 6 5 4 3 2 1
002 – 312862 – October/2019

A CIP catalogue record for this
book is available from the British Library.

ISBN: 978-0-2413-6436-9

Printed and bound in China

A WORLD OF IDEAS:
SEE ALL THERE IS TO KNOW

www.dk.com

DK

KNOWLEDGE ENCYCLOPEDIA

DINOSAUR!

Written by John Woodward
Consultant Darren Naish

Illustrators Peter Minister, Arran Lewis, Andrew Kerr,
Peter Bull, Vlad Konstantinov, James Kuether

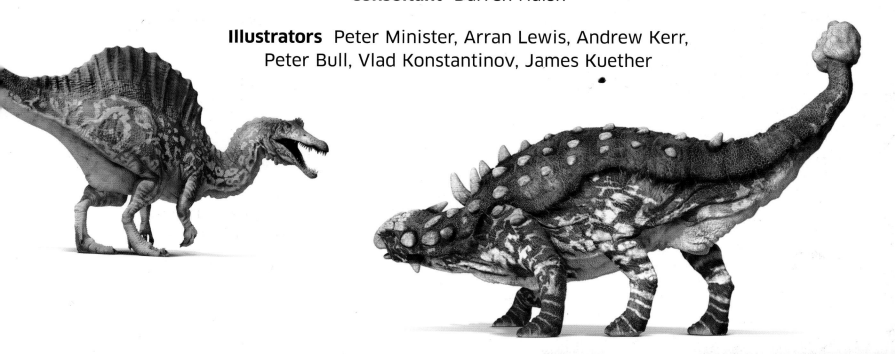

CONTENTS

THE DINOSAURS

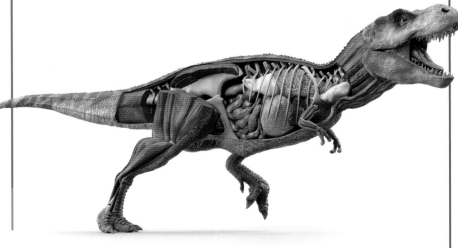

TRIASSIC LIFE

JURASSIC LIFE

CRETACEOUS LIFE

A NEW ERA

Scales and sizes
The data boxes for each prehistoric animal include a scale drawing to indicate its size (usually the maximum). This is based on the height of an average adult male, and the hand size shown below.

 1.8 m (6 ft)   18 cm (7 in)

THE DINOSAURS

The living world has evolved a dazzling diversity of life, but few animals can compete with the extinct dinosaurs for variety, size, and sheer magnificence. They ruled Earth for more than 150 million years during the Mesozoic Era, and their descendants still live all around us today.

4.6 BYA–541 MYA

This vast span of time extends from Earth's formation 4.6 billion years ago to the evolution of the first animals.

Life on Earth

The Mesozoic dinosaurs were the most spectacular animals that have ever lived. They were the product of a process of evolution that began when the first flicker of life appeared on Earth 3.8 billion years ago. But it took more than 3 billion years for life to develop beyond microscopic single cells. The earliest multi-celled life forms evolved in the oceans about 600 million years ago (MYA), and gave rise to all the living things that have appeared since. But as new life forms evolved, older ones became extinct, sometimes in catastrophic mass extinctions that reshaped the living world.

DEVONIAN

419–358 MYA

Many new types of fish evolved. Some crawled out of the water to become early amphibians.

Drepanaspis
This armoured fish was 35 cm (14 in) long and had a broad, flattened head.

Tiktaalik
The anatomy of this animal displays similarities with both fish and early amphibians.

Archaenthus
A low-growing ancestor of the tulip tree, this was one of the earliest flowering plants. It had magnolia-like flowers and lived about 100 MYA, halfway through the Cretaceous Period.

145–66 MYA

The Cretaceous saw the evolution of the first flowering plants, and many types of dinosaur. It concluded with a mass extinction that wiped out all the big dinosaurs and pterosaurs, ending the Mesozoic Era.

CRETACEOUS

201–145 MYA

During the second period of the Mesozoic Era, the dinosaurs dominated life on land. They included giant plant-eaters, hunted by powerful predators.

Cryolophosaurus
This crested dinosaur was one of the theropods – the group that included all the big meat-eaters.

KEY

■ EARLY EARTH
■ PALEOZOIC ERA
■ MESOZOIC ERA
■ CENOZOIC ERA

GEOLOGICAL TIME

The history of life is recorded by fossils in rocks that were once soft sediments such as mud. These sedimentary rocks form in layers, with older rocks beneath more recent ones. Each layer represents a span of geological time, named and given a date in millions of years ago (MYA). Seen here is Earth's geological timescale divided into divisions called "periods". Multiple periods form a larger division called an "era".

Velociraptor
The dinosaurs became much more diverse during the Cretaceous. This small, agile, feathered hunter was part of the group that gave rise to the birds.

66–23 MYA

The mass extinction that ended the Mesozoic killed off all the dinosaurs except the birds. During the new era, mammals evolved bigger forms that took the place of the vanished giants.

PALEOGENE

CAMBRIAN

541–485 MYA

The fossils of hard-shelled sea creatures start to become common during this period at the start of the Paleozoic Era.

SILURIAN

443–419 MYA
By the Silurian, the first, very simple green plants were growing on land.

SACABAMBASPIS,
AN ARMOURED FISH

ORDOVICIAN

485–443 MYA
Many types of fish evolved, along with invertebrates such as trilobites.

MARRELLA,
A SHELLED
SEA CREATURE

CARBONIFEROUS

MEGANEURA, **A TYPE OF DRAGONFLY**

358–298 MYA
Life started flourishing on land, with dense forests of early trees, ferns, mosses, and horsetails. Insects and spiders evolved, and were hunted by large amphibians.

Lepidodendron
This early tree could have been more than 30 m (100 ft) tall.

PERMIAN

298–252 MYA
The Permian saw the evolution of the first reptiles and the ancestors of modern mammals. But it ended in a catastrophic mass extinction, which destroyed 96 per cent of all species and ended the Paleozoic Era.

JURASSIC

Eudimorphodon
Early pterosaurs, such as *Eudimorphodon*, were the size of crows, but with long tails and sharp teeth.

252–201 MYA
It took millions of years for life to recover from the Permian extinction. But by the end of the Triassic Period the first dinosaurs had evolved, along with the earliest pterosaurs and mammals.

TRIASSIC

Dimetrodon
This strange, sail-backed animal looks like a reptile, but was actually related to the Permian ancestors of the mammals.

23–2 MYA
As the Paleogene Period gave way to the Neogene, many modern types of mammals and birds were appearing. By 4 MYA, upright-walking ancestors of humans were living in east Africa.

NEOGENE

Uintatherium
The rhinoceros-sized *Uintatherium* was a big plant-eating "megaherbivore" of the early Cenozoic Era.

2 MYA–present
The world entered a long ice age, with warmer phases like the one we live in today. About 350,000 years ago modern humans evolved in Africa, then spread worldwide.

QUATERNARY

Homo neanderthalensis
This species of strongly built human was adapted for life in icy climates. Neanderthals seem to have vanished by about 30,000 years ago.

NEMEGTBAATAR

VERTEBRATE EVOLUTION

All vertebrates are descended from fish. One group of bony fish evolved fleshy fins that they could use as legs, and some of these became the first four-legged animals, or tetrapods. The earliest were the amphibians, which were followed by the mammals and reptiles. One group of reptiles, the archosaurs, included the crocodilians, pterosaurs, and dinosaurs, as well as the birds.

Types of vertebrates

We usually think of the vertebrates as fish, amphibians, reptiles, birds, and mammals. But the birds can also be seen as archosaurs, a group of reptiles that includes their closest relatives – the extinct dinosaurs.

Mammals
The mammals are warm-blooded, furry, and feed their young on milk. This small insect-eater lived about 125 million years ago.

ROLFOSTEUS

Fish
The fish actually consist of three very different types of animal – primitive jawless fish, the sharks and rays, and typical bony fish.

SPINOAEQUALIS

Reptiles
By 300 million years ago early reptiles such as *Spinoaequalis* had evolved. Unlike amphibians, they had scaly, waterproof skin.

ICHTHYOSTEGA

Amphibians
Ichthyostega was one of the earliest amphibians – animals such as frogs that breathe air but usually breed in fresh water.

CARCHARODONTOSAURUS

Archosaurs
This group of reptiles includes crocodiles, pterosaurs, and dinosaurs. It also includes the birds.

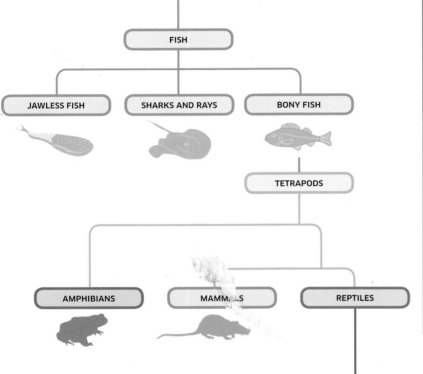

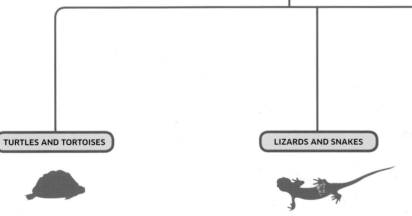

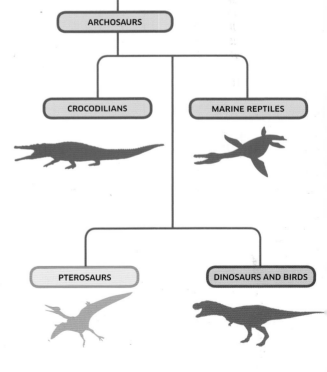

Animals with backbones

Until about 530 million years ago all the animals on planet Earth were invertebrates – creatures such as worms, snails, and crabs that do not have bony internal skeletons. But then a new type of animal appeared in the oceans, with a body strengthened by a tough rod called a notochord. This was to evolve into a backbone, formed of a chain of bones known as vertebrae. The first of these vertebrates, or animals with backbones, were fish. Some were to become the ancestors of all other vertebrates, including amphibians, reptiles, birds, and mammals.

THE VERTEBRATES MAKE UP **JUST THREE PER CENT OF ALL LIVING ANIMAL SPECIES.**

TETRAPODS

A few fish, such as modern lungfish, have four strong, fleshy fins that are rather like legs. Roughly 380 million years ago some of these lobe-finned fish were living in freshwater swamps, and began crawling out of the water to find food. They were the earliest tetrapods. They returned to the water to lay their eggs, just like most modern amphibians. These animals were the ancestors of all land vertebrates.

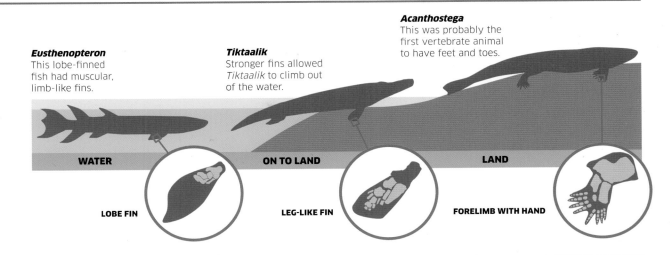

Eusthenopteron
This lobe-finned fish had muscular, limb-like fins.

Tiktaalik
Stronger fins allowed *Tiktaalik* to climb out of the water.

Acanthostega
This was probably the first vertebrate animal to have feet and toes.

WATER   ON TO LAND   LAND

LOBE FIN   LEG-LIKE FIN   FORELIMB WITH HAND

STRONG SKELETONS

The body of an aquatic vertebrate such as a marine reptile is supported by the water, so the main job of its skeleton is to anchor its muscles. But the same type of skeleton can also support the weight of a land animal. The bones are much stronger, and connected by weight-bearing joints. This adaptation permitted the evolution of land vertebrates, including giant dinosaurs.

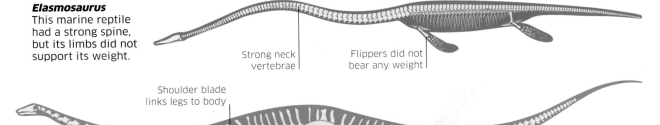

Elasmosaurus
This marine reptile had a strong spine, but its limbs did not support its weight.

Strong neck vertebrae

Flippers did not bear any weight

Shoulder blade links legs to body

Diplodocus
This dinosaur's weight was supported by massive limb bones linked to its spine.

Strong leg bones support weight

Spine is a chain of vertebrae

SUPER-SIZED ANIMALS

All the biggest land animals have been vertebrates. This is because a heavy land animal needs a strong internal skeleton to support its weight. But there is a limit, and it is likely that the giant dinosaur *Argentinosaurus* was as heavy as a land animal could possibly be. The only vertebrate that weighs more is the aquatic blue whale.

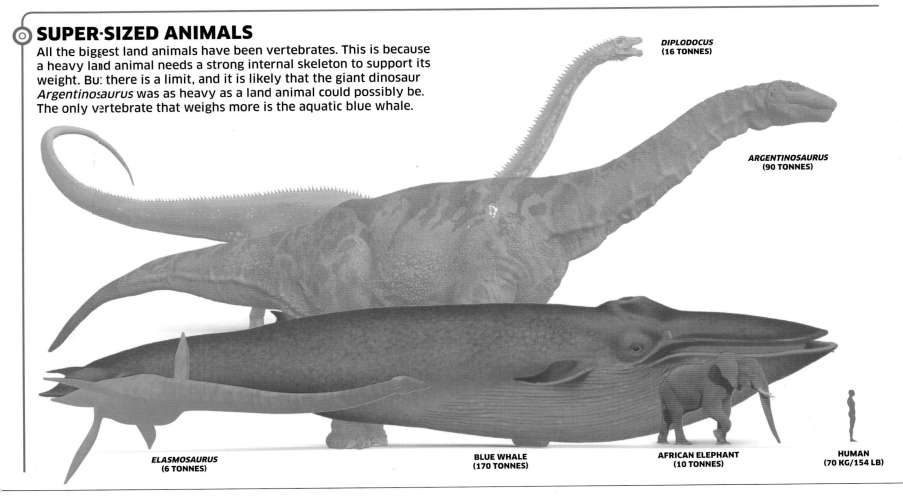

DIPLODOCUS
(16 TONNES)

ARGENTINOSAURUS
(90 TONNES)

ELASMOSAURUS
(6 TONNES)

BLUE WHALE
(170 TONNES)

AFRICAN ELEPHANT
(10 TONNES)

HUMAN
(70 KG/154 LB)

What is a dinosaur?

The first dinosaurs evolved roughly 235 million years ago, in the Middle Triassic Period. Their ancestors were small, slender archosaur reptiles that stood and walked with their legs underneath their bodies, like mammals. This high-walking stance was inherited by the dinosaurs, and was one of the factors that allowed many of them to grow so big. Many dinosaurs, including all meat-eaters, stood on two legs, balanced by the weight of their long tails. But most of the bigger plant-eaters stood on four legs. They had all the anatomical features that we see in modern vertebrate animals.

INSIDE A DINOSAUR

Because they lived so long ago, the Mesozoic dinosaurs are seen by many people as primitive animals. This is completely wrong. They thrived for 170 million years, and over that time evolution refined their anatomy to the highest degree. Their bones, muscles, and internal organs were as efficient as those of any modern animal, allowing dinosaurs like this *Tyrannosaurus rex* to evolve into the most spectacular land animals that have ever lived.

Hip bone
The massive pelvis of *Tyrannosaurus* was extremely strong.

Skin
Dinosaur skin was scaly or covered with a layer of feathers.

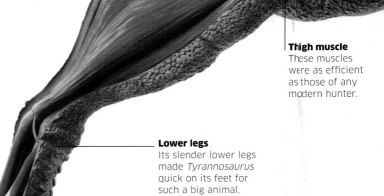

Tail
Most Mesozoic dinosaurs had long, bony, muscular tails.

Thigh muscle
These muscles were as efficient as those of any modern hunter.

WALKING TALL

The fossil skeletons of all dinosaurs have a number of features that show they walked with their legs upright beneath their bodies. They have hinge-like ankle joints, and the tops of their thigh bones are angled inwards – just like ours – to fit into open hip sockets. Other features of the bones show clear evidence of powerful muscles.

Lower legs
Its slender lower legs made *Tyrannosaurus* quick on its feet for such a big animal.

Lizard stance

Lizards usually sprawl with their legs outspread and not supporting their weight well, so their bellies are often touching the ground.

Crocodile stance

Crocodiles stand more upright than lizards, and they can use a more efficient "high walk" when they want to move fast.

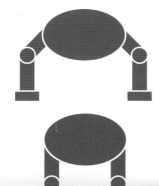

Dinosaur stance

All dinosaurs stood tall on straight legs that fully supported their weight. This is one reason why they could be so heavy.

SOME DINOSAURS, SUCH AS THIS *TYRANNOSAURUS* AND THE LONG-NECKED PLANT-EATING SAUROPODS, **WERE GIANTS, BUT MANY OTHERS WERE NO BIGGER THAN CHICKENS.**

Eyes
Tyrannosaurus had eyes that were as sharp as those of an eagle.

Brain
This was adapted for keen perception rather than high intelligence.

Teeth
This killer's teeth were strong enough to crush bone.

Jaws
Massively powerful jaws were vital for this big hunter.

Intestine
Meat-eaters had shorter intestines than plant-eaters.

Lungs
Their very efficient lungs were like those of modern birds.

Stomach
A muscular stomach helped grind food to a pulp for easy digestion.

Arms
Tyrannosaurus had tiny arms, but those of other dinosaurs were much longer and stronger.

Feet
Dinosaurs walked on their toes. Some had broad foot pads to help support their weight.

Claw
The toes were tipped with strong claws made of the same material as human toenails.

WHAT IS NOT A DINOSAUR?

The Mesozoic dinosaurs lived alongside several other types of prehistoric reptiles. They included various marine reptiles, the crocodiles and their relatives, and the flying pterosaurs with their long wings of stretched skin.

Marine reptiles
Only distantly related to the dinosaurs, the Mesozoic marine reptiles included dolphin-like ichthyosaurs, ferocious crocodile-like mosasaurs, and gigantic, carnivorous plesiosaurs, such as this massive-jawed *Liopleurodon*.

LIOPLEURODON

Pterosaurs
These winged reptiles were part of the same archosaur group as the dinosaurs. The early ones were quite small, but some of the later ones were colossal. Many had long, toothed "beaks", like this *Rhamphorhynchus*, which lived in the Middle to Late Jurassic.

RHAMPHORHYNCHUS

Dinosaur diversity

Soon after the first dinosaurs evolved in the Middle Triassic, they divided into two main types – saurischians and ornithischians. The saurischians included the long-necked, plant-eating sauropodomorphs and the mainly meat-eating theropods. The ornithischians consisted of three main groups of dinosaurs that split into five types – the dramatic-looking stegosaurs, armoured ankylosaurs, beaky ornithopods, horned and frilled ceratopsians, and thick-skulled pachycephalosaurs.

Saurischians
The word saurischian means "lizard-hipped". It refers to the fact that many of these dinosaurs had pelvic bones like those of lizards. But others did not, so this is not a reliable guide. Saurischians had longer necks than ornithischians.

EORAPTOR

The first dinosaurs
The earliest dinosaur fossils found so far date from 235 MYA. Only skeleton fragments survive, but these are enough to show that the first dinosaurs were small, agile animals. They would have looked like *Asilisaurus*, a close relative. Unlike *Asilisaurus*, however, they probably stood on two legs.

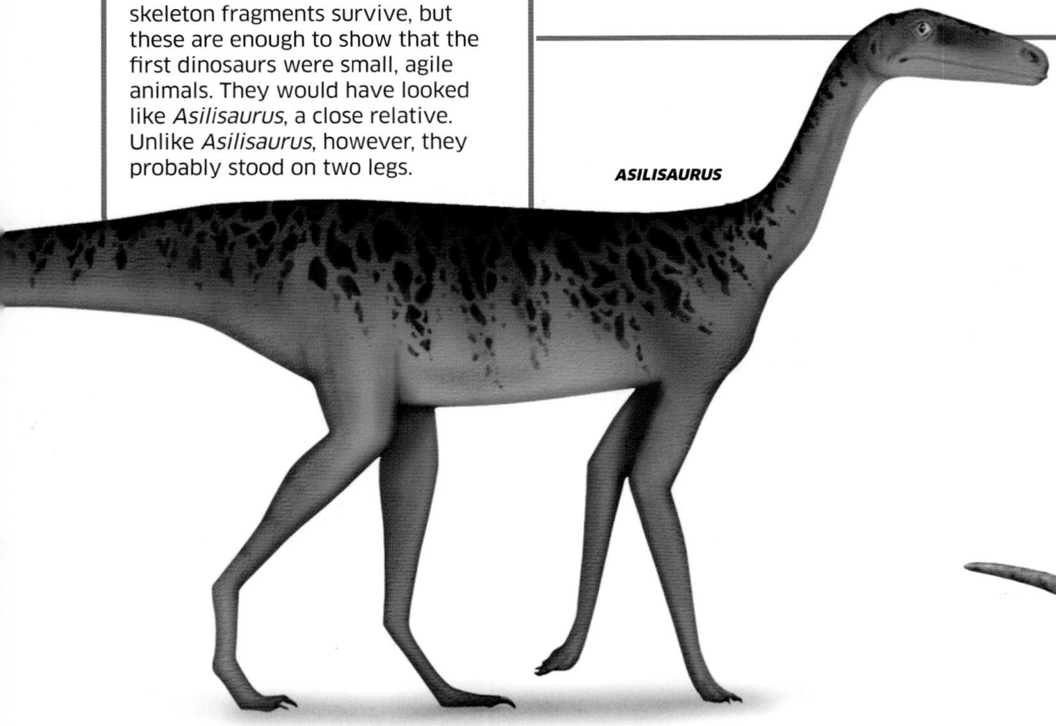

ASILISAURUS

Ornithischians
The ornithischians had beaks supported by special jaw bones. The name means "bird-hipped", because their pelvic bones were like those of birds. But, confusingly, the birds themselves are small saurischians.

HYPSILOPHODON

ALTHOUGH SCIENTISTS HAVE FOUND THE **FOSSILS OF MORE THAN 800 DIFFERENT SPECIES OF DINOSAUR,** THEY ARE SURE THAT THIS IS ONLY A SMALL FRACTION OF THE NUMBER THAT ONCE LIVED.

Theropods

The theropod group included nearly all the hunters, although some had broader diets. They all walked on their hind legs, and some became the birds. They ranged from small, feathered animals to heavily armed giants like *Tyrannosaurus*.

TYRANNOSAURUS

Sauropodomorphs

Diplodocus was a typical sauropod, with a long neck and tail, and standing on four legs. The earlier prosauropods were similar, but stood on two legs. The two types are called sauropodomorphs, which means "sauropod-shaped". They were all plant-eaters.

DIPLODOCUS

Pachycephalosaurs

These strange "boneheaded" dinosaurs are among the most mysterious ornithischians. They are famous for their massively thick skulls, which seem to have evolved to protect their brains from impact damage.

PACHYCEPHALOSAURUS

Marginocephalians

Ceratopsians

The horned dinosaurs mostly stood on four legs, and ranged from lightweights such as *Protoceratops* to giants like the famous *Triceratops*. They had big, bony frills extending from the backs of their skulls.

PROTOCERATOPS

Ornithopods

The ornithopods were among the most successful ornithischians. They included highly specialized forms such as *Corythosaurus*, which had hundreds of plant-grinding teeth.

CORYTHOSAURUS

Stegosaurs

Instantly recognizable by the rows of plates and spikes on their backs, these evolved early in the Jurassic and had mostly vanished by the Cretaceous. They used the long spikes on their tails to defend themselves.

HUAYANGOSAURUS

Thyreophorans

Ankylosaurs

The low-slung ankylosaurs were armoured with bony plates and spikes, which helped in defence against hunters. Some had heavy tail clubs that they could use as defensive weapons.

GASTONIA

Life in the Mesozoic

The very first dinosaurs evolved near the middle of the Triassic – the first of the three Periods that make up the Mesozoic Era. At first they were a minor part of the wildlife, which was dominated by bigger, more powerful reptiles such as *Postosuchus* (pages 28–29). A mass extinction at the end of the Triassic wiped out the dinosaurs' main competitors, and they rapidly evolved into the biggest, most powerful land animals of the Jurassic and Cretaceous Periods that followed. But they were not alone. Many other animals had survived the extinction, along with the plant life that supported them. These creatures formed a web of life – an ecosystem – that was very different from the living world we know today.

CHANGING CLIMATE

The average global climate in the Mesozoic was much warmer than it is now. But it was constantly changing as continents moved north or south or split apart, and as the nature of the atmosphere was altered by events such as massive volcanic eruptions.

Volcanic sunset
Dust hurled into the atmosphere by volcanoes can cool the climate by blocking some of the light from the Sun. But the dust in the air can also cause some spectacular sunsets.

SHIFTING CONTINENTS

Heat generated deep within the planet keeps the hot rock beneath Earth's crust constantly on the move. The moving rock drags on the brittle crust, and has broken it into many large plates that are very slowly pulling apart in some places and pushing together in others. This process causes earthquakes and volcanic eruptions. It also continuously reshapes the global map by moving the continents into new arrangements, and even creating new land from volcanic rock.

Volcanic landscape
The island of Java in Indonesia has been created from rock erupted by countless volcanoes over millions of years. This view over part of the island shows just a few of them, including Mount Semeru erupting in the distance.

LIVING WITH DINOSAURS

The dinosaurs were part of a rich variety of animal life that thrived in the Mesozoic. On land there were small invertebrates such as insects and spiders, amphibians such as frogs, reptiles such as lizards and crocodiles, small mammals, and flying pterosaurs. The oceans teemed with marine invertebrates, fish of all kinds, and many spectacular marine reptiles.

Land invertebrates
Insects and other invertebrates swarmed in the Mesozoic forests, where they were preyed on by animals such as lizards. This fossil dragonfly dates from the Jurassic.

LIBELLULIUM

Land reptiles
Many crocodilians and other reptiles lived alongside the dinosaurs, especially in the Triassic. This fish-eating phytosaur grew to 2 m (6.5 ft) in length.

PARASUCHUS

Marine creatures
The seas were alive with fish such as this chimaera – a relative of the sharks. They preyed on smaller fish and shellfish, and were eaten in turn by marine reptiles.

ISCHYODUS

Flying reptiles
The pterosaurs evolved in the Triassic. Some were the size of small aeroplanes. Not all were good fliers, but *Eudimorphodon* was one of the most efficient.

EUDIMORPHODON

TIMELINE

The dinosaurs appeared halfway through the Triassic and flourished for 165 million years until the end of the Mesozoic. The Cenozoic – our own era – has lasted less than half as long, which shows how successful the dinosaurs were.

ERA	MESOZOIC ERA	
PERIOD	TRIASSIC PERIOD	JURASSIC PERIOD
MILLIONS OF YEARS AGO	252	201

145

GREEN PLANET

The green landscapes that Mesozoic animals lived in were not like those we know today. Until the Cretaceous Period there were no grasses, no flowers, very few trees with broad leaves, and few trees that lost their leaves in winter. So, for most of the Mesozoic Era there were no open grasslands, and many of the plants that grew in the forests and woodlands were of types that are now rare, or even extinct.

Palaeozoic survivors
Many plants had survived from the preceding Palaeozoic Era, including primitive, simple plants like these horsetails.

Triassic clubmosses
These *Pleuromeia* plants grew worldwide in the Triassic. They belonged to a group of plants called clubmosses.

Jurassic cycadeoids
Some types of Mesozoic plants no longer exist. These Jurassic bennettitaleans look like palms, but were quite different.

Cretaceous tree ferns
Tempskya was an unusual form of tree fern with fronds sprouting from the sides of its trunk, like a redwood tree.

Dinosaur country
In the Late Jurassic, western North America was a land of lush forests, with tall trees browsed by long-necked sauropod dinosaurs. They were preyed on by hunters such as *Allosaurus* (shown here on the left).

CATASTROPHE

The Mesozoic Era ended with a mass extinction that wiped out the giant dinosaurs, pterosaurs, and many other animals. It was probably caused by an asteroid crashing into Central America, triggering a huge explosion and global chaos. But some mammals, birds, and other animals survived into a new era – the Cenozoic.

THE MESOZOIC SAW THE EVOLUTION OF THE MOST SPECTACULAR ANIMALS THAT EVER LIVED.

CRETACEOUS PERIOD

CENOZOIC ERA

0

TRIASSIC LIFE

The Triassic Period of Earth's long history started in chaos, because the world was recovering from a global catastrophe that had wiped out much of the life on Earth. Among the survivors were the animals that were to give rise to the first dinosaurs, as well as flying pterosaurs and marine reptiles.

THE TRIASSIC WORLD

The dinosaurs appeared during the first period of the Mesozoic Era – the Triassic. At this time, from 252 to 201 million years ago, most of the land on the planet was part of a single huge supercontinent, surrounded by a near-global ocean. This gigantic landmass had formed during the preceding Period, the Permian, which ended in a catastrophic mass extinction. This destroyed 96 per cent of all species, and all the animals that evolved during the Triassic were descended from the survivors.

SUPERCONTINENT

The continents are constantly being dragged around the globe by the shifting plates of Earth's crust. They have come together and split apart in different ways many times, but during the Triassic the land formed a vast supercontinent known as Pangaea. It came together some 300 million years ago, but during the late Triassic the opening Tethys Ocean started to split it in two.

PACIFIC OCEAN

NORTH AMERICA

SOUTH AMERICA

Pangaea was a huge C-shaped landmass that extended right across the Triassic globe from north to south, but there was no land at the South Pole.

The supercontinent was made up of many smaller continents that we would not recognize. The boundaries of the modern continents did not exist.

**CONTINENTS AND OCEANS
DURING THE TRIASSIC PERIOD,
252–201 MILLION YEARS AGO**

ENVIRONMENT

The Triassic was very different from our own time. At first all life was recovering from the disaster that caused the mass extinction at the end of the previous Era. The climate was profoundly affected by the way all the land formed one giant continent, and a lot of the plant life that we take for granted today did not exist.

Climate

The average global climate was very warm compared to today's 14 °C (57 °F). The regions near the centre of Pangaea were so far from the oceans that they got hardly any rain, and were barren deserts. Most of the plants and animals lived on Pangaea's milder, wetter fringes.

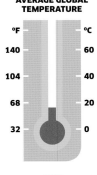

AVERAGE GLOBAL TEMPERATURE

°F	°C
140	60
104	40
68	20
32	0

17 °C
(62.6 °F)

Barren deserts
Many rocks dating from the Triassic were once desert sand dunes like these in the Sahara. They formed at the arid heart of the supercontinent.

Mild fringes
Coastal regions enjoyed a cooler climate with plenty of rain, thanks to the influence of the nearby oceans. This allowed life to flourish there.

ERA		MESOZOIC ERA	
PERIOD	TRIASSIC PERIOD	JURASSIC PERIOD	
MILLIONS OF YEARS AGO	252	201	145

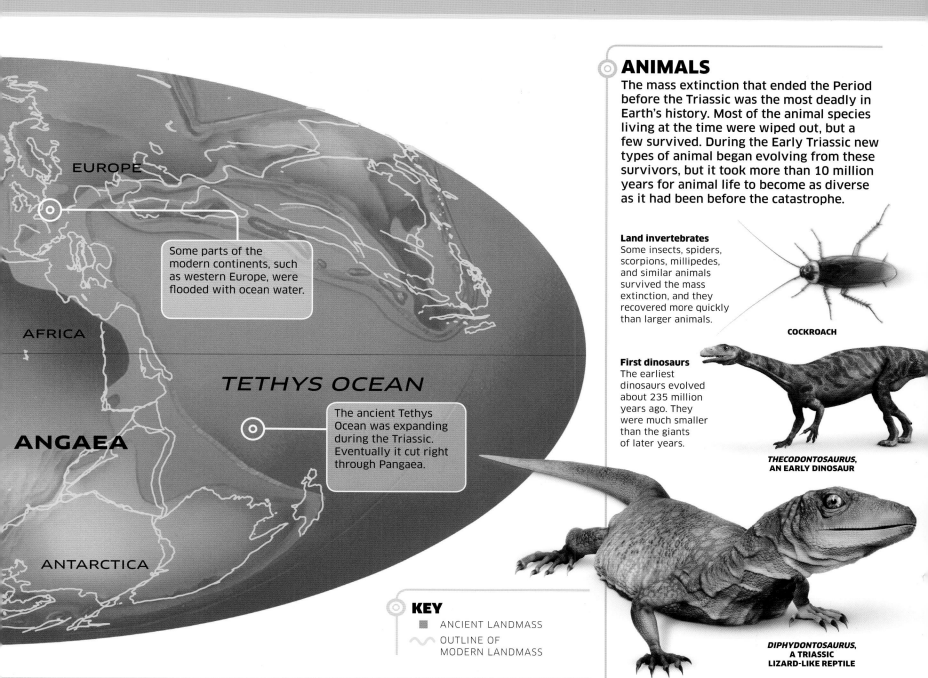

EUROPE

Some parts of the modern continents, such as western Europe, were flooded with ocean water.

AFRICA

TETHYS OCEAN

ANGAEA

The ancient Tethys Ocean was expanding during the Triassic. Eventually it cut right through Pangaea.

ANTARCTICA

KEY

- ANCIENT LANDMASS
- OUTLINE OF MODERN LANDMASS

ANIMALS

The mass extinction that ended the Period before the Triassic was the most deadly in Earth's history. Most of the animal species living at the time were wiped out, but a few survived. During the Early Triassic new types of animal began evolving from these survivors, but it took more than 10 million years for animal life to become as diverse as it had been before the catastrophe.

Land invertebrates
Some insects, spiders, scorpions, millipedes, and similar animals survived the mass extinction, and they recovered more quickly than larger animals.

COCKROACH

First dinosaurs
The earliest dinosaurs evolved about 235 million years ago. They were much smaller than the giants of later years.

THECODONTOSAURUS, AN EARLY DINOSAUR

DIPHYDONTOSAURUS, A TRIASSIC LIZARD-LIKE REPTILE

Other land reptiles
The early dinosaurs appeared in a world dominated by many other types of reptiles, including crocodiles and their relatives, turtles, and lizards.

Marine reptiles
Many reptiles such as this nothosaur hunted in the seas. They were to give rise to some of the most spectacular animals of the Mesozoic Era.

NOTHOSAURUS

Plants

During the Triassic the main plants were conifers, ginkgos, cycads, ferns, mosses, and horsetails. There were no flowering plants at all. Many types of plants took a long time to recover from the extinction at the start of the Period, especially forest trees.

Ferns
Still familiar today, these plants were a major feature of the Triassic. Most ferns can grow only in damp, shady places.

Horsetails
These primitive plants evolved about 300 million years ago. They may be the oldest surviving plant type on Earth.

Mosses
Mosses are very simple plants that soak up water from the ground like sponges, so they cannot grow very tall.

Ginkgos
The earliest of these trees lived near the beginning of the Triassic. Once common, just one species survives today.

CRETACEOUS PERIOD	CENOZOIC ERA

Fossils of this animal have been found in **Europe**, the **Middle East**, and **China**.

Long head
Long and flat, with very long jaws, the head was like that of a modern crocodile.
Flexible neck
Nothosaurus could swing its jaws sideways through the water to snap up nearby fish.
Claws
Stout claws were useful for scrambling over slippery rocks on the seashore.

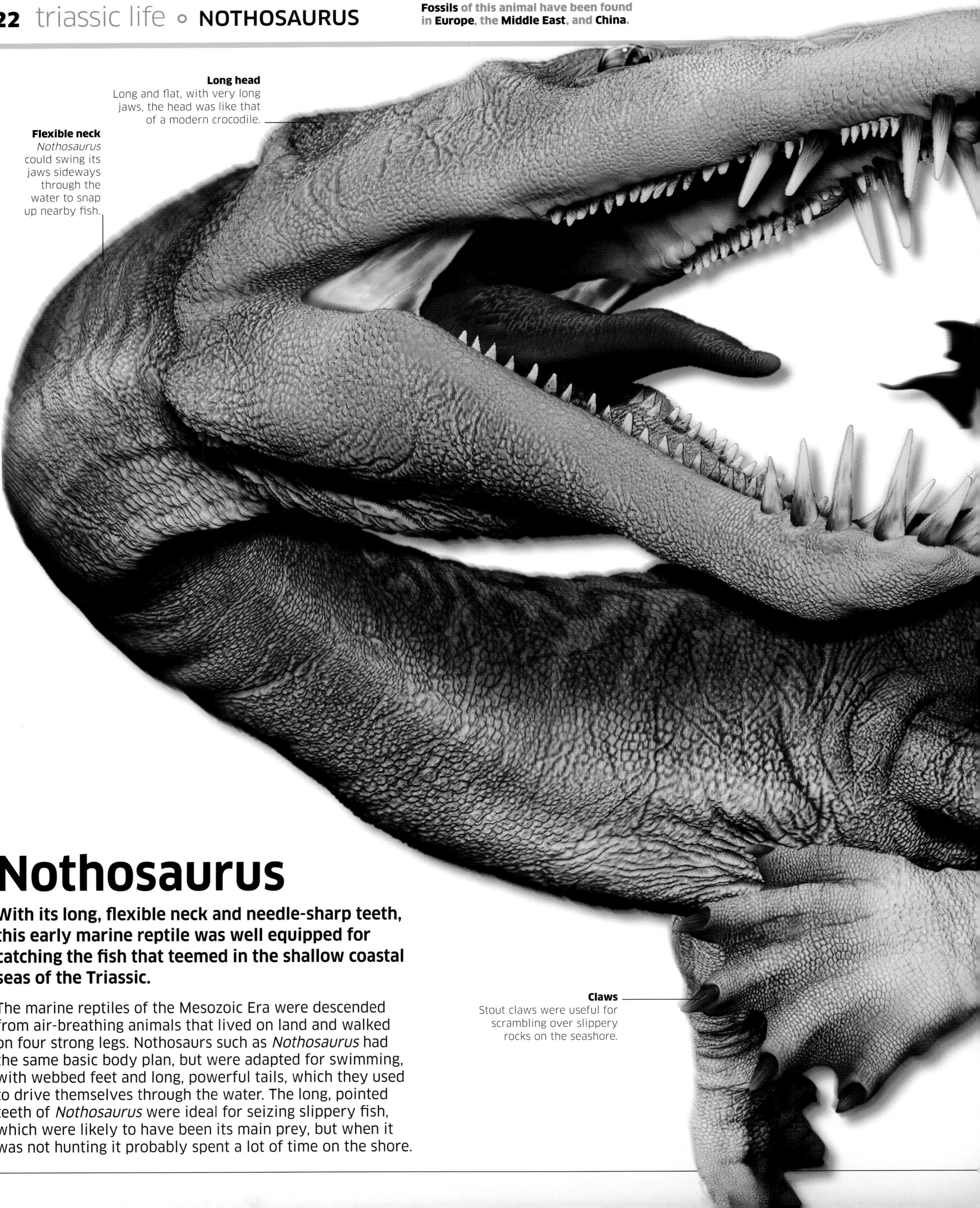

Nothosaurus

With its long, flexible neck and needle-sharp teeth, this early marine reptile was well equipped for catching the fish that teemed in the shallow coastal seas of the Triassic.

The marine reptiles of the Mesozoic Era were descended from air-breathing animals that lived on land and walked on four strong legs. Nothosaurs such as *Nothosaurus* had the same basic body plan, but were adapted for swimming, with webbed feet and long, powerful tails, which they used to drive themselves through the water. The long, pointed teeth of *Nothosaurus* were ideal for seizing slippery fish, which were likely to have been its main prey, but when it was not hunting it probably spent a lot of time on the shore.

TRIASSIC	JURASSIC	CRETACEOUS	CENOZOIC	
252 MYA	201 MYA	145 MYA	66 MYA	0

120 The number of **teeth** in the jaws of *Nothosaurus*.

23

Needle-like teeth
The sharp teeth were adapted for gripping fish, but not chewing them.

Fish prey
There were plenty of fish, squid, and other prey in Triassic oceans.

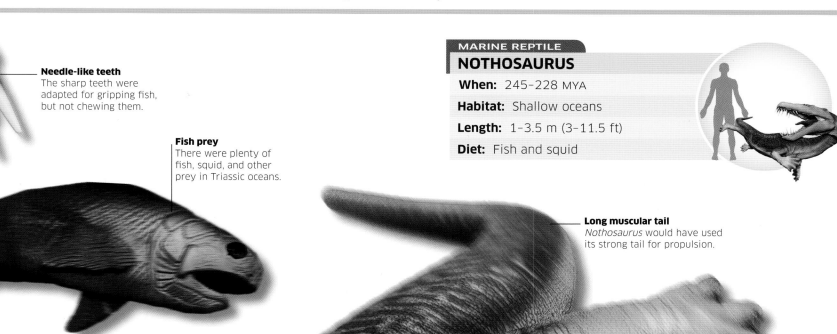

MARINE REPTILE
NOTHOSAURUS

When: 245–228 MYA

Habitat: Shallow oceans

Length: 1–3.5 m (3–11.5 ft)

Diet: Fish and squid

Long muscular tail
Nothosaurus would have used its strong tail for propulsion.

Blending in
Camouflage patterns may have hidden *Nothosaurus* from its enemies.

Smooth skin
Although scaly, the skin was smooth and well streamlined, and helped the animal to swim efficiently.

Triassic sea lion
Unlike many marine reptiles that lived later in the Mesozoic, *Nothosaurus* had four strong legs. These enabled it to walk much like a sea lion. This suggests that *Nothosaurus* lived in the same way, hunting in the ocean, but resting on beaches and rocky shores. It probably produced live young, giving birth in protected lagoons or estuaries.

Early nothosaurs hunted in the oceans at the same time as the **first dinosaurs** were walking on land.

Webbed feet
Each of the four short, strong limbs ended in five long toes, which were webbed like those of an otter. These webbed feet would have been useful on land as well as in the water.

Ferocious predator
Fierce predators like
Postosuchus (pages 28-29)
would have found
Placerias tempting prey.

Plant slicer
Big openings behind
the eye sockets
anchored very powerful
jaw muscles. The jaw
could move backwards
and forwards as well as
up and down, which
helped it cut through
tough plants.

Tusks
It is not quite clear what the
two tusks were for, but it is
probable that they were
used for digging.

Stocky build
The short, strong
body was supported
by four sturdy legs.

Placerias

Built like a hippopotamus, and with similar long tusks, this chunky herbivore was one of the most common big animals of the Late Triassic – the Epoch that saw the appearance of the first dinosaurs.

For several million years before the earliest plant-eating dinosaurs appeared, the most successful herbivores were a group of animals called dicynodonts. Their name, meaning "two dog tooth", refers to their tusk-like upper canine teeth. *Placerias* also had a parrot-like beak, used for gathering leaves and plant stems. It weighed as much as a small car, but was moderately sized compared to a dicynodont called *Lisowicia*, discovered in 2018, which was as big as an elephant.

Sturdy arms
The heavily built
arms had five strong
fingers, used as toes.

Placerias could have reached a maximum weight of **2,000 kg (4,400 lb)**.

40 The number of *Placerias* **skeletons** found at one site in Arizona, USA, **suggesting that it lived in herds.**

Placerias may have **spent part of its time in the water**, just like a **modern hippopotamus**.

25

Placerias was one of the
last dicynodonts,
which all became extinct in the Late Triassic.

MAMMAL ANCESTOR

PLACERIAS

When: 220–210 MYA

Habitat: Plains

Length: 2–3.5 m (6.5–11.5 ft)

Diet: Plants

Stumpy tail
The tail was thick but much shorter than the tail of a typical reptile.

Powerful legs
Placerias probably walked with its hind legs upright beneath its body.

Mammal ancestor

Dicynodonts, such as *Placerias*, are often described as mammal ancestors, although mammals actually evolved from a related group called the cynodonts. They all belong to a branch of the vertebrate family tree called the synapsids, which separated from the reptiles in the Carboniferous Period, almost 200 million years before the evolution of the earliest dinosaurs.

REPTILES

SYNAPSIDS

SPHENACODONTS

DICYNODONTS
(PLACERIAS)

CYNODONTS

MAMMALS

All-purpose teeth
Most of *Eoraptor*'s teeth are curved, pointed blades suitable for eating meat. But the teeth at the front of the jaw have broader crowns, and are more like those of plant-eaters. So, it is likely that *Eoraptor* ate both plants and animals.

10 kg (22 lb) – the likely weight of *Eoraptor*. This is roughly the average weight of a small child – a lot smaller than the giant dinosaurs that were to follow!

Long neck
Eoraptor's long neck was typical of the saurischian group of dinosaurs.

All-round vision
The eyes on the side of the head enabled all-round vision.

Lizard prey
Eoraptor would have had no trouble catching small animals such as lizards.

Sharp claws
Each hand had three long fingers with sharp claws, plus two short fingers.

Strong toes
Eoraptor stood on three strong toes, but had a fourth toe at the back of the foot.

Eoraptor

This was one of the earliest dinosaurs – a small, light, and agile animal no bigger than a fox, and possibly with a similar way of life. Most dinosaurs at this time resembled *Eoraptor*. It was only later that they evolved their spectacular variety of forms.

Discovered in the Triassic rocks of Argentina in 1991, the fossil bones of this animal were soon identified as those of a meat-eater. It clearly had sharp teeth and claws. Since most later dinosaurs with these features were theropods, its finders decided that *Eoraptor* was a theropod too – an ancestor of giant hunters such as *Tyrannosaurus rex*. But experts continue to disagree over the way early dinosaurs like *Eoraptor* were related to later types. Some have argued that this little dinosaur might have been more closely related to the group that includes the colossal, long-necked, plant-eating sauropods.

Eoraptor means "dawn plunderer". The "dawn" part refers to its **very early date**.

The **exact position** of *Eoraptor* in the evolution of dinosaurs **is still not known** for certain.

Its **long legs** indicate that *Eoraptor* was **a fast runner**.

27

DINOSAUR

EORAPTOR

When: 228–216 MYA

Habitat: Rocky deserts

Length: 1 m (3 ft)

Diet: Lizards, small reptiles, and plants

Balancing tail
Its long tail helped *Eoraptor* balance as it ran on its hind legs.

Exciting discovery
The first specimen of *Eoraptor* was named and described in 1993 by Paul Sereno and his colleagues. Sereno is an American paleontologist (fossil expert) who has led several expeditions in search of dinosaur fossils. At the time, *Eoraptor* was one of the oldest dinosaurs ever found.

PAUL SERENO

Scaly skin
Like most reptiles, *Eoraptor*'s skin was probably scaly.

Jaws

Easy mistake
Eoraptor lived at the same time and in the same place as a slightly bigger dinosaur, *Herrerasaurus*. *Herrerasaurus* was a theropod that looked very similar to *Eoraptor*, which explains why the scientists who first examined *Eoraptor* thought that it was a theropod too. At this stage in their evolution, all dinosaurs seem to have shared the same two-legged form.

Large hind legs

Clawed toes

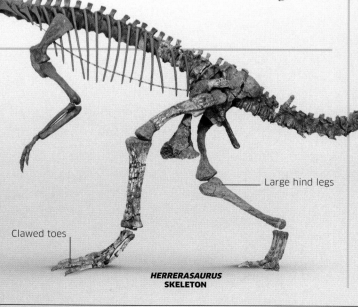

***HERRERASAURUS* SKELETON**

Valley of the Moon
The fossils of *Eoraptor* were found in the Ischigualasto National Park of Argentina. This area of barren rock has been given the name "Valley of the Moon" because it looks like a lunar landscape. During the Late Triassic, it would have been an arid, harsh, and desert-like place.

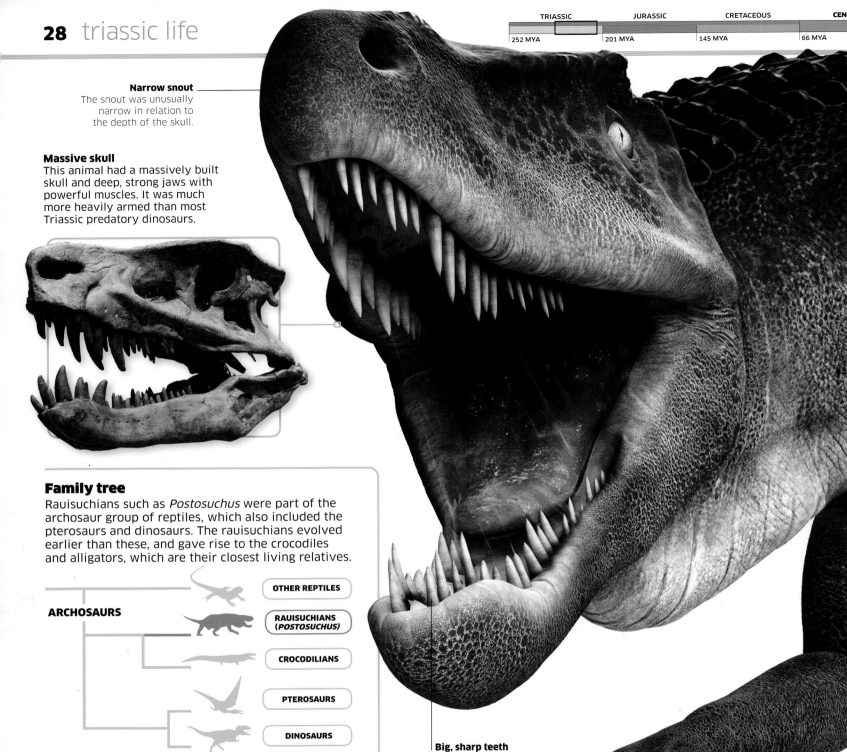

TRIASSIC	JURASSIC	CRETACEOUS	CENOZOIC
252 MYA	201 MYA	145 MYA	66 MYA 0

Narrow snout
The snout was unusually narrow in relation to the depth of the skull.

Massive skull
This animal had a massively built skull and deep, strong jaws with powerful muscles. It was much more heavily armed than most Triassic predatory dinosaurs.

Family tree

Rauisuchians such as *Postosuchus* were part of the archosaur group of reptiles, which also included the pterosaurs and dinosaurs. The rauisuchians evolved earlier than these, and gave rise to the crocodiles and alligators, which are their closest living relatives.

ARCHOSAURS

- OTHER REPTILES
- RAUISUCHIANS (*POSTOSUCHUS*)
- CROCODILIANS
- PTEROSAURS
- DINOSAURS

Ragged teeth

Postosuchus teeth were all different lengths, which was partly caused by regular tooth replacement. The teeth grew until they fell out, so the long teeth were the oldest and the short ones, the youngest. Crocodile teeth (below) are replaced in a similar way.

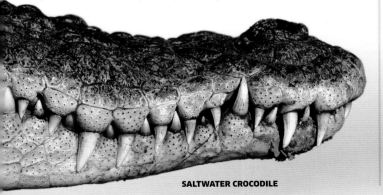

SALTWATER CROCODILE

Big, sharp teeth
The teeth were sharp, serrated blades, ideal for slicing through meat.

Short arms
The arms of *Postosuchus* were much shorter than its legs, and each hand had five fingers.

Postosuchus

Although it looks like a dinosaur, this ferocious predator was a close relative of the crocodiles. It was one of a group of reptiles that dominated life in the Triassic before the dinosaurs took over.

The biggest, most powerful land predators of the Late Triassic were reptiles called rauisuchians. *Postosuchus* was one of the biggest. It probably stood on its hind legs like a predatory dinosaur, rather than like a crocodile, and may have been almost as agile. It would have preyed on any dinosaurs it could catch, as well as dicynodonts such as *Placerias* (pages 24–25).

The name **Postosuchus** means "crocodile from Post", because its fossils were first found at Post Quarry, Texas, USA.

300 kg (661.3 lb) – the **weight of an adult Postosuchus** – equivalent to **four full-grown men**.

29

Armoured back
Its back was protected by an armour of bony scutes.

Long tail
The weight of its long tail helped balance the heavy head and jaws.

Big feet
The feet were bigger than the hands, and resemble those of modern crocodiles.

Strong legs
Postosuchus stood with its hind legs beneath its body to support its weight efficiently.

Postosuchus looked like a dinosaur because it **evolved similar features** to cope with the same way of life. This phenomenon is called "convergent evolution".

RAUISUCHIAN

POSTOSUCHUS

When: 228–204 MYA

Habitat: Woodlands

Length: 3–4.5 m (10–15 ft)

Diet: Other animals

FALSE ALARM

Sunlight gleams through the trees, flooding the forest floor with light. The loud noise of a massive sauropod rearing up to take a mouthful of leaves causes alarm nearby.

A small predator, *Coelophysis*, cannot see the source of the sound and is frightened. He sprints for cover, startling a tiny mammal searching for insects among the moss. Though he is a meat-eating dinosaur, *Coelophysis* is not going to chance being in the path of one of the bigger killers prowling these Triassic forests.

All-round view
The eyes of *Plateosaurus* were high on the sides of its head, giving an all-round view so it could watch out for enemies.

Flexible neck
Its long, flexible neck allowed *Plateosaurus* to browse and feed high in the trees.

Slicing teeth
The upper leaf-shaped teeth overlapped the lower ones like scissor blades for slicing vegetation.

Sure-footed
Plateosaurus stood on the five toes of each sturdy hind limb, and could probably run quite fast. The inner toe bones were much longer and stronger than the outer ones, and were equipped with stout claws.

35 virtually complete skeletons of *Plateosaurus* were found in a single quarry in southern Germany – plus the scattered bones of at least 70 more that died at the same site.

TRIASSIC	JURASSIC	CRETACEOUS	CENOZOIC
252 MYA	201 MYA	145 MYA	66 MYA	0

Some *Plateosaurus* adults were **twice the size** of others, a difference that is very odd for a dinosaur.

33

DINOSAUR
PLATEOSAURUS

When: 216–204 MYA

Habitat: Forests and swamps

Length: 10 m (33 ft)

Diet: Plants

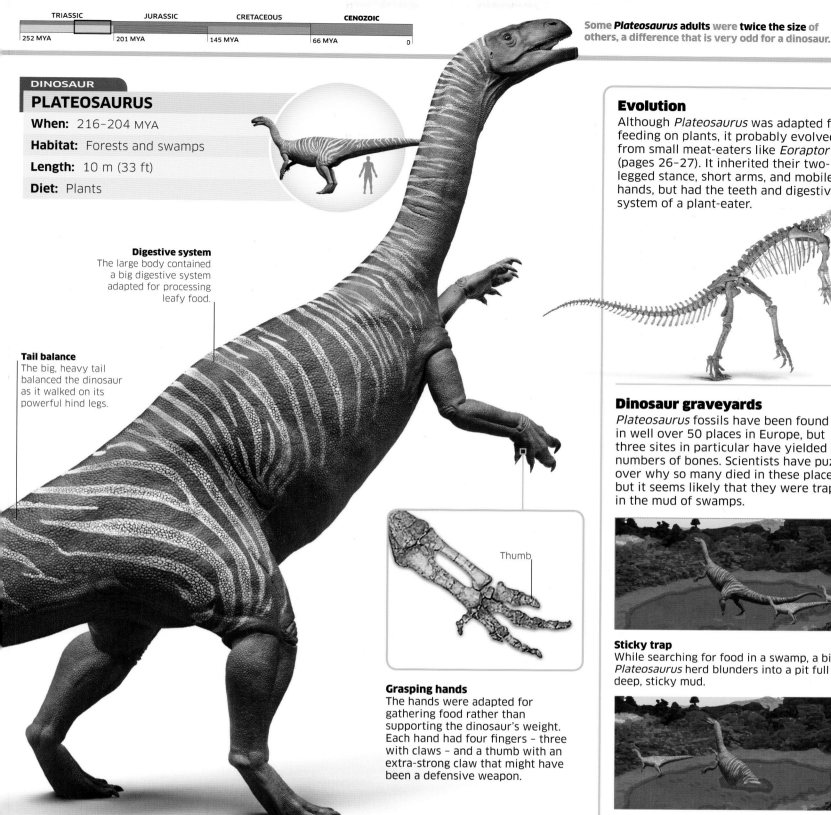

Digestive system
The large body contained a big digestive system adapted for processing leafy food.

Tail balance
The big, heavy tail balanced the dinosaur as it walked on its powerful hind legs.

Thumb

Grasping hands
The hands were adapted for gathering food rather than supporting the dinosaur's weight. Each hand had four fingers – three with claws – and a thumb with an extra-strong claw that might have been a defensive weapon.

Plateosaurus

One of the first fossil dinosaurs to be discovered, this plant-eater was a sauropodomorph, a type of dinosaur closely related to the biggest land animals that ever lived, the long-necked sauropods.

Early sauropodomorphs like this one were smaller and lighter than the sauropods, though *Plateosaurus* was one of the biggest. They walked on their hind legs and used their hands to gather food. *Plateosaurus* seems to have been quite common in the region that is now northern and central Europe. Scientists have found more than 100 well-preserved skeletons since the first fossils were discovered in Germany in 1834.

Evolution
Although *Plateosaurus* was adapted for feeding on plants, it probably evolved from small meat-eaters like *Eoraptor* (pages 26–27). It inherited their two-legged stance, short arms, and mobile hands, but had the teeth and digestive system of a plant-eater.

Dinosaur graveyards
Plateosaurus fossils have been found in well over 50 places in Europe, but three sites in particular have yielded huge numbers of bones. Scientists have puzzled over why so many died in these places, but it seems likely that they were trapped in the mud of swamps.

Sticky trap
While searching for food in a swamp, a big *Plateosaurus* herd blunders into a pit full of deep, sticky mud.

Lucky escape
The lighter animals escape, but the bigger, heavy ones cannot. The more they struggle, the deeper they sink.

Fossilization
The trapped animals drown and sink out of sight of scavengers. Over millions of years they are fossilized.

	TRIASSIC	JURASSIC	CRETACEOUS	CENOZOIC
252 MYA	201 MYA	145 MYA	66 MYA	0

Complex teeth

Fossils show that *Eudimorphodon* had needle-like teeth at the tips of its jaws, plus many smaller, multi-pointed teeth that formed long blades for slicing up prey.

Sharp claws

The fingers of its hands had sharp claws.

Wing structure

Pterosaur wings were made of skin reinforced by many slender, pliable stiffening fibres. The stiffened membrane was backed up by sheets of muscle that modified the wing profile to make it more efficient. The muscle was fuelled by a network of blood vessels.

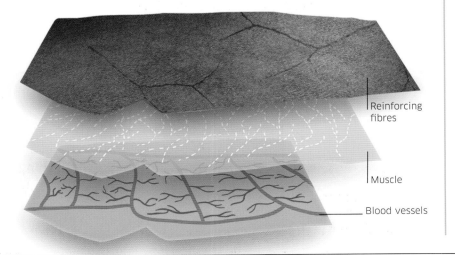

Reinforcing fibres

Muscle

Blood vessels

FOSSILS OF *DICELLOPYGE*, A TRIASSIC FISH

Fish diet

The pterosaur's sharp-pointed teeth would have been ideal for gripping slippery, struggling fish, and the stomachs of *Eudimorphodon* fossils contain scales very like the ones visible on these fossil Triassic fish. This makes it likely that fish were its main prey.

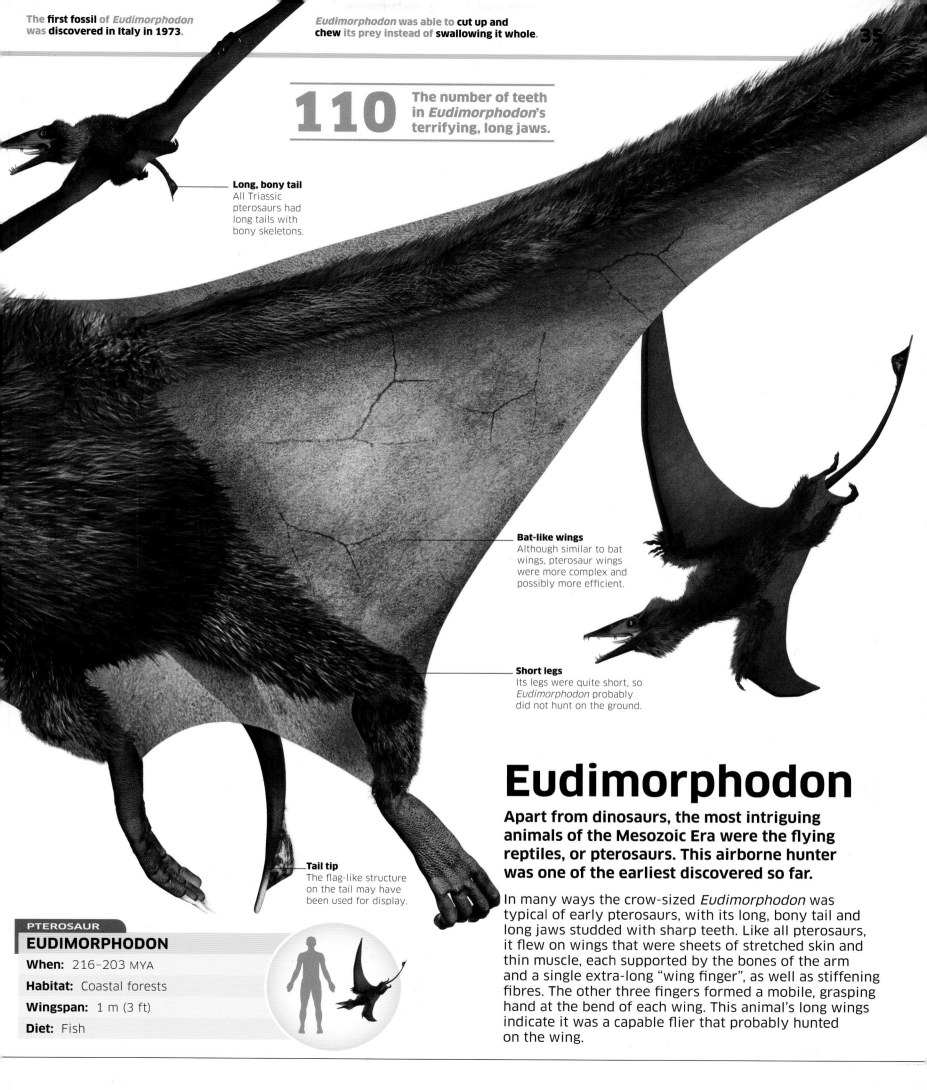

The **first fossil** of *Eudimorphodon* was **discovered in Italy in 1973**.

Eudimorphodon was able to **cut up and chew** its prey instead of **swallowing it whole**.

110
The number of teeth in *Eudimorphodon*'s terrifying, long jaws.

Long, bony tail
All Triassic pterosaurs had long tails with bony skeletons.

Bat-like wings
Although similar to bat wings, pterosaur wings were more complex and possibly more efficient.

Short legs
Its legs were quite short, so *Eudimorphodon* probably did not hunt on the ground.

Tail tip
The flag-like structure on the tail may have been used for display.

PTEROSAUR
EUDIMORPHODON

When: 216–203 MYA

Habitat: Coastal forests

Wingspan: 1 m (3 ft)

Diet: Fish

Eudimorphodon

Apart from dinosaurs, the most intriguing animals of the Mesozoic Era were the flying reptiles, or pterosaurs. This airborne hunter was one of the earliest discovered so far.

In many ways the crow-sized *Eudimorphodon* was typical of early pterosaurs, with its long, bony tail and long jaws studded with sharp teeth. Like all pterosaurs, it flew on wings that were sheets of stretched skin and thin muscle, each supported by the bones of the arm and a single extra-long "wing finger", as well as stiffening fibres. The other three fingers formed a mobile, grasping hand at the bend of each wing. This animal's long wings indicate it was a capable flier that probably hunted on the wing.

TRIASSIC		JURASSIC		CRETACEOUS		CENOZOIC	
252 MYA		201 MYA		145 MYA		66 MYA	0

High tail
Strong tendons linking the bones of the dinosaur's tail held it high off the ground.

Isanosaurus

Some of the most famous dinosaurs, and certainly the biggest, were the colossal long-necked sauropods that supported their immense weight on four legs. _Isanosaurus_ was one of the earliest – much smaller than the later giants, but with the same basic body plan.

The first sauropodomorphs were small, agile animals. They gave rise to larger, heavier types such as _Plateosaurus_ (pages 32–33), which were specialized for eating plants, but still walked on two legs. Towards the end of the Triassic these were replaced by true sauropods like _Isanosaurus_, which walked on all fours, but could still rear up on their hind legs to feed.

Leg bone
The thigh bones are relatively straight compared to those of the earlier prosauropods. This shows that _Isanosaurus_ was adapted for walking on all four pillar-like legs, rather than just on its hind legs.

Full stretch
Although it almost certainly walked on all four feet, _Isanosaurus_ would have stood up on its sturdy hind legs to gather leaves from tall trees. Its front limbs were less heavily built than its hind legs, and it had mobile fingers which it could use to grasp branches for support. This feeding technique was also used by many sauropods that evolved later in the Mesozoic.

Only a few bones of _Isanosaurus_ have survived as fossils, but they include a vital leg bone that shows **it walked on all fours.**

Strong legs
Most of the animal's weight was carried by its massive hind legs.

The **only known specimen** of *Isanosaurus* was **not fully grown**, so we **don't know how big it might have become**.

Isanosaurus was named after the **Isan region** of northeast Thailand, **where its fossils were found**.

37

DINOSAUR

ISANOSAURUS

When: 219–199 MYA

Habitat: Woodlands

Length: 6 m (20 ft)

Diet: Leaves

Spiky crest
Isanosaurus may have had a spiky dorsal crest.

Short neck
The neck was short compared to the necks of later sauropods.

Simple teeth
This animal's skull and jaw have not been found, but it probably had small, simple teeth.

Mobile fingers
Although adapted for walking, the fingers were still quite mobile.

Bulky body
Its big body contained a large digestive system for processing its leafy diet.

Heavyweight herds
Fossilized footprint trackways show that many of the later sauropods travelled together in herds, like modern bison. *Isanosaurus* probably did the same, for mutual protection from enemies such as meat-eating theropod dinosaurs.

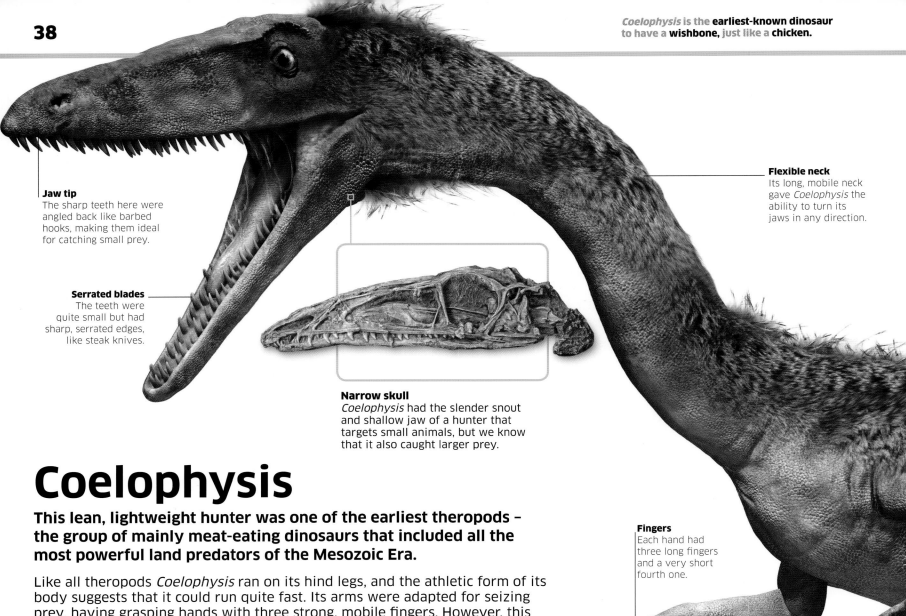

Jaw tip
The sharp teeth here were angled back like barbed hooks, making them ideal for catching small prey.

Serrated blades
The teeth were quite small but had sharp, serrated edges, like steak knives.

Flexible neck
Its long, mobile neck gave *Coelophysis* the ability to turn its jaws in any direction.

Narrow skull
Coelophysis had the slender snout and shallow jaw of a hunter that targets small animals, but we know that it also caught larger prey.

Fingers
Each hand had three long fingers and a very short fourth one.

Coelophysis

This lean, lightweight hunter was one of the earliest theropods – the group of mainly meat-eating dinosaurs that included all the most powerful land predators of the Mesozoic Era.

Like all theropods *Coelophysis* ran on its hind legs, and the athletic form of its body suggests that it could run quite fast. Its arms were adapted for seizing prey, having grasping hands with three strong, mobile fingers. However, this dinosaur probably relied more on its long, narrow, lightly built jaws, which were specialized for catching small animals such as lizards, early mammals, and large insects. The teeth at the tip of its upper jaw may have been specially adapted for plucking small burrowing animals from their holes.

Ghost Ranch bone bed

We know a lot about *Coelophysis* because hundreds of its skeletons were found together in a "bone bed" at Ghost Ranch, New Mexico, USA in 1947. It is not clear why so many died at once at this particular place. It is possible that groups of these dinosaurs were attracted to an isolated waterhole during a drought, but then drowned in a catastrophic flash flood triggered by a sudden storm.

Gathering crowd
On a hot summer day, thirsty groups of *Coelophysis* gather at the one place that still has drinkable water.

Deadly wave
A massive thunderstorm causes torrential rain. Water surges downhill in a wave that drowns all the dinosaurs.

Fossil evidence
The flood carries mud that buries the bodies. Over millions of years the mud turns to rock, fossilizing the bones.

Hunting together

If *Coelophysis* did live in groups, as the Ghost Ranch fossils suggest, then the animals may have hunted together to give them an advantage with larger prey. This wolf pack, for example, is working together to attack dangerous musk oxen, which a single wolf would not dare to tackle. But wolves are much smarter than *Coelophysis* would have been, so such tactics may not have been likely.

TRIASSIC	JURASSIC	CRETACEOUS	CENOZOIC
252 MYA	201 MYA	145 MYA	66 MYA	0

1998 In this year, a *Coelophysis* skull was carried into space aboard the Space Shuttle *Endeavour*.

39

500

Coelophysis skeletons were found together at the Ghost Ranch site in New Mexico, USA.

DINOSAUR
COELOPHYSIS

When: 216–200 MYA

Habitat: Desert plains

Length: 3 m (10 ft)

Diet: Other animals

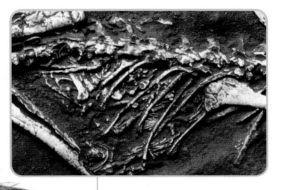

Inside the stomach
The stomach regions of some fossil *Coelophysis* skeletons contain the remains of their prey. One such discovery appeared to be the skeleton of a juvenile *Coelophysis*, and was originally seen as evidence of cannibalism. The bones were later shown to be those of a crocodile-type reptile, but it is possible that *Coelophysis* really was a cannibal after all. In 2009, the bones of a baby *Coelophysis* were discovered inside the skull of an adult.

Long tail
Like nearly all dinosaurs that stood on two legs, *Coelophysis* balanced itself with a long tail.

Tough skin
The skin was probably covered by an outer layer of small, protective scales, but it is possible that *Coelophysis* had feathers.

Tagging along
Coelophysis may have hunted in family groups, so the young could learn from their parents.

Strong toes
Coelophysis stood on three toes with stout claws. A fourth, much shorter toe on the inside of the foot was raised off the ground.

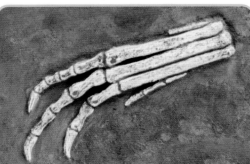

JURASSIC LIFE

For most of the Triassic, the dinosaurs had been just a minor part of the wildlife. But the Jurassic Period saw them evolve into a spectacular variety of forms, ranging from earth-shaking giants to agile, feathered hunters the size of crows. They dominated a world that teemed with all kinds of animal life.

THE JURASSIC WORLD

The Jurassic Period of the Mesozoic Era lasted from 201 to 145 million years ago. During this time the supercontinent Pangaea split in two, changing the climate and allowing lush vegetation to spread over much more of the land. The rich plant growth supported many animals of different kinds, especially the dinosaurs, which became the dominant land animals. They included huge plant-eaters, powerful hunters, and small feathered dinosaurs that were to evolve into the first birds.

North America was almost surrounded by water. The ocean that was to become the north Atlantic was opening up, pushing Laurasia away from Gondwana.

PACIFIC OCEAN

LAURASIA

NORTH AMERICA

An opening rift in Earth's crust extended the Tethys Ocean westwards between North America and Africa, forcing them apart to create the "proto-Atlantic Ocean".

SOUTH AMERICA

GONDWANA

Gondwana was still a massive landmass, with deserts at its heart. The animals here evolved in different ways from those on the northern supercontinent.

CONTINENTS AND OCEANS DURING THE JURASSIC PERIOD, 201–145 MILLION YEARS AGO

TWO SUPERCONTINENTS

The supercontinent Pangaea had started to break up in the Triassic Period, but the Jurassic saw it split into two parts – the northern supercontinent of Laurasia and the southern supercontinent of Gondwana. They were separated by the tropical Tethys Ocean. Many of the continental margins and even interiors were flooded by ocean water, creating thousands of islands.

◎ ENVIRONMENT

The Triassic had ended with a mass extinction, and although it was not as severe as the previous one, this killed off roughly half the species living at the time. Its cause is still not known, but its effects on the environment do not seem to have lasted very long, and life was soon flourishing on land and in the oceans.

Climate
The break-up of Pangaea into two parts had a dramatic effect on the climate. Much of the land was nearer the ocean, so conditions became damper and milder. It was very warm during the Early and Middle Jurassic, but cooler in the Late Jurassic.

AVERAGE GLOBAL TEMPERATURE

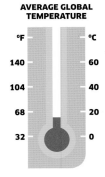

°F	°C
140	60
104	40
68	20
32	0

16.5 °C
(61.7 °F)

Temperate rainforests
Lush, ferny forests were typical of the warm, wet Jurassic. They provided plenty of food for the big plant-eating dinosaurs that evolved at this time.

Tropical islands
The warmer climate made sea levels rise. Parts of the continents became flooded with warm, shallow seas dotted with tropical islands.

ERA		MESOZOIC ERA	
PERIOD	TRIASSIC PERIOD	JURASSIC PERIOD	
MILLIONS OF YEARS AGO	252	201	145

EUROPE

Shallow seas covered many parts of central Laurasia. They turned the higher parts into islands, and may have divided the continent in two.

TETHYS OCEAN

FRICA

Together with its western arm, which was turning into the Atlantic Ocean, the Tethys Ocean separated the northern lands of Laurasia from Gondwana.

ANTARCTICA

ANIMALS

The extinction at the end of the Triassic killed off a lot of animal life, but the survivors were soon flourishing in the warm, moist climate. In particular, the dinosaurs benefited from the destruction of their main reptile competitors and, along with the flying pterosaurs, they soon came to dominate animal life on land.

CYLINDROTEUTHIS, A LARGE BELEMNITE

Marine invertebrates
The shallow shelf seas on the continental margins were rich habitats for marine animals such as ammonites and belemnites (extinct relatives of squid).

Land invertebrates
Insects such as the dragonfly *Libellulium* swarmed in the lush Jurassic forests, along with spiders and other land invertebrates. But there were still no nectar-feeding insects such as bees and butterflies.

LIBELLULIUM

Giant dinosaurs
The dinosaurs diversified into many different types, including giant sauropods like *Barapasaurus*, plated stegosaurs, many powerful meat-eating theropods, and the earliest, primitive birds.

BARAPASAURUS

Marine reptiles
The teeming marine life in the oceans was hunted by voracious ichthyosaurs, plesiosaurs, and other marine reptiles such as *Dakosaurus* – a distant relative of the crocodiles.

DAKOSAURUS

KEY

■ ANCIENT LANDMASS
〜 OUTLINE OF MODERN LANDMASS

Plants

The plant life of the Jurassic was more lush and widespread than in the Triassic, but otherwise it was very similar. There were still no flowering plants, and no grass, but there were vast forests of ginkgos, cycads, and conifers of various kinds.

Ferns
The warm, wet Jurassic climate was ideal for these primitive but very successful plants, which thrived in the shady forests.

Conifers
The landscape was dominated by tall conifer trees. Some were very like the modern Chilean pine, or monkey puzzle.

Cycads
Palm-like cycads were common in the Jurassic forests. We know that they were eaten by many dinosaurs.

Ginkgos
Fossils preserving their fan-shaped leaves show that ginkgos were widespread throughout the Jurassic Period.

TRIASSIC   JURASSIC   CRETACEOUS   **CENOZOIC**

252 MYA   201 MYA   145 MYA   66 MYA   0

Megazostrodon

No bigger than a mouse, this creature was one of the earliest mammals. It lived right at the beginning of the Jurassic, when the dinosaurs were just beginning to dominate life on land.

Megazostrodon was such an early mammal that some experts prefer to see it as a link between true mammals and their cynodont ancestors. However, it had most of the features of true mammals, including fur and a set of teeth that were of different shapes and suitable for different jobs – cutting, piercing, slicing, and chewing. It would have preyed on worms, insects, spiders, and similar small animals, very like a modern shrew.

Like all mammals that can see and hunt in the dark, *Megazostrodon* probably could **not see well in colour.**

Sensitive ears
The structure of its brain shows that *Megazostrodon* had acute hearing.

Large eyes
Megazostrodon had big eyes that may have helped it hunt at night, when most of its enemies were asleep.

Teeth
Its sharp teeth were adapted for seizing small animals and cutting them up.

Most of **what we know about this animal's senses is** based on the **shape of its brain**.

It is likely that this small mammal **dug burrows to hide in** during the day.

The **main enemies** of *Megazostrodon* were probably **small meat-eating dinosaurs**.

45

Furry body
Thick fur helped stop its body heat escaping, saving vital energy.

Low profile
The fur would have been camouflaged to hide this animal from its enemies.

Specialized teeth

Its jaws contained four types of teeth – nipping incisors at the front, pointed canines, and larger premolars and molars for chewing its food.

Incisor   Premolar

Canine   Molar   **LOWER JAW**

Egg-laying mammal

Although a mammal, *Megazostrodon* would have laid leathery-shelled eggs. A few modern mammals do this, including this Australian duck-billed platypus. When the eggs hatched, the tiny, toothless babies would have fed on milk provided by their mother.

Five-toed feet
It had five toes on each foot, with sharp claws for holding down prey.

Low crouch
Megazostrodon crouched low to the ground, ready to spring up and out of trouble.

MAMMAL

MEGAZOSTRODON

When: 199–196 MYA

Habitat: Woodlands

Length: 10 cm (4 in)

Diet: Small animals

Scaly tail
Megazostrodon probably had a naked, scaly tail, very like the tail of a modern rat.

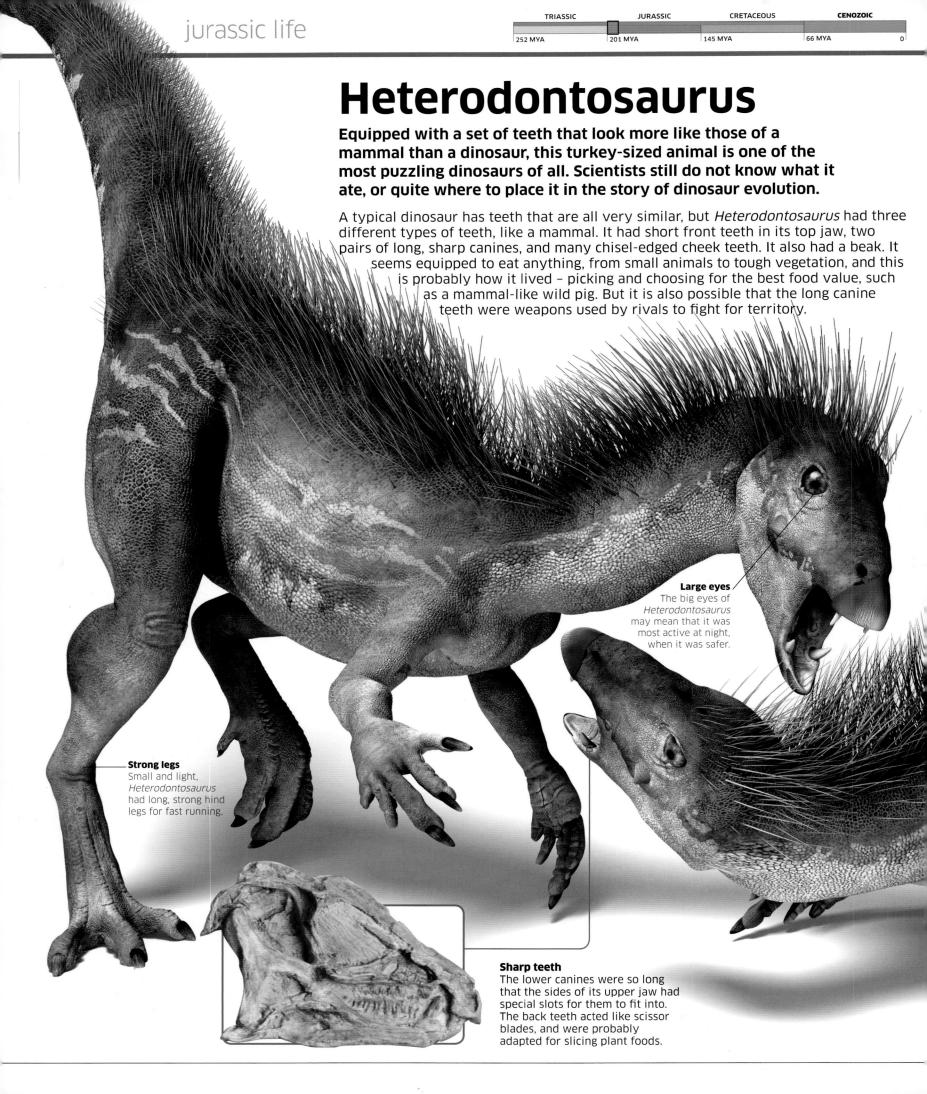

Heterodontosaurus

Equipped with a set of teeth that look more like those of a mammal than a dinosaur, this turkey-sized animal is one of the most puzzling dinosaurs of all. Scientists still do not know what it ate, or quite where to place it in the story of dinosaur evolution.

A typical dinosaur has teeth that are all very similar, but *Heterodontosaurus* had three different types of teeth, like a mammal. It had short front teeth in its top jaw, two pairs of long, sharp canines, and many chisel-edged cheek teeth. It also had a beak. It seems equipped to eat anything, from small animals to tough vegetation, and this is probably how it lived – picking and choosing for the best food value, such as a mammal-like wild pig. But it is also possible that the long canine teeth were weapons used by rivals to fight for territory.

Large eyes
The big eyes of *Heterodontosaurus* may mean that it was most active at night, when it was safer.

Strong legs
Small and light, *Heterodontosaurus* had long, strong hind legs for fast running.

Sharp teeth
The lower canines were so long that the sides of its upper jaw had special slots for them to fit into. The back teeth acted like scissor blades, and were probably adapted for slicing plant foods.

It is possible that this dinosaur used its **long teeth** to **crack into ancient termite nests**.

Heterodontosaurus means **"different toothed lizard".**

47

Some think *Heterodontosaurus* was a hunter that used its sharp teeth to
kill quite big animals
and rip them apart, like a theropod.

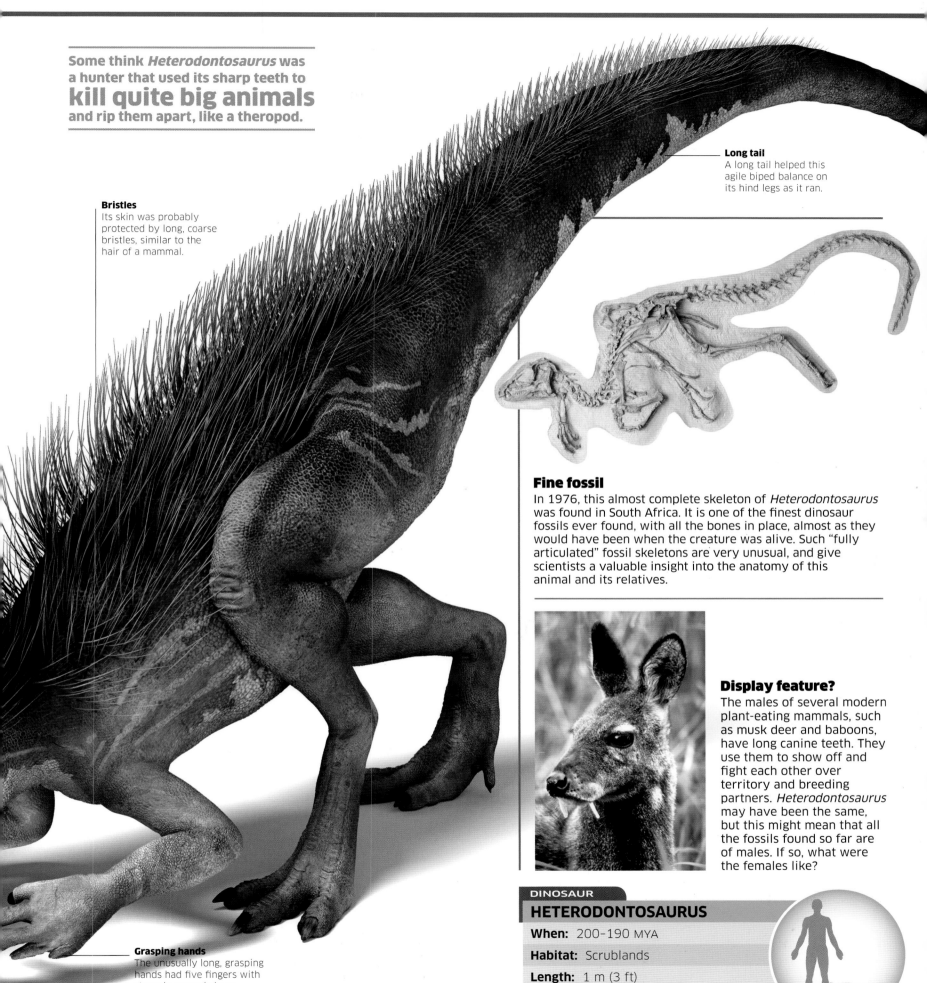

Bristles
Its skin was probably protected by long, coarse bristles, similar to the hair of a mammal.

Long tail
A long tail helped this agile biped balance on its hind legs as it ran.

Fine fossil
In 1976, this almost complete skeleton of *Heterodontosaurus* was found in South Africa. It is one of the finest dinosaur fossils ever found, with all the bones in place, almost as they would have been when the creature was alive. Such "fully articulated" fossil skeletons are very unusual, and give scientists a valuable insight into the anatomy of this animal and its relatives.

Display feature?
The males of several modern plant-eating mammals, such as musk deer and baboons, have long canine teeth. They use them to show off and fight each other over territory and breeding partners. *Heterodontosaurus* may have been the same, but this might mean that all the fossils found so far are of males. If so, what were the females like?

Grasping hands
The unusually long, grasping hands had five fingers with strongly curved claws.

DINOSAUR
HETERODONTOSAURUS
When: 200–190 MYA

Habitat: Scrublands

Length: 1 m (3 ft)

Diet: Plants, tubers, and insects

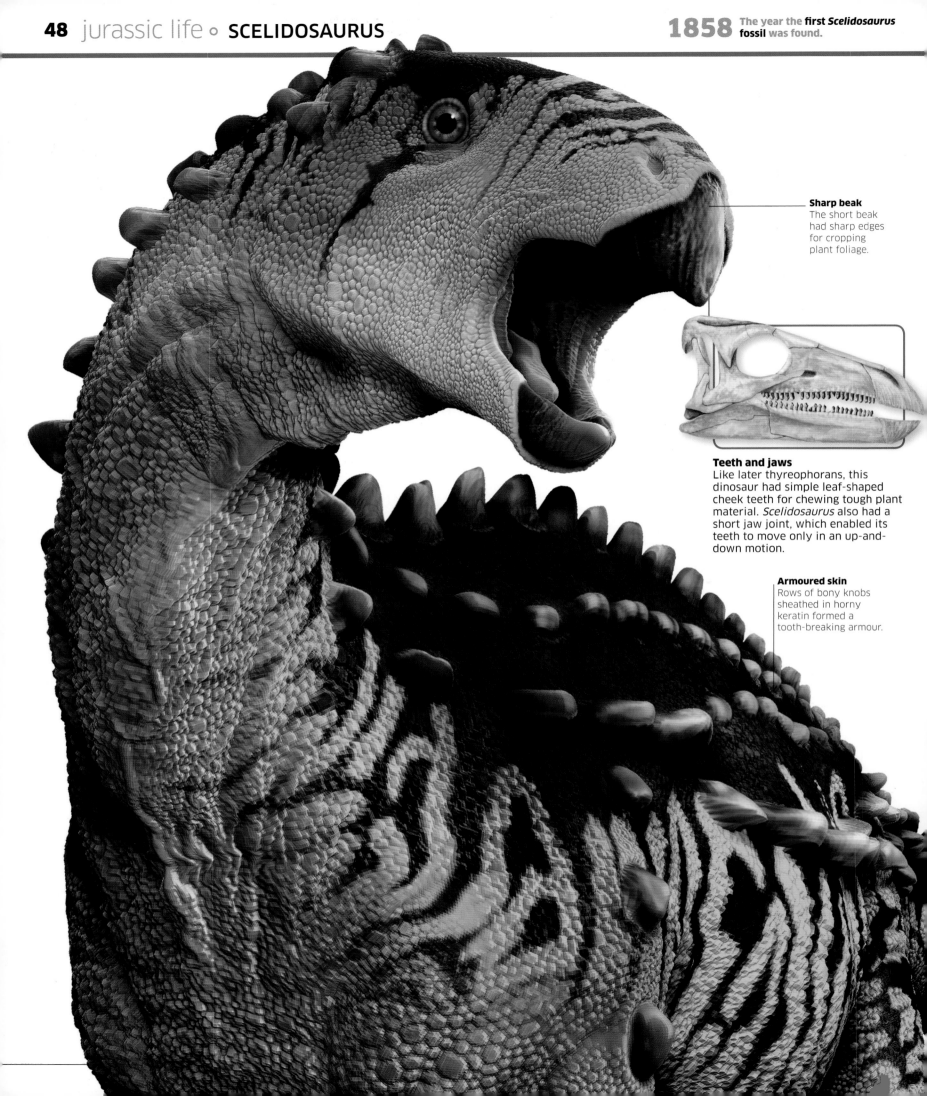

1858 The year the **first** *Scelidosaurus* **fossil** was found.

Sharp beak
The short beak had sharp edges for cropping plant foliage.

Teeth and jaws
Like later thyreophorans, this dinosaur had simple leaf-shaped cheek teeth for chewing tough plant material. *Scelidosaurus* also had a short jaw joint, which enabled its teeth to move only in an up-and-down motion.

Armoured skin
Rows of bony knobs sheathed in horny keratin formed a tooth-breaking armour.

TRIASSIC | JURASSIC | CRETACEOUS | CENOZOIC
252 MYA | 201 MYA | 145 MYA | 66 MYA | 0

This was **one of the first** dinosaurs to be **scientifically described** and named.

49

Scelidosaurus

The chunky, four-footed *Scelidosaurus* was a member of a group of dinosaurs called the thyreophorans – beaked plant-eaters that developed tough, bony defences against hungry, sharp-toothed predators.

In the Early Jurassic, the main enemies of plant-eating dinosaurs were lightly built hunters with sharp-edged teeth, like knife blades. Such teeth were ideal for slicing through soft flesh, but likely to snap if they hit hard bone. This encouraged the evolution of a group of dinosaurs with bony plates, called scutes, embedded in their skin. *Scelidosaurus* was among the earliest of these armoured dinosaurs.

DINOSAUR

SCELIDOSAURUS

When: 196–183 MYA

Habitat: Forests

Length: 4 m (13 ft)

Diet: Low-growing plants

The bones of the first *Scelidosaurus* fossil to be found were largely hidden in hard limestone **for more than 100 years,** until scientists in the 1960s decided to to dissolve the surrounding rock with acid.

Good vision
High-set eyes gave good, all-round vision.

Spiky tail
Sharp-edged bony plates on the tail made a useful defensive weapon.

Blunt claws
The hind feet had four long toes, each tipped with a tough claw. The bony core of each claw has survived as a fossil, but it would have supported a much longer sheath of keratin – the material that your fingernails are made of.

First toe, with claw

Second toe

Third toe

Fourth toe

Fossilized ankle bones

Sturdy front limbs
Its long, strong forelimbs show that this animal walked on all four feet.

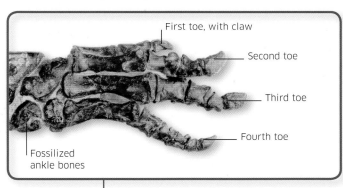

STEGOSAURS

SCUTELLOSAURUS — SCELIDOSAURUS

NODOSAURIDS

ANKYLOSAURS

ANKYLOSAURIDS

Thyreophoran evolution
The first thyreophorans such as *Scutellosaurus* walked on two legs. Over time they became bigger and heavier, and all later ones, *Scelidosaurus* included, walked on all fours. At some point they split into two groups: the stegosaurs with their tall back plates, and the heavily armoured ankylosaurs that included club-tailed ankylosaurids and spiny nodosaurids. Some think that *Scelidosaurus* was an early ankylosaur.

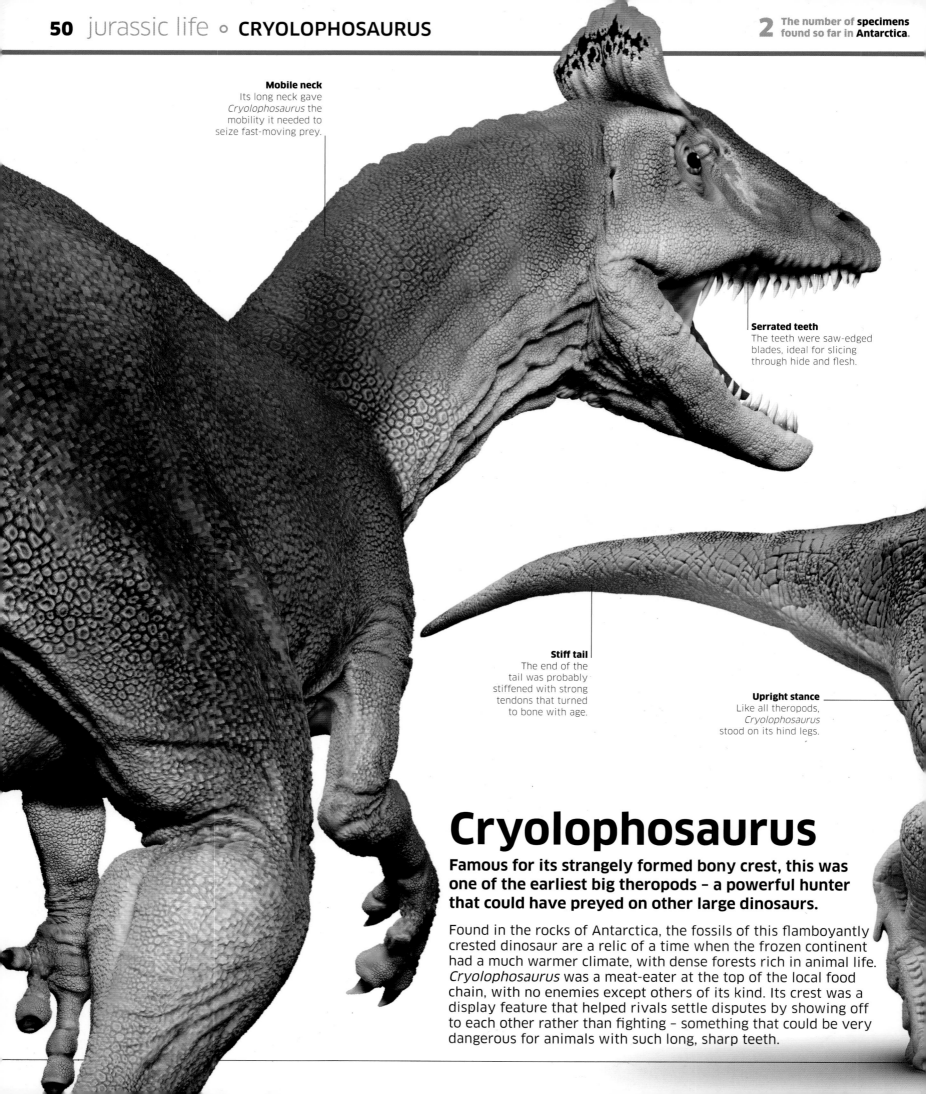

50 jurassic life ○ **CRYOLOPHOSAURUS**

2 The number of **specimens** found so far in **Antarctica**.

Mobile neck
Its long neck gave *Cryolophosaurus* the mobility it needed to seize fast-moving prey.

Serrated teeth
The teeth were saw-edged blades, ideal for slicing through hide and flesh.

Stiff tail
The end of the tail was probably stiffened with strong tendons that turned to bone with age.

Upright stance
Like all theropods, *Cryolophosaurus* stood on its hind legs.

Cryolophosaurus

Famous for its strangely formed bony crest, this was one of the earliest big theropods – a powerful hunter that could have preyed on other large dinosaurs.

Found in the rocks of Antarctica, the fossils of this flamboyantly crested dinosaur are a relic of a time when the frozen continent had a much warmer climate, with dense forests rich in animal life. *Cryolophosaurus* was a meat-eater at the top of the local food chain, with no enemies except others of its kind. Its crest was a display feature that helped rivals settle disputes by showing off to each other rather than fighting – something that could be very dangerous for animals with such long, sharp teeth.

TRIASSIC	JURASSIC	CRETACEOUS	CENOZOIC
252 MYA	201 MYA	145 MYA	66 MYA	0

Only **parts** of this dinosaur have been discovered so far, and the fossils are **difficult to collect** from hard rock.

51

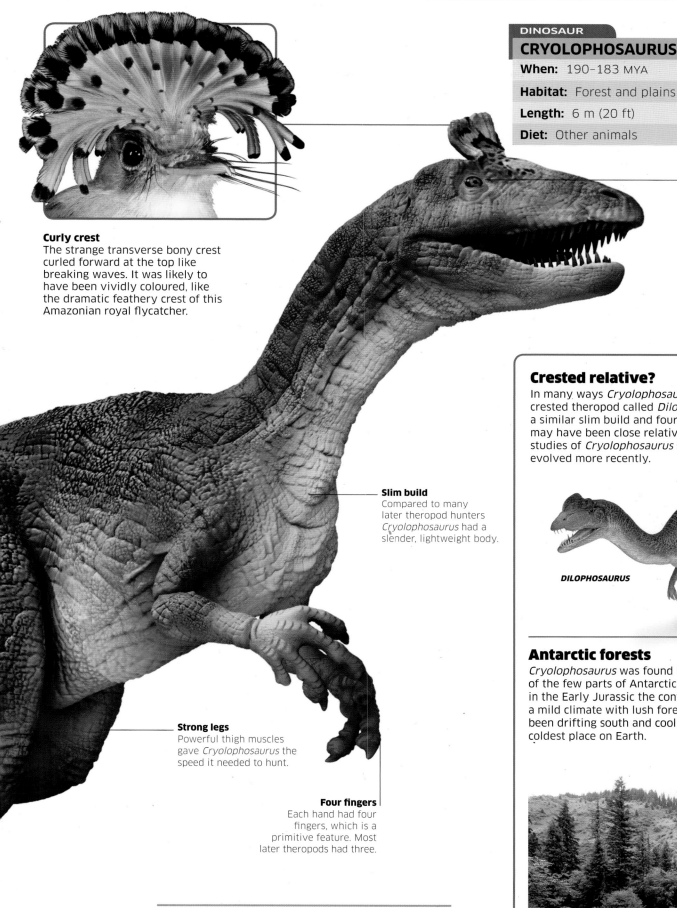

DINOSAUR

CRYOLOPHOSAURUS

When: 190–183 MYA

Habitat: Forest and plains

Length: 6 m (20 ft)

Diet: Other animals

Curly crest
The strange transverse bony crest curled forward at the top like breaking waves. It was likely to have been vividly coloured, like the dramatic feathery crest of this Amazonian royal flycatcher.

Side-facing eyes
Its eyes did not face forwards, so its binocular vision for seeing in depth was not very good.

Slim build
Compared to many later theropod hunters *Cryolophosaurus* had a slender, lightweight body.

Strong legs
Powerful thigh muscles gave *Cryolophosaurus* the speed it needed to hunt.

Four fingers
Each hand had four fingers, which is a primitive feature. Most later theropods had three.

Crested relative?
In many ways *Cryolophosaurus* is very like another crested theropod called *Dilophosaurus*, which had a similar slim build and four-fingered hands. They may have been close relatives, but detailed studies of *Cryolophosaurus* suggest that it evolved more recently.

DILOPHOSAURUS

Antarctic forests
Cryolophosaurus was found in the Transantarctic Mountains in one of the few parts of Antarctica that is not covered by thick ice. But in the Early Jurassic the continent was nearer the equator, and had a mild climate with lush forests like these in western China. It has been drifting south and cooling down ever since, and is now the coldest place on Earth.

The scientists who found the first fossil skull of this animal called it "*Elvisaurus*" because its crest reminded them of rock singer
Elvis Presley's hairstyle.

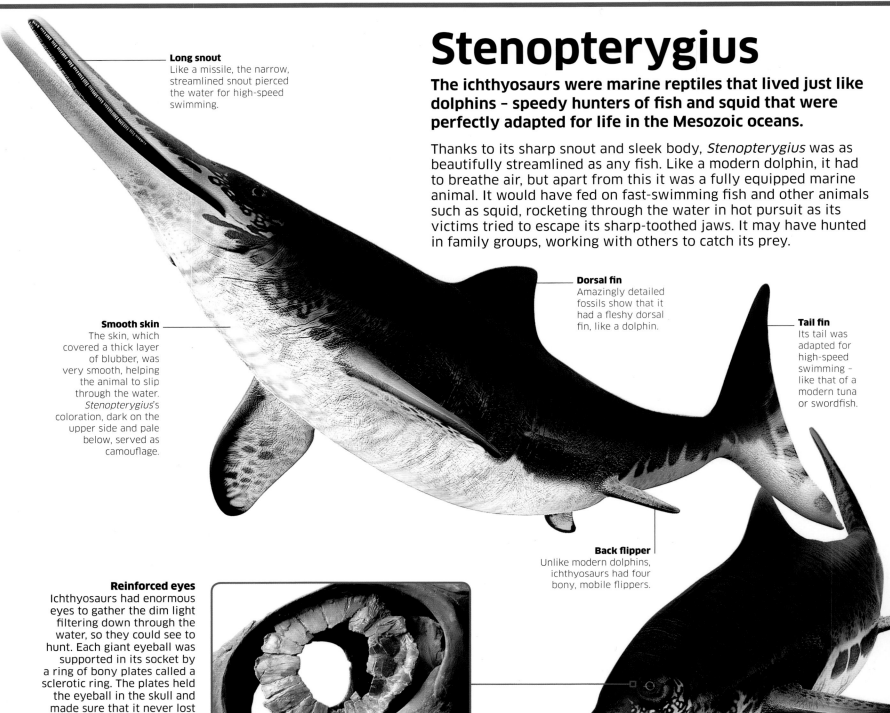

Stenopterygius

The ichthyosaurs were marine reptiles that lived just like dolphins – speedy hunters of fish and squid that were perfectly adapted for life in the Mesozoic oceans.

Thanks to its sharp snout and sleek body, *Stenopterygius* was as beautifully streamlined as any fish. Like a modern dolphin, it had to breathe air, but apart from this it was a fully equipped marine animal. It would have fed on fast-swimming fish and other animals such as squid, rocketing through the water in hot pursuit as its victims tried to escape its sharp-toothed jaws. It may have hunted in family groups, working with others to catch its prey.

Long snout
Like a missile, the narrow, streamlined snout pierced the water for high-speed swimming.

Smooth skin
The skin, which covered a thick layer of blubber, was very smooth, helping the animal to slip through the water. *Stenopterygius*'s coloration, dark on the upper side and pale below, served as camouflage.

Dorsal fin
Amazingly detailed fossils show that it had a fleshy dorsal fin, like a dolphin.

Tail fin
Its tail was adapted for high-speed swimming – like that of a modern tuna or swordfish.

Back flipper
Unlike modern dolphins, ichthyosaurs had four bony, mobile flippers.

Reinforced eyes
Ichthyosaurs had enormous eyes to gather the dim light filtering down through the water, so they could see to hunt. Each giant eyeball was supported in its socket by a ring of bony plates called a sclerotic ring. The plates held the eyeball in the skull and made sure that it never lost its perfect spherical shape, which was vital for clear, undistorted vision.

Live birth

We know that *Stenopterygius* gave birth to live young, because several fossils have been preserved with the remains of young inside their mother. This one even shows how they were born – tail-first, just like baby dolphins, so that they did not drown before they could take their first breath at the surface. Since they were fully marine animals that never returned to land, ichthyosaurs could not lay eggs like most other reptiles. They had to give birth at sea, producing babies that could fend for themselves as soon as they were born.

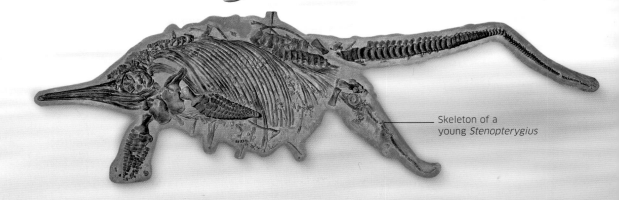

Skeleton of a young *Stenopterygius*

MARINE REPTILE
STENOPTERYGIUS

When: 183–176 MYA

Habitat: Shallow oceans

Length: 2–4 m (6.5–13 ft)

Diet: Fish and squid

Sharp teeth
Slender jaws bristled with small, sharp teeth that were ideal for catching fish.

Front flipper
Each flipper was a modified arm or leg, supported by many bones arranged to form a flat plate. They were mainly used for steering as the ichthyosaur drove itself through the water with its tail.

50 kph (31 mph) – the likely maximum speed that *Stenopterygius* achieved as it surged through the water after its prey.

Monolophosaurus

This powerful hunter was similar to many other theropod dinosaurs except for one feature – the big, knobbly crest capping its snout. The crest's bony core was hollow, so it might have acted as a soundbox that made the dinosaur's calls extra-loud!

Although it lived in the Middle Jurassic, *Monolophosaurus* was an early type of theropod, belonging to a group that evolved after *Coelophysis* (pages 38–39) and its Triassic relatives, but before big Jurassic hunters such as *Allosaurus* (pages 72–73). Only one fossil specimen has been found, in China in 1984, and it has several odd features that make its exact place in the evolution of dinosaurs difficult to pin down. But it must have been an impressive animal, and would have been one of the most feared predators of its time.

Knife-edged teeth
The teeth were meat-slicing blades with sharp, serrated edges.

Long neck
Monolophosaurus had a long, mobile neck with a good range of movement.

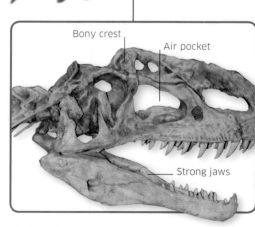

Bony crest

Air pocket

Strong jaws

Skull and crest
The crest was part of the skull, which was taller than usual because of large air pockets in the bones of the snout. The cavities kept its weight down, and may have added resonance to the animal's calls in the same way that the hollow body of a guitar makes its strings sound louder.

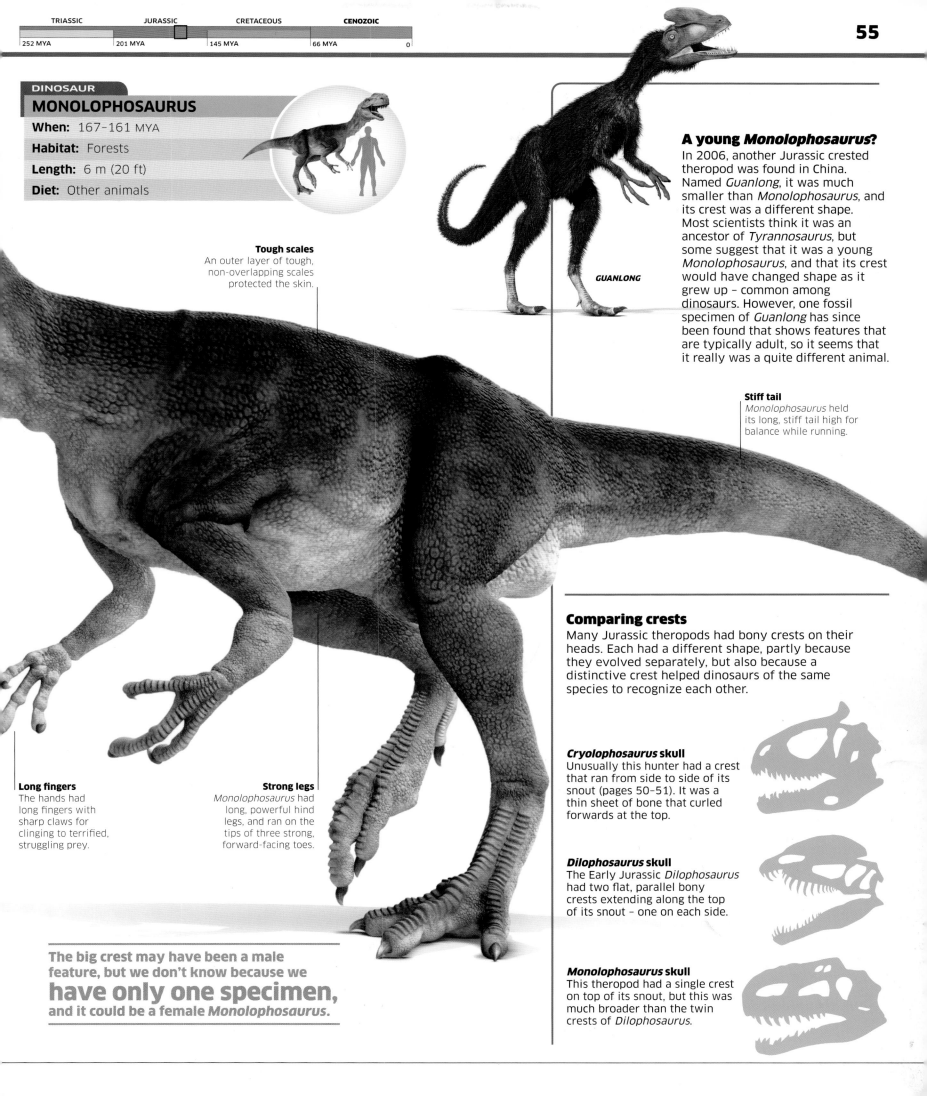

DINOSAUR
MONOLOPHOSAURUS

When: 167–161 MYA

Habitat: Forests

Length: 6 m (20 ft)

Diet: Other animals

A young *Monolophosaurus*?

In 2006, another Jurassic crested theropod was found in China. Named *Guanlong*, it was much smaller than *Monolophosaurus*, and its crest was a different shape. Most scientists think it was an ancestor of *Tyrannosaurus*, but some suggest that it was a young *Monolophosaurus*, and that its crest would have changed shape as it grew up – common among dinosaurs. However, one fossil specimen of *Guanlong* has since been found that shows features that are typically adult, so it seems that it really was a quite different animal.

GUANLONG

Tough scales
An outer layer of tough, non-overlapping scales protected the skin.

Stiff tail
Monolophosaurus held its long, stiff tail high for balance while running.

Comparing crests

Many Jurassic theropods had bony crests on their heads. Each had a different shape, partly because they evolved separately, but also because a distinctive crest helped dinosaurs of the same species to recognize each other.

Long fingers
The hands had long fingers with sharp claws for clinging to terrified, struggling prey.

Strong legs
Monolophosaurus had long, powerful hind legs, and ran on the tips of three strong, forward-facing toes.

***Cryolophosaurus* skull**
Unusually this hunter had a crest that ran from side to side of its snout (pages 50–51). It was a thin sheet of bone that curled forwards at the top.

***Dilophosaurus* skull**
The Early Jurassic *Dilophosaurus* had two flat, parallel bony crests extending along the top of its snout – one on each side.

The big crest may have been a male feature, but we don't know because we
have only one specimen,
and it could be a female *Monolophosaurus*.

***Monolophosaurus* skull**
This theropod had a single crest on top of its snout, but this was much broader than the twin crests of *Dilophosaurus*.

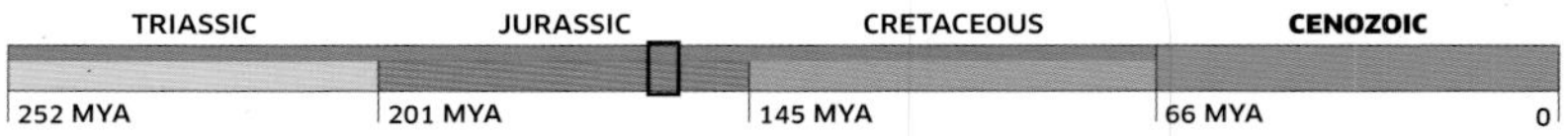

Liopleurodon

Some of the most fearsome predators that have ever existed lived not on land, but in the oceans. They were the pliosaurs – true sea monsters with massive, immensely strong jaws.

Pliosaurs, such as *Liopleurodon*, were big-jawed relatives of long-necked plesiosaurs such as *Albertonectes* (pages 110–111). They swam in the same way, driving themselves through the water with four flippers, but pliosaurs were specialized for hunting big animals, including their plesiosaur relatives. *Liopleurodon* was probably an ambush killer that used its speed to surge out of the depths, seize its prey in its teeth and, if necessary, rip it to pieces.

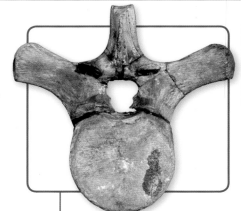

Back bones
The spine of a *Liopleurodon* was made up of massive vertebrae (back bones), the size of dinner plates.

Tail
The tail was quite short, and probably played no part in driving the animal through the water.

Swimming style
Liopleurodon probably used its four long flippers to "fly" though the water, beating them up and down rather like a modern sea turtle. It would have beaten them together, sweeping both pairs down then raising them. Experiments show that this could have given the animal terrific acceleration for pursuing and catching its prey.

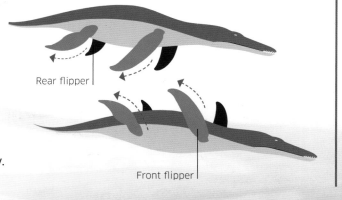

Rear flipper

Front flipper

Swift swimmer
A layer of fat beneath the smooth, scaly skin improved streamlining for more efficient swimming.

1.5 m (5 ft) – the length of the largest *Liopleurodon* skull found so far. Most of that length is jaw, studded with huge, very deep-rooted, spike-shaped teeth.

15 m (49.25 ft) – the **length of the biggest-known pliosaurs**, which had skulls up to 2.4 m (7.75 ft) long.

The **swimming technique of pliosaurs** was tested by building a **swimming robot**.

57

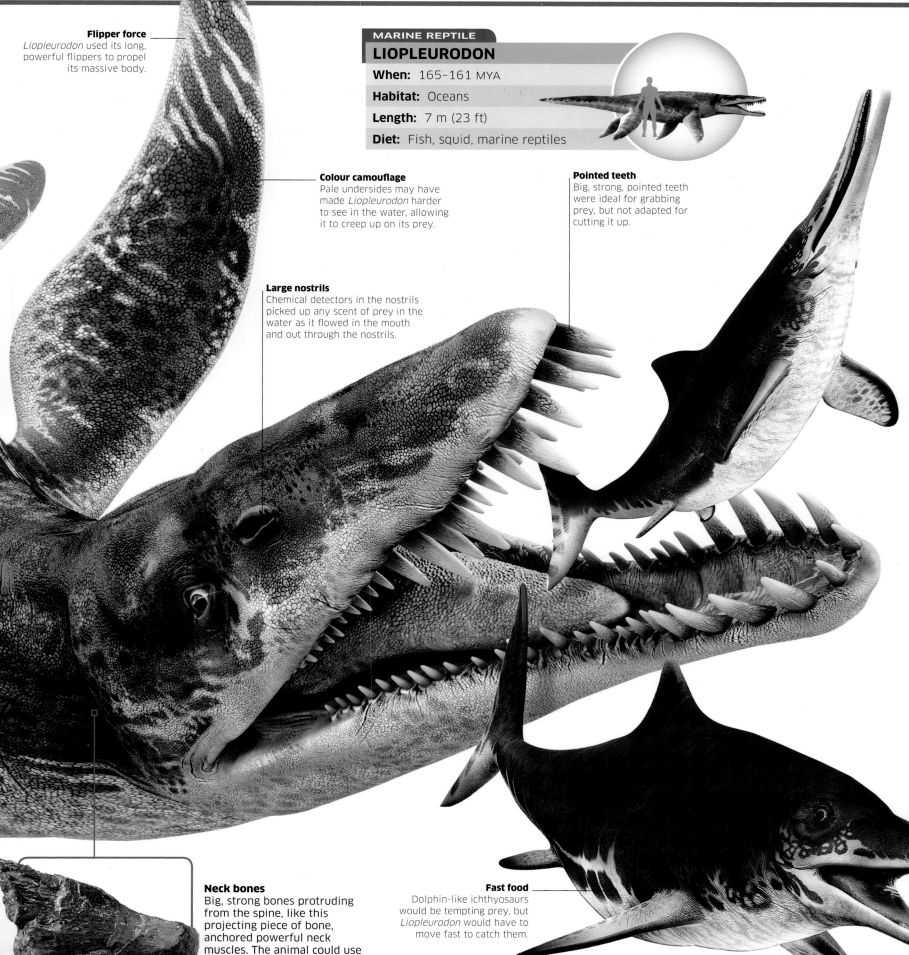

Flipper force
Liopleurodon used its long, powerful flippers to propel its massive body.

MARINE REPTILE
LIOPLEURODON
When: 165–161 MYA
Habitat: Oceans
Length: 7 m (23 ft)
Diet: Fish, squid, marine reptiles

Colour camouflage
Pale undersides may have made *Liopleurodon* harder to see in the water, allowing it to creep up on its prey.

Pointed teeth
Big, strong, pointed teeth were ideal for grabbing prey, but not adapted for cutting it up.

Large nostrils
Chemical detectors in the nostrils picked up any scent of prey in the water as it flowed in the mouth and out through the nostrils.

Neck bones
Big, strong bones protruding from the spine, like this projecting piece of bone, anchored powerful neck muscles. The animal could use these muscles to swing its jaws from side to side to tear its victims apart.

Fast food
Dolphin-like ichthyosaurs would be tempting prey, but *Liopleurodon* would have to move fast to catch them.

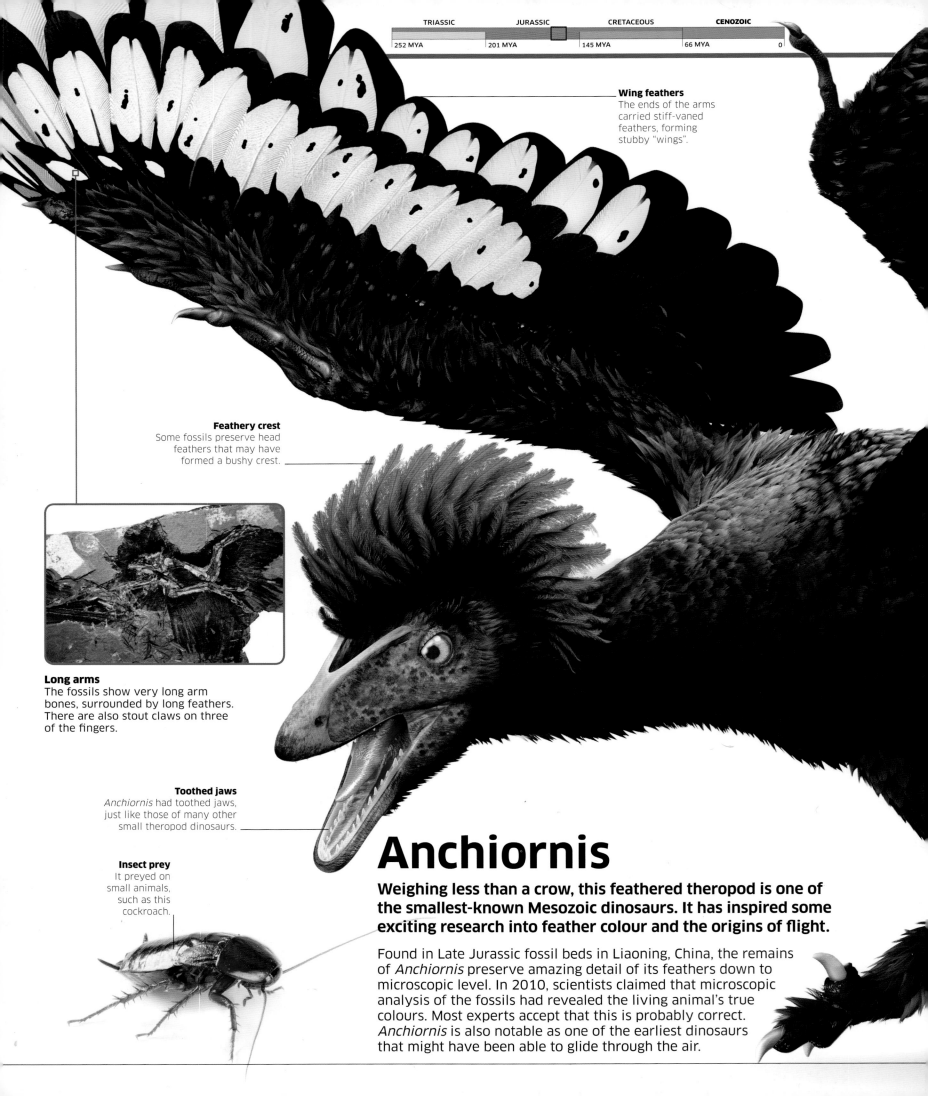

Wing feathers
The ends of the arms carried stiff-vaned feathers, forming stubby "wings".

Feathery crest
Some fossils preserve head feathers that may have formed a bushy crest.

Long arms
The fossils show very long arm bones, surrounded by long feathers. There are also stout claws on three of the fingers.

Toothed jaws
Anchiornis had toothed jaws, just like those of many other small theropod dinosaurs.

Insect prey
It preyed on small animals, such as this cockroach.

Anchiornis

Weighing less than a crow, this feathered theropod is one of the smallest-known Mesozoic dinosaurs. It has inspired some exciting research into feather colour and the origins of flight.

Found in Late Jurassic fossil beds in Liaoning, China, the remains of *Anchiornis* preserve amazing detail of its feathers down to microscopic level. In 2010, scientists claimed that microscopic analysis of the fossils had revealed the living animal's true colours. Most experts accept that this is probably correct. *Anchiornis* is also notable as one of the earliest dinosaurs that might have been able to glide through the air.

The name *Anchiornis* means "near bird", which is a good description of its nature.

59

DINOSAUR

ANCHIORNIS

When: 161–155 MYA

Habitat: Woodlands

Length: 50 cm (20 in)

Diet: Small animals

255
The number of fossil specimens of *Anchiornis* held in Chinese museums.

Getting down to details

The fossils of *Anchiornis* are amazingly detailed, but they have been crushed and flattened by the fossilization process. This makes the details hard to interpret, and scientists are still trying to discover what some of them may mean.

Glider
Anchiornis may have used its short feathered wings to glide or parachute to the ground, much like the flying squirrel today.

Fully feathered legs
The fringe of stiff-vaned feathers on its legs may have helped *Anchiornis* glide.

Sharp claws
The feathered feet had sharp-clawed toes similar to those of *Velociraptor* (pages 108–109).

Colour clues
Fossilized microscopic structures called melanosomes (left) indicate that *Anchiornis* was likely to have been mostly grey and black, with reddish head feathers and white wing feathers that featured black specks.

ALLOSAURUS ATTACK

Peacefully browsing on delicious, crunchy pine needles, a *Stegosaurus* is not aware of the stealthy approach of a hungry, heavily armed *Allosaurus* until it is almost too late.

Bursting from the cover of the trees that edge the lake on this Jurassic floodplain, the *Allosaurus* launches its attack, startling a nearby *Archaeopteryx* as well as the stegosaur. But *Stegosaurus* is no soft target. Its long tail spikes are lethal weapons, and it knows how to use them. If the hunter puts a foot wrong, the next few minutes could be its last.

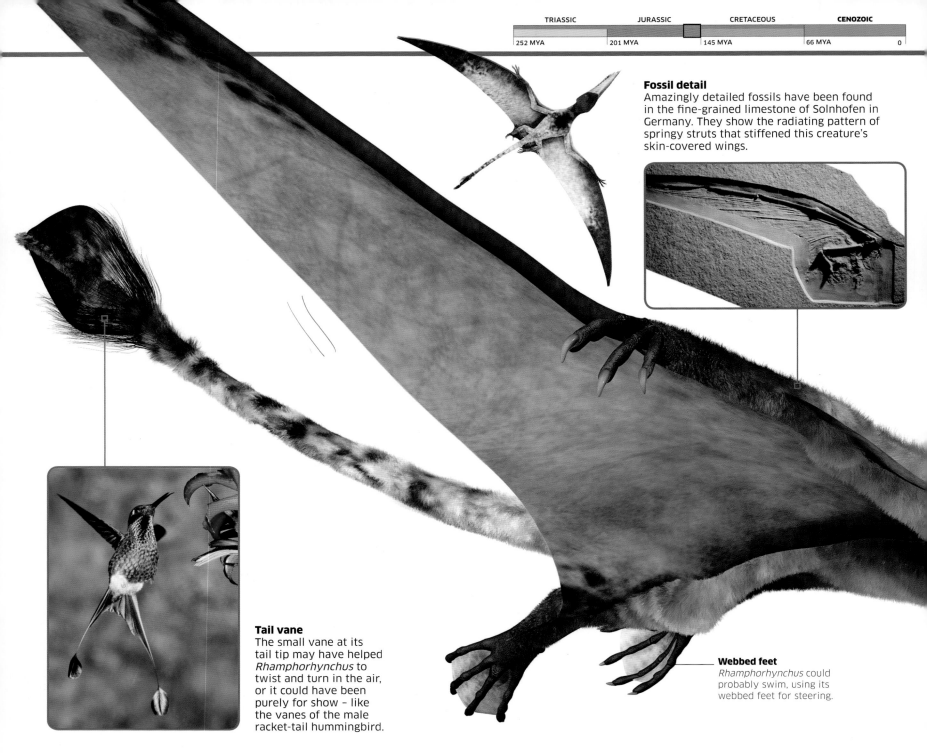

Fossil detail
Amazingly detailed fossils have been found in the fine-grained limestone of Solnhofen in Germany. They show the radiating pattern of springy struts that stiffened this creature's skin-covered wings.

Tail vane
The small vane at its tail tip may have helped *Rhamphorhynchus* to twist and turn in the air, or it could have been purely for show – like the vanes of the male racket-tail hummingbird.

Webbed feet
Rhamphorhynchus could probably swim, using its webbed feet for steering.

Fatal attraction
We know that *Rhamphorhynchus* preyed on fish because some of its fossils have fish bones in their stomachs. One contains a fish nearly as long as its own body, which shows that it always swallowed its food whole – even very big prey. But some fish fought back, or even tried to eat the pterosaur. This amazing fossil shows a *Rhamphorhynchus* (left) with its wing in the jaws of a big, spear-nosed fish called *Aspidorhynchus* (right). As they both sank, the pterosaur drowned, and the fish became entangled in its prey and was unable to pull itself free, so it died too.

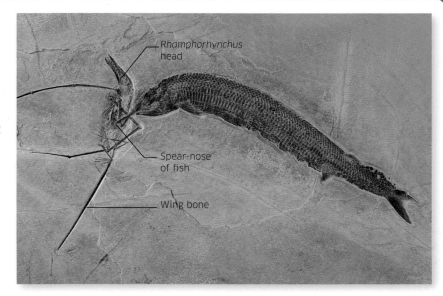

Rhamphorhynchus head

Spear-nose of fish

Wing bone

100 or more fossil specimens
of *Rhamphorhynchus* have been found, so scientists know more about it than almost any other pterosaur.

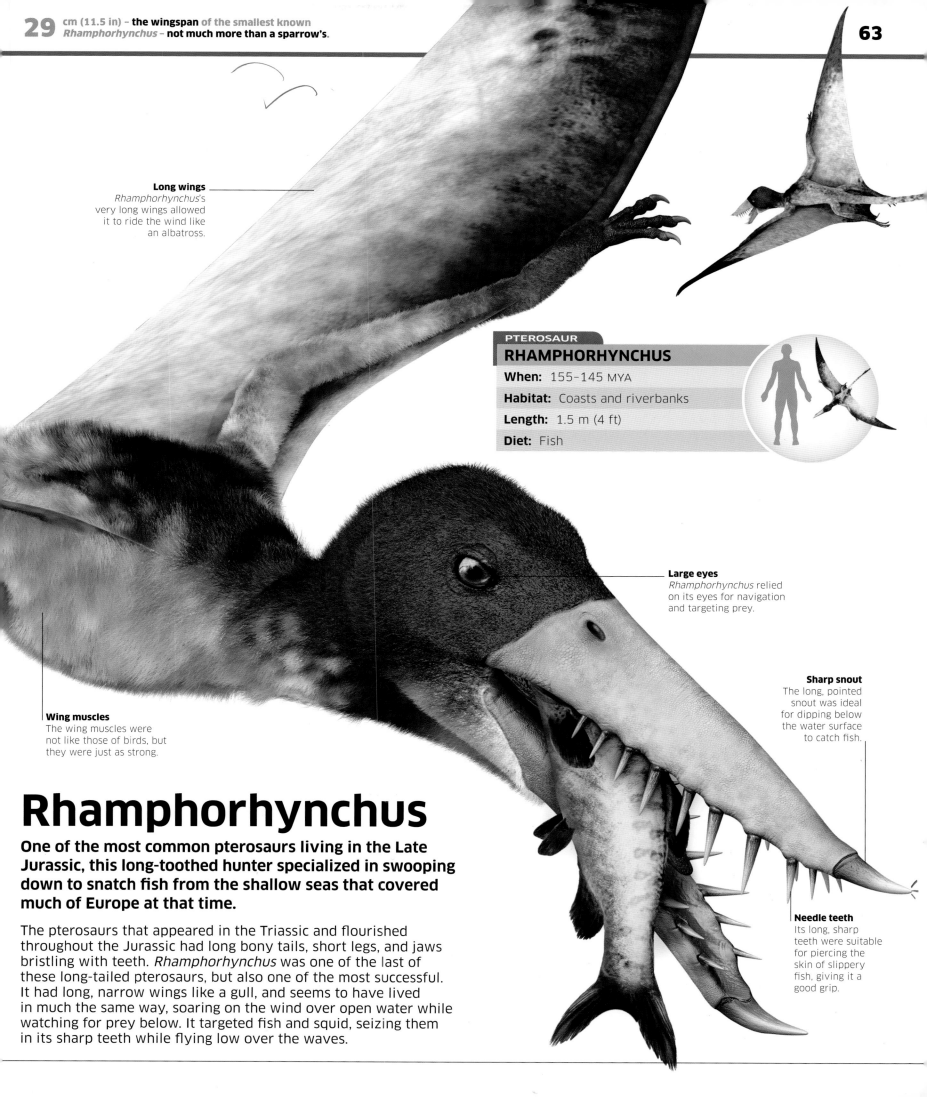

Long wings
Rhamphorhynchus's very long wings allowed it to ride the wind like an albatross.

PTEROSAUR
RHAMPHORHYNCHUS

When: 155–145 MYA

Habitat: Coasts and riverbanks

Length: 1.5 m (4 ft)

Diet: Fish

Large eyes
Rhamphorhynchus relied on its eyes for navigation and targeting prey.

Sharp snout
The long, pointed snout was ideal for dipping below the water surface to catch fish.

Wing muscles
The wing muscles were not like those of birds, but they were just as strong.

Rhamphorhynchus

One of the most common pterosaurs living in the Late Jurassic, this long-toothed hunter specialized in swooping down to snatch fish from the shallow seas that covered much of Europe at that time.

The pterosaurs that appeared in the Triassic and flourished throughout the Jurassic had long bony tails, short legs, and jaws bristling with teeth. *Rhamphorhynchus* was one of the last of these long-tailed pterosaurs, but also one of the most successful. It had long, narrow wings like a gull, and seems to have lived in much the same way, soaring on the wind over open water while watching for prey below. It targeted fish and squid, seizing them in its sharp teeth while flying low over the waves.

Needle teeth
Its long, sharp teeth were suitable for piercing the skin of slippery fish, giving it a good grip.

TRIASSIC	JURASSIC		CRETACEOUS	CENOZOIC	
252 MYA	201 MYA		145 MYA	66 MYA	0

Kentrosaurus

A smaller relative of the famous *Stegosaurus*, this Late Jurassic dinosaur was even more spectacular, thanks to its dramatic double row of dorsal plates and long, sharp spines.

By the Middle Jurassic, the thyreophoran dinosaurs such as *Scelidosaurus* (pages 48–49) had split into two distinct groups – the heavily armoured ankylosaurs, and the stegosaurs, with their bony dorsal plates and spikes. *Kentrosaurus* was one of the spikiest of these stegosaurs. Its fossils have been found in the Late Jurassic rocks of Tanzania in East Africa. Long, sharp spines must have been a very effective defence, and its spiky tail was a formidable weapon. But the plates and spines were also very impressive display features.

Dorsal plates
The plates and spikes were bony osteoderms embedded in the skin, and not attached to the skeleton. In this restored fossil they are supported by strong metal rods.

Small head
Like all stegosaurs, *Kentrosaurus* had a small skull, with a tiny space for its brain. This dinosaur gathered leafy food with a sharp beak, slicing it finely with leaf-shaped teeth to make it easier to digest.

Although *Kentrosaurus* weighed as much as a horse, it had a plum-sized brain.

Neck
A flexible neck gave its head plenty of mobility for feeding.

Front legs
This animal is in a defensive crouch, but would normally have stood up straight.

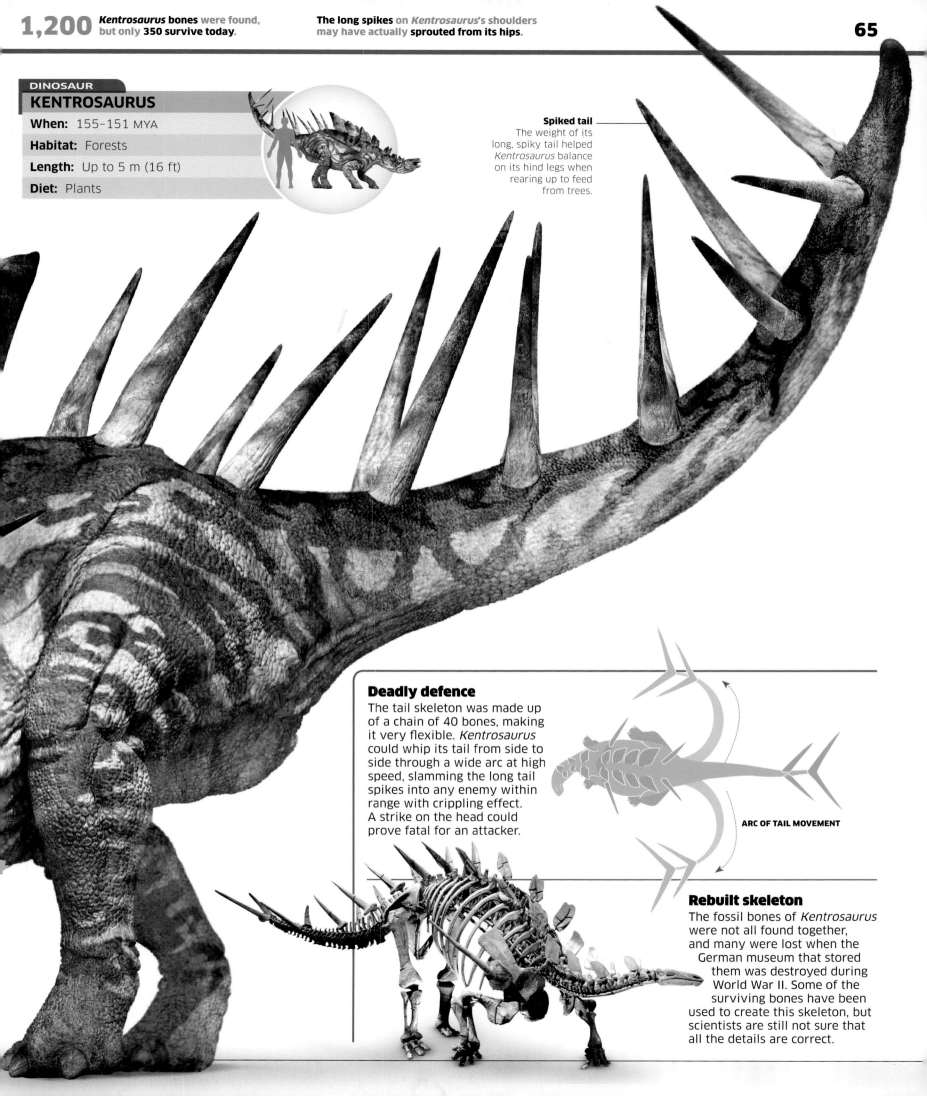

1,200 *Kentrosaurus* **bones** were found, but only **350 survive today**.

The long spikes on *Kentrosaurus*'s shoulders may have actually **sprouted from its hips**.

65

DINOSAUR
KENTROSAURUS

When: 155–151 MYA

Habitat: Forests

Length: Up to 5 m (16 ft)

Diet: Plants

Spiked tail
The weight of its long, spiky tail helped *Kentrosaurus* balance on its hind legs when rearing up to feed from trees.

Deadly defence
The tail skeleton was made up of a chain of 40 bones, making it very flexible. *Kentrosaurus* could whip its tail from side to side through a wide arc at high speed, slamming the long tail spikes into any enemy within range with crippling effect. A strike on the head could prove fatal for an attacker.

ARC OF TAIL MOVEMENT

Rebuilt skeleton
The fossil bones of *Kentrosaurus* were not all found together, and many were lost when the German museum that stored them was destroyed during World War II. Some of the surviving bones have been used to create this skeleton, but scientists are still not sure that all the details are correct.

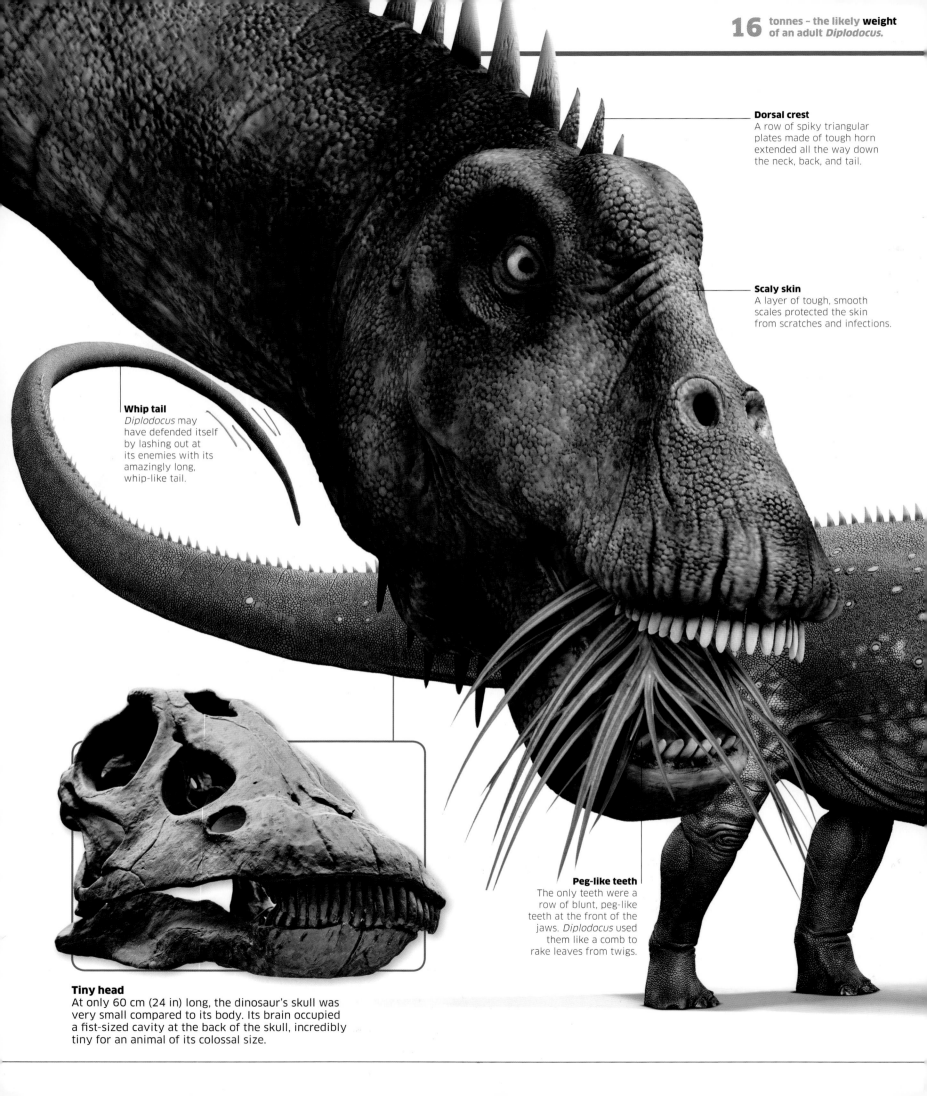

Dorsal crest
A row of spiky triangular plates made of tough horn extended all the way down the neck, back, and tail.

Scaly skin
A layer of tough, smooth scales protected the skin from scratches and infections.

Whip tail
Diplodocus may have defended itself by lashing out at its enemies with its amazingly long, whip-like tail.

Peg-like teeth
The only teeth were a row of blunt, peg-like teeth at the front of the jaws. *Diplodocus* used them like a comb to rake leaves from twigs.

Tiny head
At only 60 cm (24 in) long, the dinosaur's skull was very small compared to its body. Its brain occupied a fist-sized cavity at the back of the skull, incredibly tiny for an animal of its colossal size.

TRIASSIC	JURASSIC	CRETACEOUS	CENOZOIC
252 MYA	201 MYA	145 MYA	66 MYA	0

356 The **number of bones** in one *Diplodocus* skeleton.

67

DINOSAUR
DIPLODOCUS

When: 154–150 MYA

Habitat: Plains with tall trees

Length: 33 m (108 ft)

Diet: Tree foliage

Diplodocus

Unbelievably long though this dinosaur may be, it was not the biggest sauropod that ever lived. Several other kinds were even bigger. But *Diplodocus* skeletons are the most complete giant sauropod skeletons yet discovered.

The long-necked sauropods that evolved during the Jurassic Period were gigantic plant-eaters, specialized for gathering leaves from the tops of tall trees. These leaves were tough and woody, like pine needles, making them hard to digest, but the massive bodies of sauropods contained huge digestive systems that processed the leaves for a long time to extract nutrients. This worked so well that *Diplodocus* did not need to chew the leaves at all, increasing the amount it could eat.

Long neck
The long neck was supported by at least 15 vertebrae. *Diplodocus* probably held its neck at a 45-degree angle, but could raise it higher to browse in the treetops.

Small head
Big eyes and a long, flat lower jaw are the main features of the comparatively small head.

Despite its immense weight, *Diplodocus* could
rear up on its hind legs
to reach the highest branches.

Weight-bearing legs
The weight of the body was supported by four thick, pillar-like legs, resembling those of elephants.

Thumb claw
Each front foot had a single large claw.

Incredible length
The biggest complete *Diplodocus* skeleton is an amazing 27 m (88 ft) in length. However, other *Diplodocus* bones have been found that must have belonged to even bigger animals which could have been 33 m (108 ft) long. That's the length of three US school buses!

DIPLODOCUS

US SCHOOL BUS 11 M (36 FT) LONG

0	11 M (36 FT)	22 M (72 FT)	33 M (108 FT)

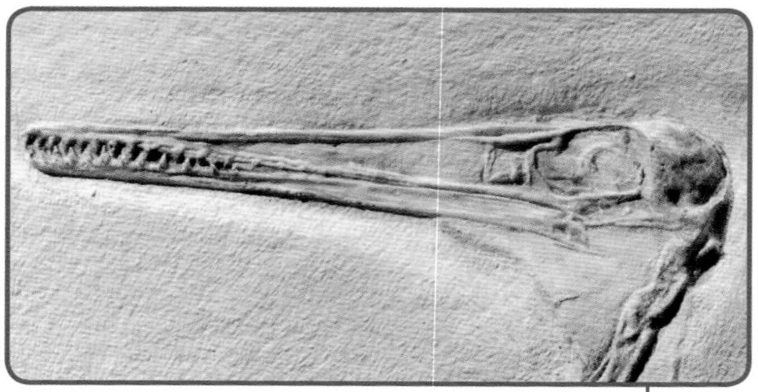

The name *Pterodactyl* is Greek **for "wing finger",** after the elongated fourth finger that supported each wing.

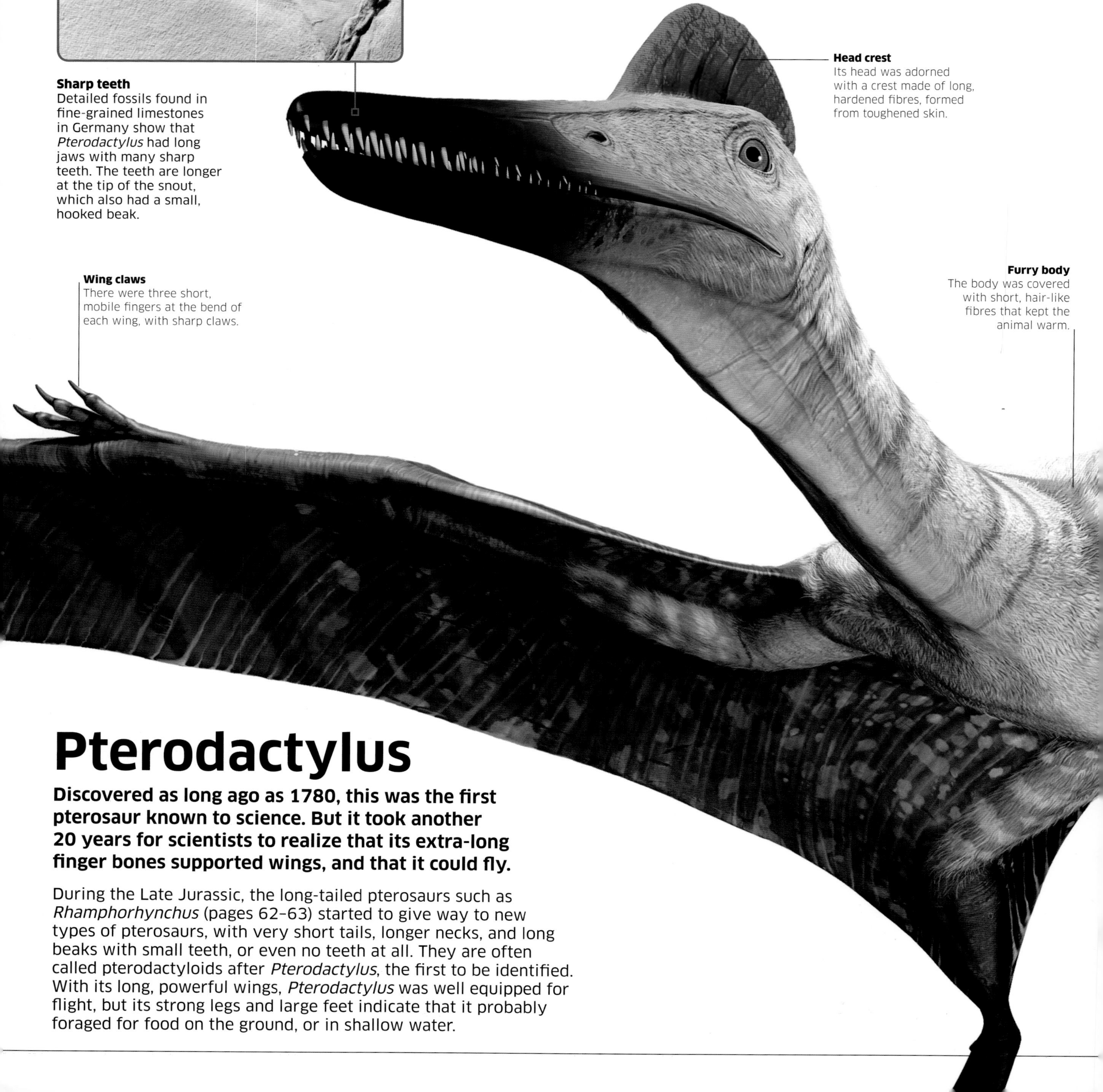

Sharp teeth
Detailed fossils found in fine-grained limestones in Germany show that *Pterodactylus* had long jaws with many sharp teeth. The teeth are longer at the tip of the snout, which also had a small, hooked beak.

Head crest
Its head was adorned with a crest made of long, hardened fibres, formed from toughened skin.

Wing claws
There were three short, mobile fingers at the bend of each wing, with sharp claws.

Furry body
The body was covered with short, hair-like fibres that kept the animal warm.

Pterodactylus

Discovered as long ago as 1780, this was the first pterosaur known to science. But it took another 20 years for scientists to realize that its extra-long finger bones supported wings, and that it could fly.

During the Late Jurassic, the long-tailed pterosaurs such as *Rhamphorhynchus* (pages 62–63) started to give way to new types of pterosaurs, with very short tails, longer necks, and long beaks with small teeth, or even no teeth at all. They are often called pterodactyloids after *Pterodactylus*, the first to be identified. With its long, powerful wings, *Pterodactylus* was well equipped for flight, but its strong legs and large feet indicate that it probably foraged for food on the ground, or in shallow water.

27 The number of good **fossil specimens** of *Pterodactylus* **known to science**.

69

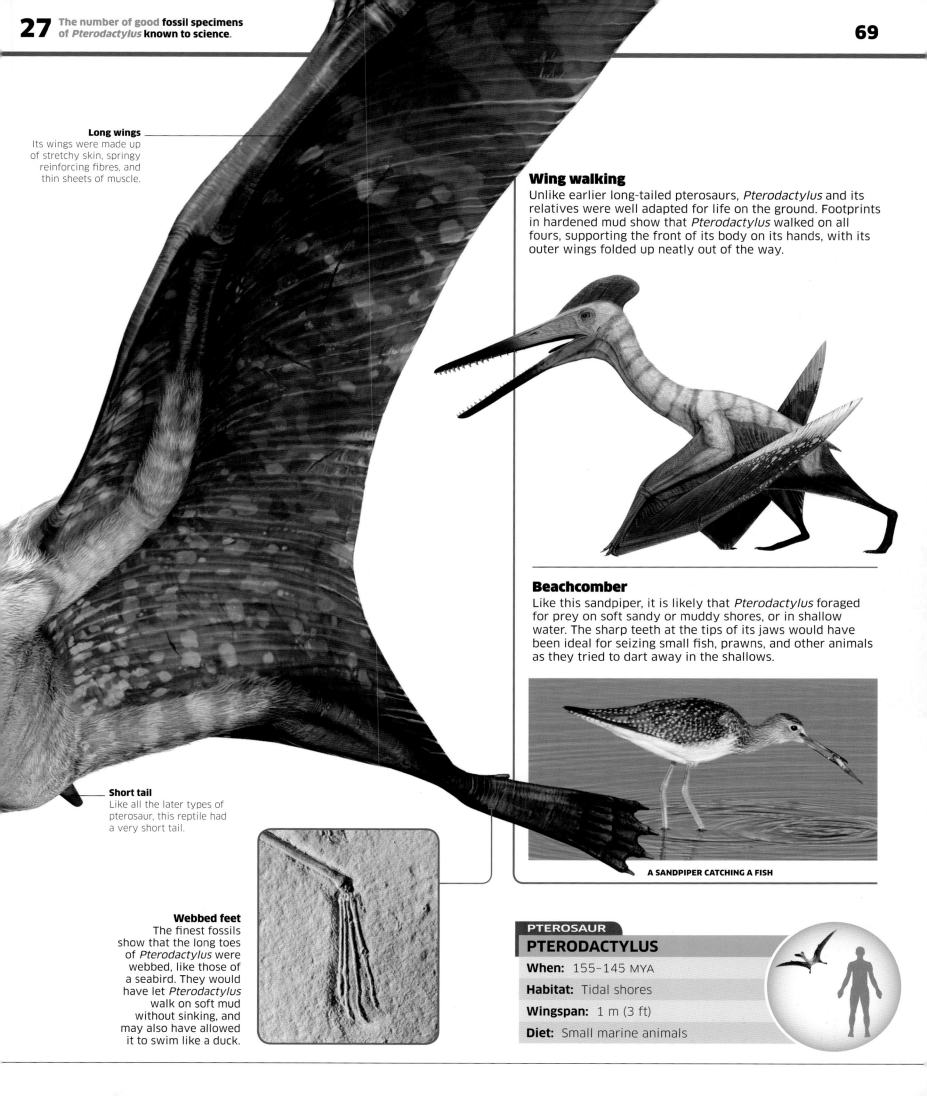

Long wings
Its wings were made up of stretchy skin, springy reinforcing fibres, and thin sheets of muscle.

Wing walking
Unlike earlier long-tailed pterosaurs, *Pterodactylus* and its relatives were well adapted for life on the ground. Footprints in hardened mud show that *Pterodactylus* walked on all fours, supporting the front of its body on its hands, with its outer wings folded up neatly out of the way.

Beachcomber
Like this sandpiper, it is likely that *Pterodactylus* foraged for prey on soft sandy or muddy shores, or in shallow water. The sharp teeth at the tips of its jaws would have been ideal for seizing small fish, prawns, and other animals as they tried to dart away in the shallows.

A SANDPIPER CATCHING A FISH

Short tail
Like all the later types of pterosaur, this reptile had a very short tail.

Webbed feet
The finest fossils show that the long toes of *Pterodactylus* were webbed, like those of a seabird. They would have let *Pterodactylus* walk on soft mud without sinking, and may also have allowed it to swim like a duck.

PTEROSAUR
PTERODACTYLUS

When: 155–145 MYA

Habitat: Tidal shores

Wingspan: 1 m (3 ft)

Diet: Small marine animals

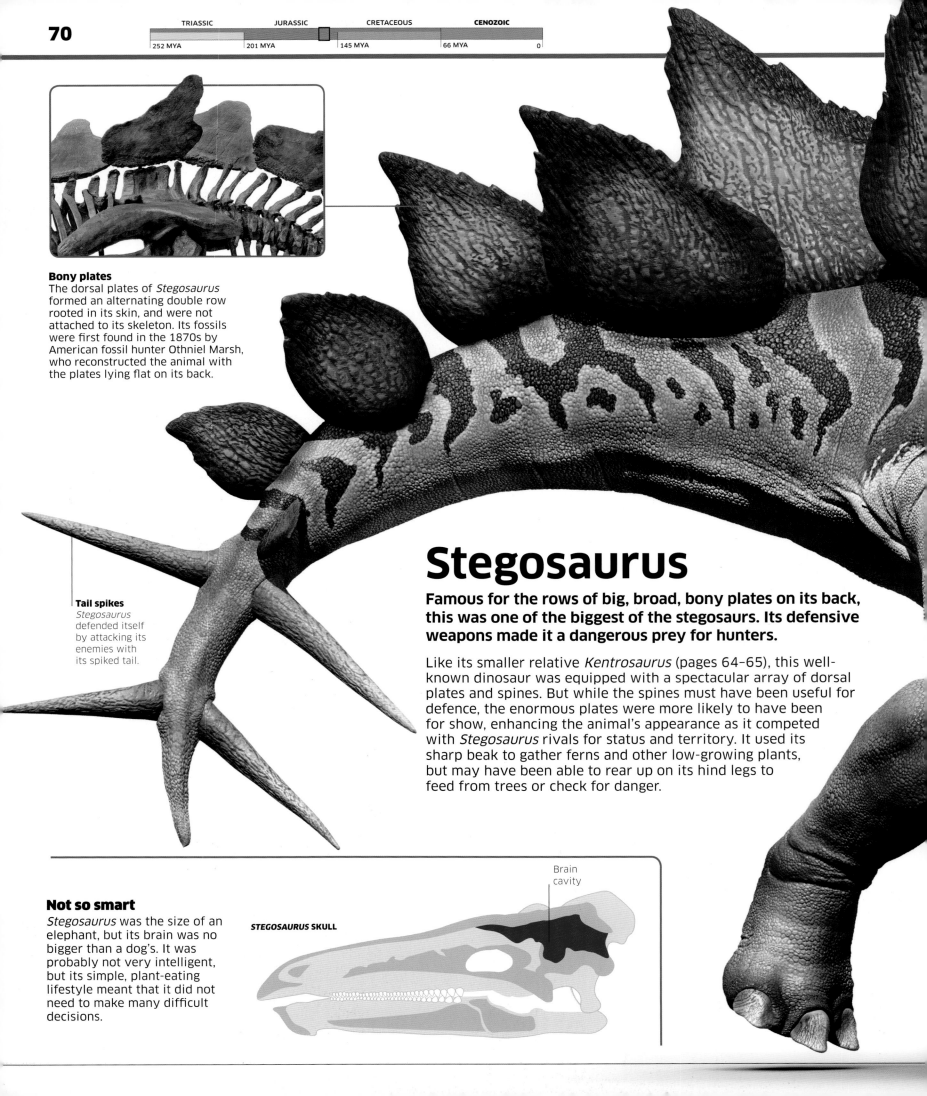

Bony plates

The dorsal plates of *Stegosaurus* formed an alternating double row rooted in its skin, and were not attached to its skeleton. Its fossils were first found in the 1870s by American fossil hunter Othniel Marsh, who reconstructed the animal with the plates lying flat on its back.

Tail spikes

Stegosaurus defended itself by attacking its enemies with its spiked tail.

Stegosaurus

Famous for the rows of big, broad, bony plates on its back, this was one of the biggest of the stegosaurs. Its defensive weapons made it a dangerous prey for hunters.

Like its smaller relative *Kentrosaurus* (pages 64–65), this well-known dinosaur was equipped with a spectacular array of dorsal plates and spines. But while the spines must have been useful for defence, the enormous plates were more likely to have been for show, enhancing the animal's appearance as it competed with *Stegosaurus* rivals for status and territory. It used its sharp beak to gather ferns and other low-growing plants, but may have been able to rear up on its hind legs to feed from trees or check for danger.

Not so smart

Stegosaurus was the size of an elephant, but its brain was no bigger than a dog's. It was probably not very intelligent, but its simple, plant-eating lifestyle meant that it did not need to make many difficult decisions.

STEGOSAURUS SKULL

Brain cavity

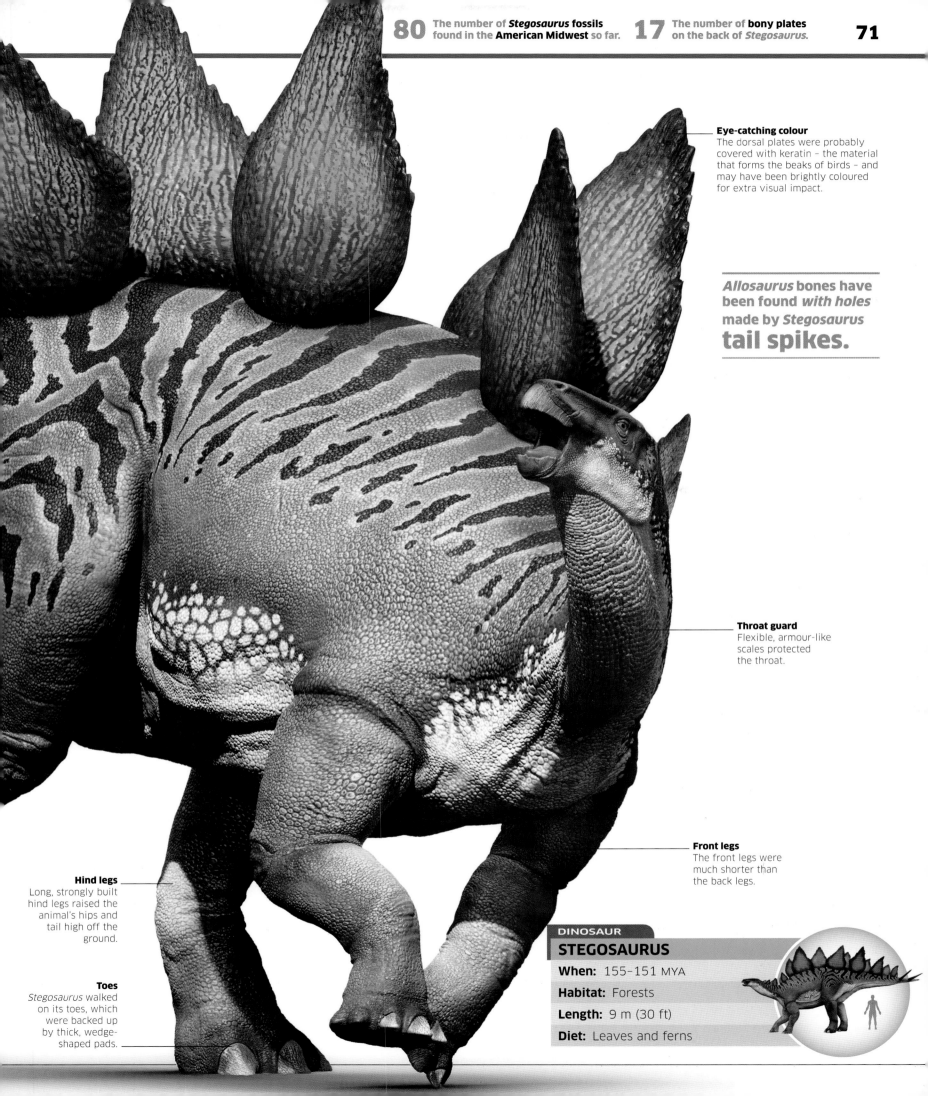

80 The number of *Stegosaurus* fossils found in the **American Midwest** so far.

17 The number of **bony plates** on the back of *Stegosaurus*.

71

Eye-catching colour
The dorsal plates were probably covered with keratin – the material that forms the beaks of birds – and may have been brightly coloured for extra visual impact.

Allosaurus **bones have been found** *with holes* **made by** *Stegosaurus* **tail spikes.**

Throat guard
Flexible, armour-like scales protected the throat.

Hind legs
Long, strongly built hind legs raised the animal's hips and tail high off the ground.

Front legs
The front legs were much shorter than the back legs.

Toes
Stegosaurus walked on its toes, which were backed up by thick, wedge-shaped pads.

DINOSAUR
STEGOSAURUS

When: 155–151 MYA

Habitat: Forests

Length: 9 m (30 ft)

Diet: Leaves and ferns

Short horns
Bony projections above and in front of the eyes would have supported a pair of short horns.

Side view
Although *Allosaurus*'s eyes mostly faced sideways, the animal's range of forward vision was sufficient for hunting.

Knife-edged teeth
The strong but narrow skull was armed with more than 70 teeth, each with a sharp, serrated edge, like that of a steak knife. The teeth were continually replaced, so they never got the chance to wear out and lose their edge.

Allosaurus

This fearsome hunter was one of the most common big predators of Late Jurassic North America. Armed with a mouthful of sharp, lacerating teeth, it was a mortal enemy of the rhino-sized *Stegosaurus* (pages 70–71), and may even have attacked the young of giant sauropods such as *Diplodocus* (pages 66–67).

As the biggest plant-eating dinosaurs evolved into larger and larger forms during the Jurassic, their predators grew bigger too. *Allosaurus* was one of the most powerful, and was clearly specialized for attacking and eating super-sized prey. The scars left by its teeth on their bones are convincing evidence of that, although exactly how it subdued its victims is still being debated. The fossil evidence also show that its prey fought back, making every hunt a potential life-or-death struggle.

Powerful claw
Massively strong, sharp, hooked claws on three-fingered hands show that *Allosaurus* used its arms to grapple with struggling prey, pinning it down to stop it escaping.

Judging from tooth marks on some *Allosaurus* bones, **these dinosaurs sometimes ate each other.**

46 The number of *Allosaurus* specimens found in a **single quarry** in Utah, USA.

73

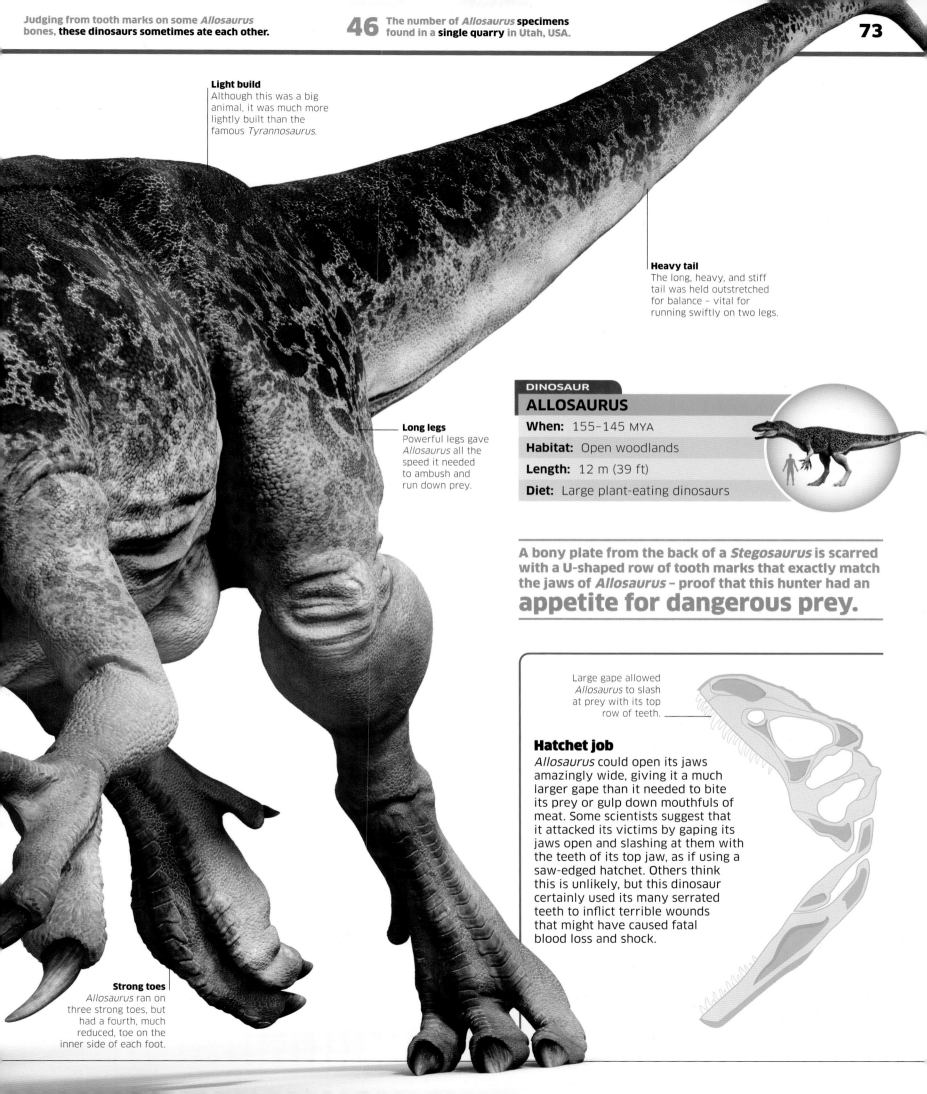

Light build
Although this was a big animal, it was much more lightly built than the famous *Tyrannosaurus*.

Heavy tail
The long, heavy, and stiff tail was held outstretched for balance – vital for running swiftly on two legs.

Long legs
Powerful legs gave *Allosaurus* all the speed it needed to ambush and run down prey.

DINOSAUR
ALLOSAURUS

When: 155–145 MYA

Habitat: Open woodlands

Length: 12 m (39 ft)

Diet: Large plant-eating dinosaurs

A bony plate from the back of a *Stegosaurus* is scarred with a U-shaped row of tooth marks that exactly match the jaws of *Allosaurus* – proof that this hunter had an
appetite for dangerous prey.

Large gape allowed *Allosaurus* to slash at prey with its top row of teeth.

Hatchet job
Allosaurus could open its jaws amazingly wide, giving it a much larger gape than it needed to bite its prey or gulp down mouthfuls of meat. Some scientists suggest that it attacked its victims by gaping its jaws open and slashing at them with the teeth of its top jaw, as if using a saw-edged hatchet. Others think this is unlikely, but this dinosaur certainly used its many serrated teeth to inflict terrible wounds that might have caused fatal blood loss and shock.

Strong toes
Allosaurus ran on three strong toes, but had a fourth, much reduced, toe on the inner side of each foot.

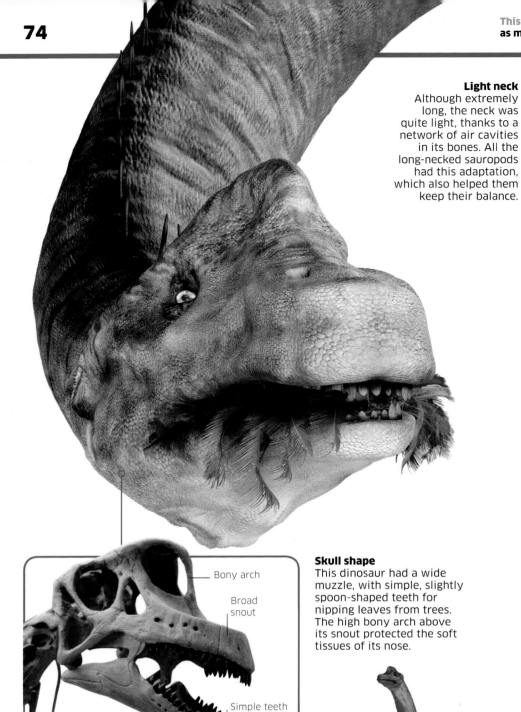

Light neck
Although extremely long, the neck was quite light, thanks to a network of air cavities in its bones. All the long-necked sauropods had this adaptation, which also helped them keep their balance.

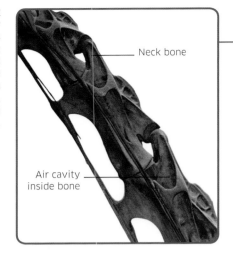

Neck bone

Air cavity inside bone

Skull shape
This dinosaur had a wide muzzle, with simple, slightly spoon-shaped teeth for nipping leaves from trees. The high bony arch above its snout protected the soft tissues of its nose.

Bony arch

Broad snout

Simple teeth

Giraffatitan

The name of this giant plant-eating dinosaur describes it perfectly, because it was like a colossal giraffe. Its astoundingly high reach allowed it to browse in the Jurassic treetops without lifting a foot from the ground.

Giraffatitan was a sauropod, like *Diplodocus* (pages 66–67), but it was built along different lines. Instead of rearing up on its hind legs to reach into the treetops to feed, it could simply use its very long neck to reach the leaves while standing on extra-long front legs that raised the front end of its body higher than the back end. It was one of the tallest dinosaurs that ever lived. *Giraffatitan* was an African relative of the similar *Brachiosaurus* from America. Fossil remains of *Giraffatitan*'s skull show us what its teeth were like, so we know how this massive animal probably fed.

High and mighty
The very long neck and extended front legs of this sauropod enabled it to reach up to 15 m (49 ft) above ground level to gather young, tender leaves. You would need a fire engine ladder to look it in the eye. A similar large sauropod called *Sauroposeidon* may have been even taller, but its remains are too fragmentary to be sure.

Walking tall
A modern giraffe is specialized for feeding from the tops of tall trees. Thanks to its long neck and long legs, the biggest giraffe can reach up to 5 m (16 ft) to gather foliage beyond the reach of other leaf-eaters. *Giraffatitan* had the same basic adaptations, but its front legs were longer than its hind legs, raising the level of its shoulders to give it the highest possible reach.

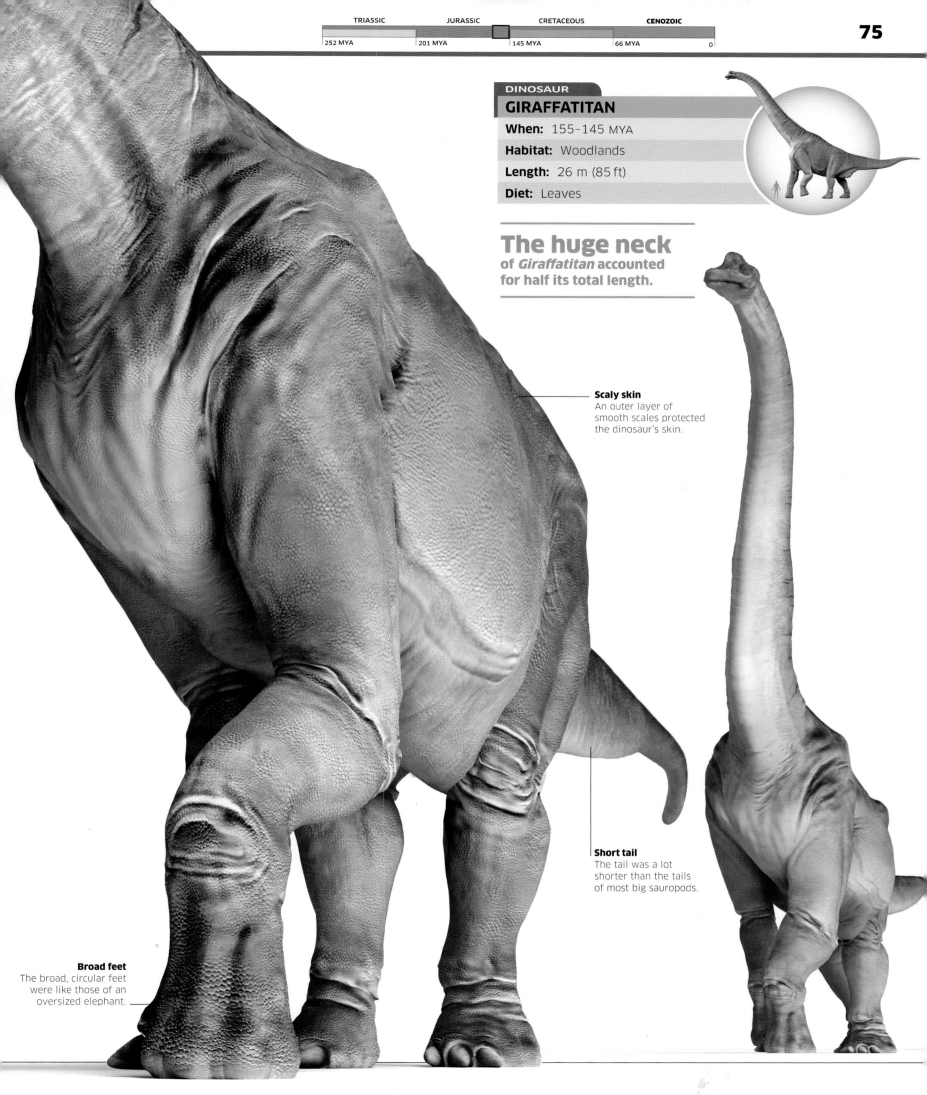

DINOSAUR
GIRAFFATITAN

When: 155–145 MYA

Habitat: Woodlands

Length: 26 m (85 ft)

Diet: Leaves

The huge neck
of *Giraffatitan* accounted
for half its total length.

Scaly skin
An outer layer of
smooth scales protected
the dinosaur's skin.

Short tail
The tail was a lot
shorter than the tails
of most big sauropods.

Broad feet
The broad, circular feet
were like those of an
oversized elephant.

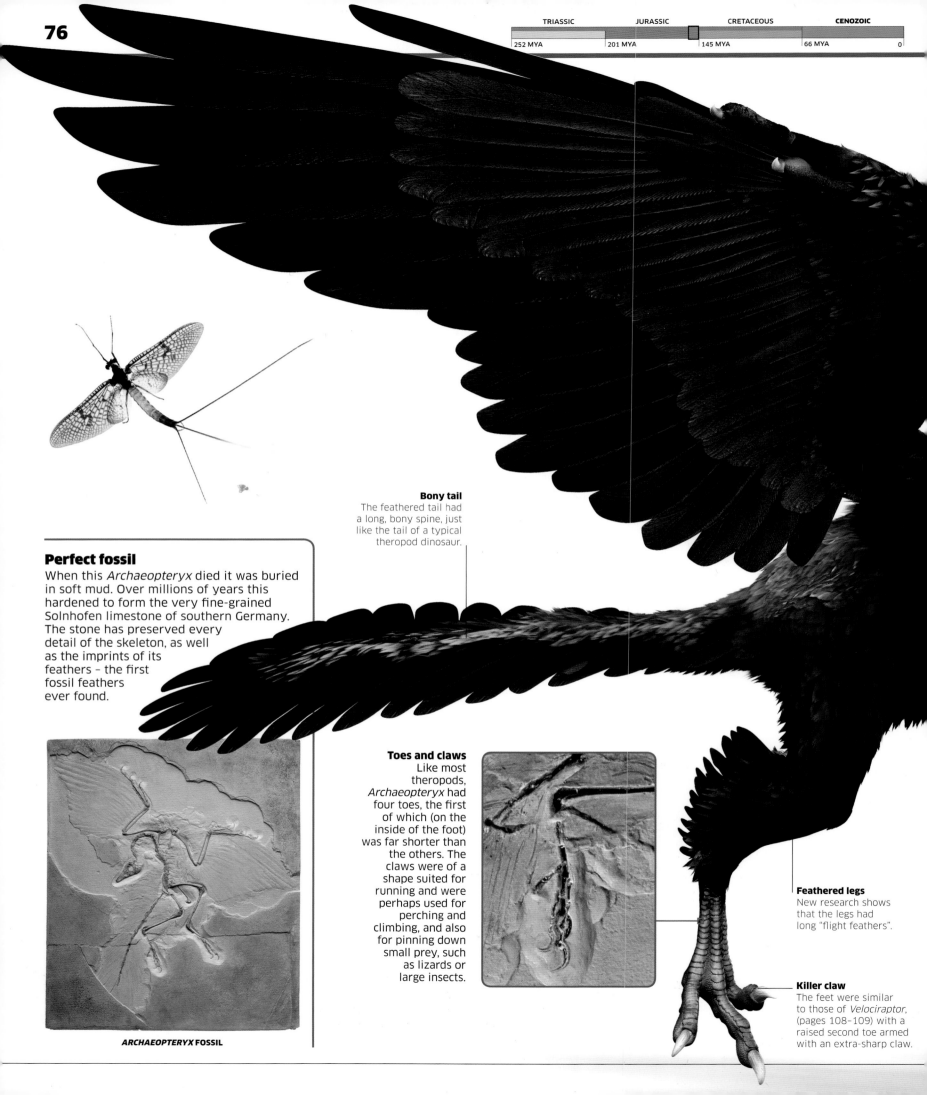

TRIASSIC		JURASSIC		CRETACEOUS		CENOZOIC	
252 MYA		201 MYA		145 MYA		66 MYA	0

Bony tail
The feathered tail had a long, bony spine, just like the tail of a typical theropod dinosaur.

Perfect fossil

When this *Archaeopteryx* died it was buried in soft mud. Over millions of years this hardened to form the very fine-grained Solnhofen limestone of southern Germany. The stone has preserved every detail of the skeleton, as well as the imprints of its feathers – the first fossil feathers ever found.

Toes and claws
Like most theropods, *Archaeopteryx* had four toes, the first of which (on the inside of the foot) was far shorter than the others. The claws were of a shape suited for running and were perhaps used for perching and climbing, and also for pinning down small prey, such as lizards or large insects.

Feathered legs
New research shows that the legs had long "flight feathers".

Killer claw
The feet were similar to those of *Velociraptor*, (pages 108–109) with a raised second toe armed with an extra-sharp claw.

ARCHAEOPTERYX FOSSIL

Archaeopteryx was **distantly related** to fast, agile hunters such as ***Deinonychus*** and ***Velociraptor***.

The name *Archaeopteryx* means **"ancient wing"**.

77

Short wings
The wings were quite short, but long enough for brief flights.

Wing claws
Like most other theropod dinosaurs of its time, *Archaeopteryx* had powerful three-clawed hands. It may have used them to seize prey, or to scramble through the branches of trees and shrubs.

DINOSAUR

ARCHAEOPTERYX

When: 151–146 MYA

Habitat: Wooded islands

Length: 45 cm (1.5 ft)

Diet: Insects and small reptiles

Bony jaws
The toothed jaws were heavier than the beak of a modern bird.

Sharp teeth
Its small, pointed teeth were ideal for catching small animals.

Flight muscles
A shallow breastbone shows that *Archaeopteryx*'s flight muscles must have been quite small.

Flying prey
Slow-flying insects like this mayfly were possible prey.

Archaeopteryx

When the first fossils of this animal were found in 1861, they clearly showed that it had feathers like a bird. But its bones were just like those of many small Mesozoic dinosaurs.

Unlike a modern bird, *Archaeopteryx* had teeth, claws on its wings, and a bony tail. It was very like many of the feathered but flightless theropod dinosaurs found recently in China, except that its wings were longer and the wing feathers were the same basic shape as those of flying birds. *Archaeopteryx* could probably fly, if not very well, which would make it the earliest known flying dinosaur. Its place on the bird family tree has been questioned, but most scientists agree that this is where it belongs.

10 The total number of *Archaeopteryx* fossils discovered so far.

CRETACEOUS LIFE

The final Period of the Mesozoic Era was the heyday of the dinosaurs. As the Jurassic supercontinents broke up to form many smaller continents, the dinosaurs became even more diverse and amazing. The Cretaceous also saw the evolution of the biggest flying animals that have ever lived.

THE CRETACEOUS WORLD

About 145 million years ago, the Jurassic Period ended with an event that caused the extinction of a lot of marine life, but had less impact on land. This marked the beginning of the Cretaceous, which lasted until the end of the Mesozoic Era, 66 million years ago. During this long span of time the continents split up even more, and life evolved differently on each landmass. This created a wider diversity of species – and in particular it led to the evolution of many new types of dinosaur.

CHANGING WORLD

Laurasia and Gondwana started to break up during the Cretaceous. The opening Atlantic Ocean pulled America away from Asia and Africa, and India became a separate continent surrounded by water. At first high sea levels flooded some parts of these continents, disguising their outlines. But by the end of the Cretaceous the continents we know today were becoming recognizable.

ARCTIC OCEAN

NORTH AMERICA

North America was divided by a north-south seaway that occupied what are now the prairies.

NORTH ATLANTIC OCEAN

PACIFIC OCEAN

North and South America were divided by the Caribbean Sea, and not linked at any point.

SOUTH AMERICA

The south Atlantic Ocean opened up, dragging South America away from Africa.

SOUTH ATLANTIC OCEAN

CONTINENTS AND OCEANS DURING THE CRETACEOUS PERIOD, 145–66 MILLION YEARS AGO

◎ ENVIRONMENT

The break-up of the continents in the Cretaceous created a wider variety of environments for life. Each continent had its own physical features and climatic conditions, ranging from tropical to almost polar. This made the plants and animals isolated on each continent evolve in different ways, into new species.

Climate

This was a time of mainly warm, mild climates, with remains of palm trees found as far north as Alaska. But towards the end of the period average global temperatures fell, possibly because some continental regions had moved nearer to the poles.

AVERAGE GLOBAL TEMPERATURE

°F	°C
140	60
104	40
68	20
32	0

18 °C
(64.4 °F)

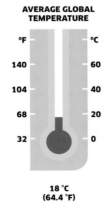

Woodlands
Dense tropical forests and more open woodlands were widespread, with new types of trees and smaller plants living among the dominant conifers.

Arid scrub
Regions such as the heart of Asia were deserts and semi-deserts, with scrubby vegetation. The fringes of these regions eventually became grasslands.

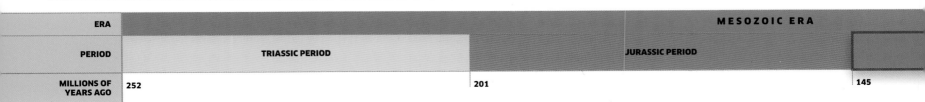

ERA	MESOZOIC ERA		
PERIOD	TRIASSIC PERIOD	JURASSIC PERIOD	
MILLIONS OF YEARS AGO	252	201	145

EURASIA

Asia was rotating clockwise and Africa was moving north, bringing them closer together.

TETHYS OCEAN

AFRICA

Australia was still attached to Antarctica, and both were close to the cold South Pole.

INDIA

ANTARCTICA

⊙ KEY

- ▬ ANCIENT LANDMASS
- ∿ OUTLINE OF MODERN LANDMASS

⊙ ANIMALS

The animal life of the Cretaceous Period was similar to that of the Jurassic. But it became more diverse as the continents broke up because populations of animals separated by water could not interbreed. Many different types of dinosaur evolved as a result. There were also new types of smaller animal, especially insects specialized for feeding from flowers.

Land invertebrates
The appearance of flowers containing sugary nectar led to the evolution of many nectar-feeders, such as butterflies and bees. Spiders and other small animals were also abundant.

SPIDER PRESERVED IN AMBER

EOMAIA,
A PLACENTAL MAMMAL

Mammals
Small mammals had existed since the Triassic, but the Cretaceous saw the evolution of the first placental mammals – the group that is most common today.

Dinosaurs
Many specialized types of dinosaur evolved, including a wide variety of feathered theropods, such as *Alxasaurus*.

ALXASAURUS

Marine life
Big marine reptiles were still the top oceanic predators, but were challenged by other hunters, including sharks such as *Hybodus*. The sharks preyed on fish and various invertebrates, such as ammonites.

HYBODUS

Plants

The Cretaceous saw a dramatic change in plant life, with the evolution of flowering plants and, eventually, grasses. But until the end of the period these flowering plants were outnumbered by the conifers, ferns, cycads, and ginkgos surviving from the Jurassic.

Ferns
These shade-loving plants were abundant in the forests, and a vital food source for many plant-eating dinosaurs.

Conifers
Needle-leafed conifers such as sequoia were the dominant trees, but broad-leafed trees were getting more common.

Ginkgos
As flowering plants, including trees, gained ground at the end of the period, ginkgos and cycads were becoming rarer.

Flowering plants
By the end of the Cretaceous many landscapes were dotted with early flowers such as magnolias and waterlilies.

Sharp edge

Worn-down tooth

Beak made of
hard keratin

Simple teeth
The leaf-shaped teeth are typical
of early plant-eating dinosaurs.
The animal used them to chew
plants gathered with its sharp beak.

Narrow head
The skull was tall
and quite narrow, with
high-set eyes that gave
a wide field of vision.

Scaly skin
An outer layer of tough
scales protected the
skin from scratches
and infections.

Iguanodon

**This elephant-sized plant-eater was one of the first
dinosaurs to be named, back in 1825 – when most
scientists had no idea that such animals had ever lived.**

In 1822, English amateur geologist Gideon Mantell found some fossil
teeth that seemed to belong to a giant lizard. They looked like those of
an oversized iguana, and in 1825 it was officially named *Iguanodon* –
one of the first dinosaurs to be named. Then, in 1878, many complete
skeletons with similar teeth were found in Belgium. The fossils revealed
that *Iguanodon* was a big ornithopod dinosaur that spent most of its time
walking on all fours, eating plants such as horsetails, cycads, and conifers.

Thumb
spike

Central fingers
bound together

Mobile
fifth finger

Hoof-like
claw

All-purpose hand
Although built more like an arm,
the front limb was long enough
to support part of the animal's
weight. The three middle fingers
held the animal up, the thumb
was armed with a sharp spike,
and the fifth finger was able
to move freely.

Joined fingers
The three middle fingers were
bound together with flesh.

38 skeletons of *Iguanodon* were found in a **single Belgian coal mine** in 1878.

Iguanodon probably used its **stout thumb spike** as a defensive weapon.

3 tonnes is the **average weight** of *Iguanodon* – about **twice** the weight of a **car**.

83

Stiff tail
The weight of the head and upper body was balanced by a long, stiff, and heavy tail.

Large, strong hind limb
Most of the weight of *Iguanodon* was supported by its massively built hind limbs.

DINOSAUR
IGUANODON

When: 130–125 MYA

Habitat: Forests

Length: 9 m (29.5 ft)

Diet: Plants

Gideon Mantell
Like many early paleontologists, Gideon Mantell was not a professional. He was a country doctor who collected fossils in his spare time. Either he, or his wife Mary, found the big fossil teeth in a quarry in southern England. But it took three years for other scientists to agree that they belonged to the dinosaur that he named *Iguanodon*.

Interpretations
The fossils described by Mantell were clearly the remains of a big reptile. But they were just a few teeth and bones, so the shape of the animal was a mystery. At first, it was seen as a giant, sprawling lizard. When complete *Iguanodon* skeletons were found in 1878, they were reconstructed sitting on their tails like kangaroos. We now think that it was a part-time quadruped.

IDEAS ABOUT *IGUANODON*'S STANCE

1854
SQUAT QUADRUPED

1878
KANGAROO STANCE

MODERN-DAY IDEA
PART-TIME QUADRUPED

Camouflage colours
Using feather analysis, scientists reconstructed this dinosaur's colour pattern, which provided camouflage.

This tiny theropod was the first feathered dinosaur to be found that was clearly **not a bird, and did not fly.**

Pointed snout
Sinosauropteryx had a long, pointed snout with small, sharp-edged teeth.

Small prey
Sinosauropteryx hunted lizards, insects, and other small animals such as this centipede.

Short arms
Its arms and hands were relatively short, but useful for grabbing prey.

Feathery pelt
Under a microscope, the fossil fuzz has a wavy form that shows it was soft and pliable. It would have looked and felt furry, but was actually made up of short, branched, flexible feathers.

Sinosauropteryx

The fossils of this small, fast, agile hunter caused a sensation when they were discovered in China in 1996. They clearly showed that *Sinosauropteryx* was covered with some sort of fuzz – demolishing the idea that all typical dinosaurs had naked, scaly skins.

The bones of similar small theropods had been found in other parts of the world, but until the discovery of *Sinosauropteryx*, we had no idea that the living animals had fuzzy pelts. In fact, the fuzz consisted of simple feathers, very like those of some flightless birds. Since the feathers were so short, it is likely that this dinosaur needed them as insulation, to keep warm while searching the woodlands of Early Cretaceous China for prey.

64 The number of **bones in the extra-long tail** of *Sinosauropteryx*.

Sinosauropteryx was first discovered in 1996 by a **farmer and part-time fossil hunter** in Liaoning Province, China.

Another specimen has **several unlaid eggs** in its body, so **it was clearly a female**. **85**

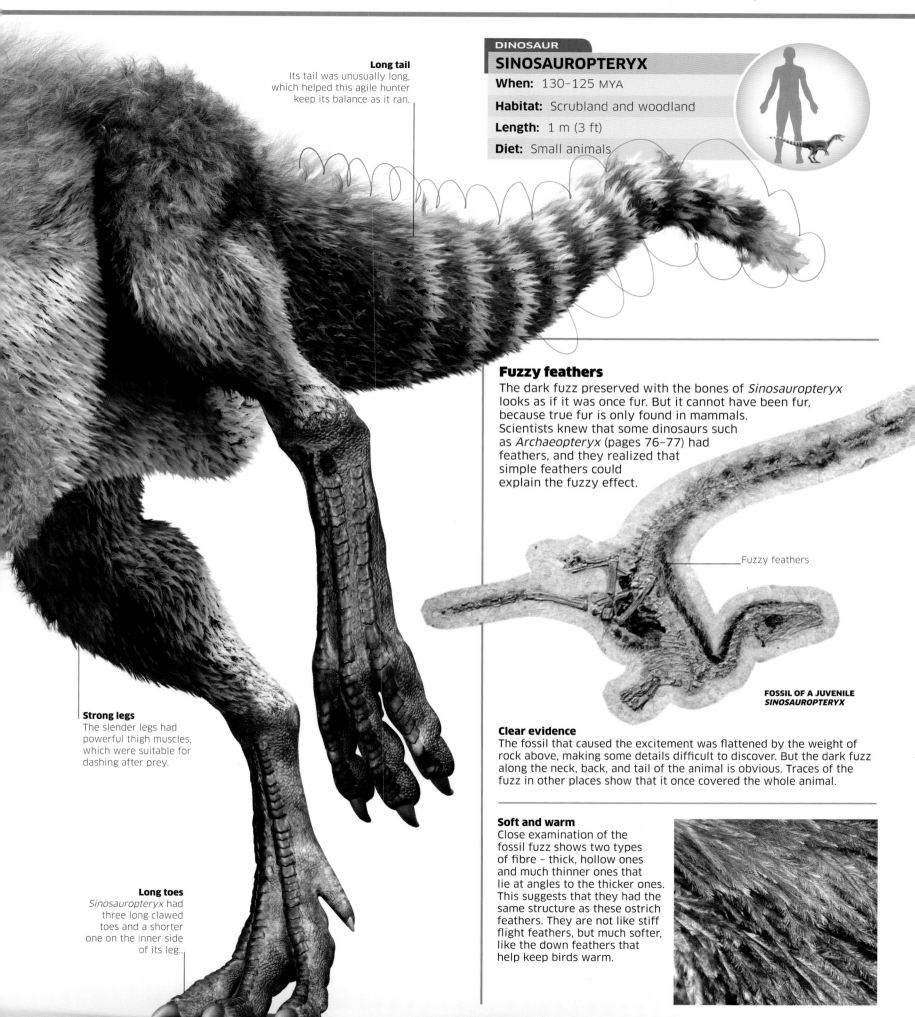

Long tail
Its tail was unusually long, which helped this agile hunter keep its balance as it ran.

DINOSAUR
SINOSAUROPTERYX

When: 130–125 MYA

Habitat: Scrubland and woodland

Length: 1 m (3 ft)

Diet: Small animals

Fuzzy feathers
The dark fuzz preserved with the bones of *Sinosauropteryx* looks as if it was once fur. But it cannot have been fur, because true fur is only found in mammals. Scientists knew that some dinosaurs such as *Archaeopteryx* (pages 76–77) had feathers, and they realized that simple feathers could explain the fuzzy effect.

Fuzzy feathers

FOSSIL OF A JUVENILE SINOSAUROPTERYX

Strong legs
The slender legs had powerful thigh muscles, which were suitable for dashing after prey.

Clear evidence
The fossil that caused the excitement was flattened by the weight of rock above, making some details difficult to discover. But the dark fuzz along the neck, back, and tail of the animal is obvious. Traces of the fuzz in other places show that it once covered the whole animal.

Soft and warm
Close examination of the fossil fuzz shows two types of fibre – thick, hollow ones and much thinner ones that lie at angles to the thicker ones. This suggests that they had the same structure as these ostrich feathers. They are not like stiff flight feathers, but much softer, like the down feathers that help keep birds warm.

Long toes
Sinosauropteryx had three long clawed toes and a shorter one on the inner side of its leg.

Repenomamus

One of the biggest Mesozoic mammals yet found, the badger-sized *Repenomamus* was a meat-eater that would have competed with small dinosaurs for prey – and even killed and eaten them.

Most of the mammals that lived in the Mesozoic Era were the size of shrews or rats, and lived on seeds or small creatures such as insects. But *Repenomamus* was much bigger, and probably hunted other vertebrates. It had powerful jaws and sharp teeth, and one specimen has been found with a baby *Psittacosaurus* (pages 92–93) in its stomach. *Repenomamus* may have found this already dead, and eaten it, but it could easily have tracked its prey down and killed it.

Furry tail
its fossils show that *Repenomamus* had a short, flexible tail, probably covered with fur.

Strong legs
Its legs were short and strong, allowing the mammal to forage for food over a wide area.

Broad feet
This mammal walked on the soles of its broad feet, like a badger or skunk.

In life, the baby *Psittacosaurus* **found in the stomach** of one of the fossils would have been less than 15 cm (6 in) long.

Like many hunters, *Repenomamus* probably also ate fruits, nuts, insects, and worms.

This type of mammal is called a triconodont because its **back teeth have three dull, conical points**.

Its **fossils** were found in China, **near those of many small, feathered dinosaurs**.

87

Furry body
Its long, bulky body had a coat of warm fur, just like that of a modern mammal.

Whiskers
Repenomamus probably had long, sensitive whiskers, much like those of a modern cat.

Jaws and teeth
Repenomamus had big, pointed teeth at the front of its strong jaws, but quite small, blunt chewing teeth. This suggests that it was a predator, not a bone-crushing scavenger.

MAMMAL

REPENOMAMUS

When: 130–125 MYA

Habitat: Woodlands

Length: 1 m (3 ft)

Diet: Small animals and fruits

Strong skull and jaw

Flexible backbone

Mesozoic devil
In size, shape, and probable strength, *Repenomamus* was similar to the modern Tasmanian devil. The "devil" owes its name to its ferocity, but it also eats a lot of dead animals. It is likely that *Repenomamus* was more of an active hunter.

TASMANIAN DEVIL

Fossil evidence
Two species of this animal have been found, one much bigger than the other. This fossil of the biggest, *Repenomamus giganticus*, shows it lying curled up on its side with its tail tucked under its belly. The specimen with the baby dinosaur in its stomach belonged to an even smaller species, so *Repenomamus giganticus* (above) would have been able to kill and eat much bigger prey.

Short hind leg

TRIASSIC | JURASSIC | CRETACEOUS | CENOZOIC
252 MYA | 201 MYA | 145 MYA | 66 MYA | 0

100 *Hypsilophodon* fossils have been found on a single site on the Isle of Wight in Britain.

Tail
The long, stiff tail helped *Hypsilophodon* keep its balance as it ran on its long legs.

Camouflage colours
Its colours would have helped *Hypsilophodon* hide from its enemies.

Long legs
Its long, muscular hind legs gave *Hypsilophodon* a great deal of speed.

Sharp claw
Each foot had four long toes with long, sharp claws. *Hypsilophodon* may have used these for digging up juicy roots to eat, and they would have given a good grip on the soft ground of the woodlands that were its likely habitat.

Named in 1869, *Hypsilophodon* was one of the **first small dinosaurs** known to science.

When the first fossil skeleton was found, people **thought it was a young *Iguanodon***.

89

Small body
It did not have room for a big gut, so *Hypsilophodon* would have avoided eating bulky, low-nutrient foods.

Narrow beak
It had a sharp, narrow beak for selecting young, tender leaves and shoots that were easy to digest.

Large eyes
Hypsilophodon had big eyes supported by rings of bony plates called sclerotic rings. This may indicate that it was active at night. The eyes faced sideways for good all-round vision, allowing it to watch for danger as it fed.

Five-fingered hand
The hands had five fingers, but the fifth one was very small.

DINOSAUR
HYPSILOPHODON

When: 130–125 MYA

Habitat: Open woodlands

Length: 1.5 m (5 ft)

Diet: Plants

A tree dinosaur?
In the early 20th century some scientists thought that *Hypsilophodon* was able to climb trees, using its toes to grip branches. Danish researcher Gerhard Heilmann even suggested that it lived up trees all the time, like this tree kangaroo. But in 1971 a careful study of *Hypsilophodon*'s bones showed that this was impossible, and we are now sure that it lived on the ground.

Hypsilophodon

Small, light, and agile, this elegant plant-eater was similar to many other small dinosaurs that lived alongside their giant relatives, staying well hidden from big predators.

During the Cretaceous the ornithopod dinosaurs evolved a variety of specialized forms, such as the heavyweight *Iguanodon* (pages 82–83) and its relatives. But smaller, less-specialized ornithopods were still very successful, perhaps because they could live in many different habitats. *Hypsilophodon* was typical of these small plant-eaters. It would have spent most of its time looking for food in the dense undergrowth of open woodlands, where it could hide from its enemies – but could run fast to escape danger if it had to.

Slicing teeth
Like other ornithopods, *Hypsilophodon* had a beak, but it also had five pointed front teeth on each side of its upper jaw. The fan-shaped back teeth worked like scissor blades, with the lower ones closing inside the upper ones to slice food.

Hypsilophodon's slicing teeth may have been self-sharpening.

TRIASSIC	JURASSIC	CRETACEOUS	CENOZOIC
252 MYA	201 MYA	145 MYA	66 MYA 0

Confuciusornis

Hundreds of fossils of this feathered dinosaur have been found in the rocks of Liaoning, China. They show that bird-like creatures were flying in flocks more than 120 million years ago.

At first glance *Confuciusornis* looks like a modern bird, with a toothless beak, long wings, overlapping flight feathers, and no long, bony tail. But it also had big claws at the bend of each wing, and no normal tail feathers, though some fossils show long tail streamers that were probably for show. The wings of this creature had much longer outer flight feathers than those of earlier birds, but *Confuciusornis* seems to have had small flight muscles, limiting its flying ability.

Long primary feathers
The outer wing feathers were as long as those of modern flying birds.

Clawed fingers
Powerful claws on its wings may have helped *Confuciusornis* scramble through trees.

The amazing number of *Confuciusornis* fossils found in one ancient lake bed may have made up a flock that was killed at once by a cloud of poisonous volcanic gas.

Stout beak
Confuciusornis had a strong beak, like this Australian kookaburra. It probably had a similar diet of small animals, and one specimen has been found with fish bones in its stomach.

The **name *Confuciusornis*** combines the **Greek word for "bird"** with the name of the **Chinese philosopher Confucius**.

500 **fossils** of *Confuciusornis* are held in a **single Chinese museum**.

91

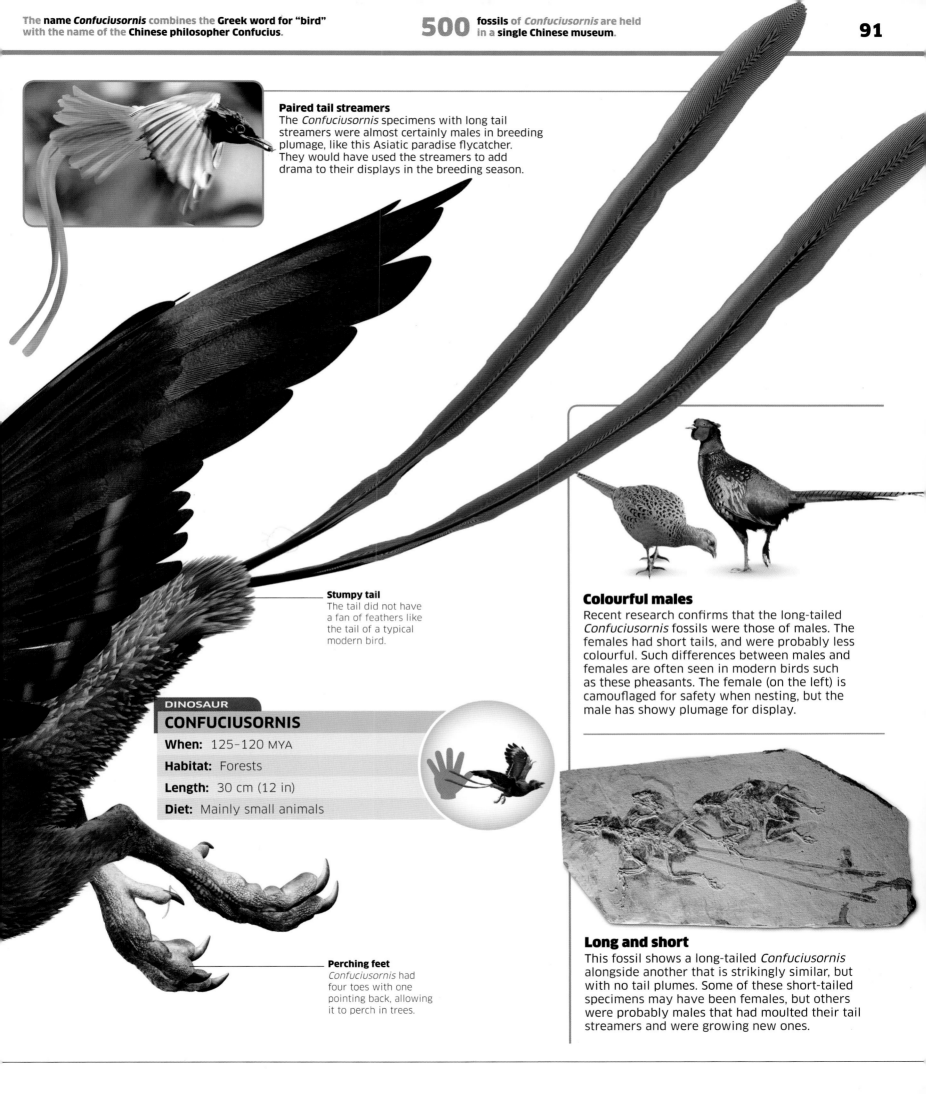

Paired tail streamers
The *Confuciusornis* specimens with long tail streamers were almost certainly males in breeding plumage, like this Asiatic paradise flycatcher. They would have used the streamers to add drama to their displays in the breeding season.

Stumpy tail
The tail did not have a fan of feathers like the tail of a typical modern bird.

DINOSAUR

CONFUCIUSORNIS

When: 125–120 MYA

Habitat: Forests

Length: 30 cm (12 in)

Diet: Mainly small animals

Colourful males
Recent research confirms that the long-tailed *Confuciusornis* fossils were those of males. The females had short tails, and were probably less colourful. Such differences between males and females are often seen in modern birds such as these pheasants. The female (on the left) is camouflaged for safety when nesting, but the male has showy plumage for display.

Perching feet
Confuciusornis had four toes with one pointing back, allowing it to perch in trees.

Long and short
This fossil shows a long-tailed *Confuciusornis* alongside another that is strikingly similar, but with no tail plumes. Some of these short-tailed specimens may have been females, but others were probably males that had moulted their tail streamers and were growing new ones.

Cheek horns
Horn-like bony growths projected from the cheeks.

Parrot-like beak
The name *Psittacosaurus* means "parrot lizard", and refers to its narrow, parrot-like beak. The animal would have used its beak to gather plant food, which probably included a lot of seeds. The beak may also have made a good nutcracker!

Psittacosaurus

A small, early relative of giant horned dinosaurs such as the famous *Triceratops* (pages 138–139), the parrot-beaked *Psittacosaurus* was one of the most common and successful plant-eating dinosaurs of Early Cretaceous China, with at least nine different species.

The ceratopsians were a group of ornithischian dinosaurs known for their horns and big, bony neck frills. Most of them lived in the Late Cretaceous. They were large, heavy animals that stood on four legs, but early types such as *Psittacosaurus* were much smaller, and ran on their hind legs. Like all ceratopsians, *Psittacosaurus* had a narrow beak and sharp back teeth that sliced its food like scissors. But its strangest feature was the flamboyant brush of long bristles that seems to have sprouted from the top of its tail.

Some scientists think that *Psittacosaurus* spent a lot of time in the water, like an otter or beaver.

Of the 400 known *Psittacosaurus* fossils, just one shows bristles on its tail.

34 *Psittacosaurus* baby fossils were found in one nest, all killed by a burrow collapse or a volcano eruption.

93

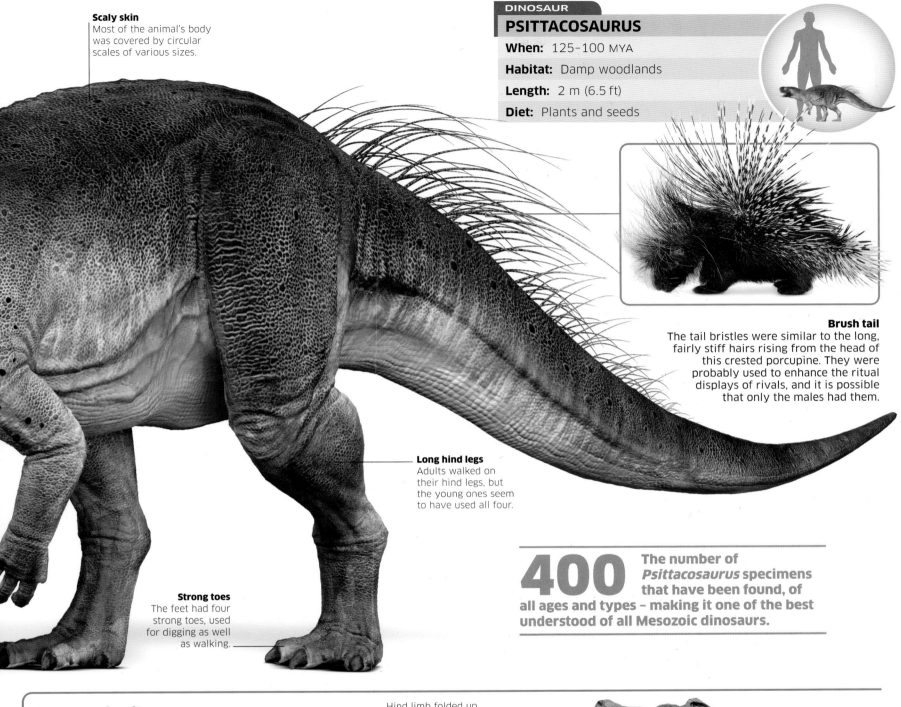

Scaly skin
Most of the animal's body was covered by circular scales of various sizes.

DINOSAUR
PSITTACOSAURUS

When: 125–100 MYA

Habitat: Damp woodlands

Length: 2 m (6.5 ft)

Diet: Plants and seeds

Brush tail
The tail bristles were similar to the long, fairly stiff hairs rising from the head of this crested porcupine. They were probably used to enhance the ritual displays of rivals, and it is possible that only the males had them.

Long hind legs
Adults walked on their hind legs, but the young ones seem to have used all four.

Strong toes
The feet had four strong toes, used for digging as well as walking.

400 The number of *Psittacosaurus* specimens that have been found, of all ages and types – making it one of the best understood of all Mesozoic dinosaurs.

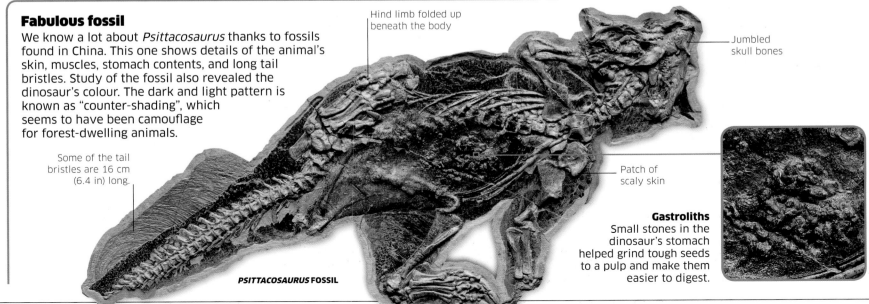

Fabulous fossil
We know a lot about *Psittacosaurus* thanks to fossils found in China. This one shows details of the animal's skin, muscles, stomach contents, and long tail bristles. Study of the fossil also revealed the dinosaur's colour. The dark and light pattern is known as "counter-shading", which seems to have been camouflage for forest-dwelling animals.

Hind limb folded up beneath the body

Jumbled skull bones

Some of the tail bristles are 16 cm (6.4 in) long.

Patch of scaly skin

Gastroliths
Small stones in the dinosaur's stomach helped grind tough seeds to a pulp and make them easier to digest.

PSITTACOSAURUS FOSSIL

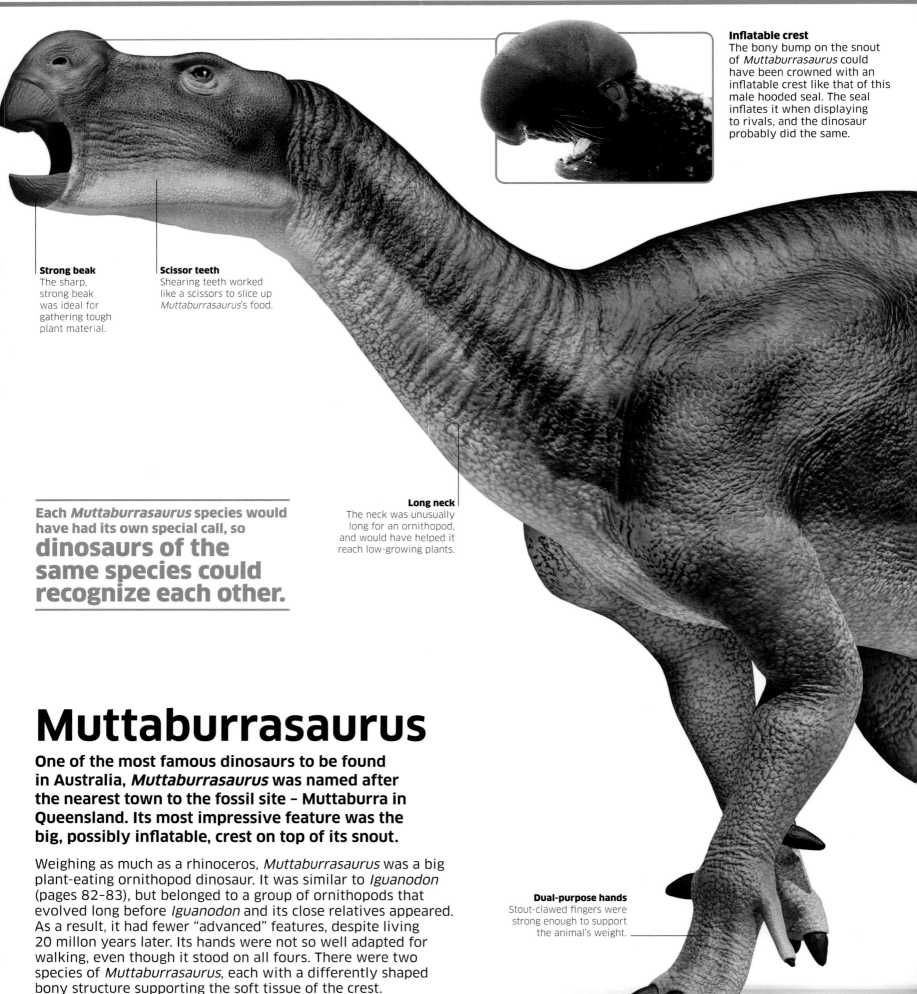

Inflatable crest
The bony bump on the snout of *Muttaburrasaurus* could have been crowned with an inflatable crest like that of this male hooded seal. The seal inflates it when displaying to rivals, and the dinosaur probably did the same.

Strong beak
The sharp, strong beak was ideal for gathering tough plant material.

Scissor teeth
Shearing teeth worked like a scissors to slice up *Muttaburrasaurus*'s food.

Each *Muttaburrasaurus* species would have had its own special call, so **dinosaurs of the same species could recognize each other.**

Long neck
The neck was unusually long for an ornithopod, and would have helped it reach low-growing plants.

Muttaburrasaurus

One of the most famous dinosaurs to be found in Australia, *Muttaburrasaurus* was named after the nearest town to the fossil site – Muttaburra in Queensland. Its most impressive feature was the big, possibly inflatable, crest on top of its snout.

Weighing as much as a rhinoceros, *Muttaburrasaurus* was a big plant-eating ornithopod dinosaur. It was similar to *Iguanodon* (pages 82–83), but belonged to a group of ornithopods that evolved long before *Iguanodon* and its close relatives appeared. As a result, it had fewer "advanced" features, despite living 20 millon years later. Its hands were not so well adapted for walking, even though it stood on all fours. There were two species of *Muttaburrasaurus*, each with a differently shaped bony structure supporting the soft tissue of the crest.

Dual-purpose hands
Stout-clawed fingers were strong enough to support the animal's weight.

It is possible that **only males had a crest**, and **used it to intimidate rival males**.

Like many plant-eaters, *Muttaburrasaurus* probably **lived in large herds**.

Some scientists once thought that this dinosaur **ate meat as well as plants**.

95

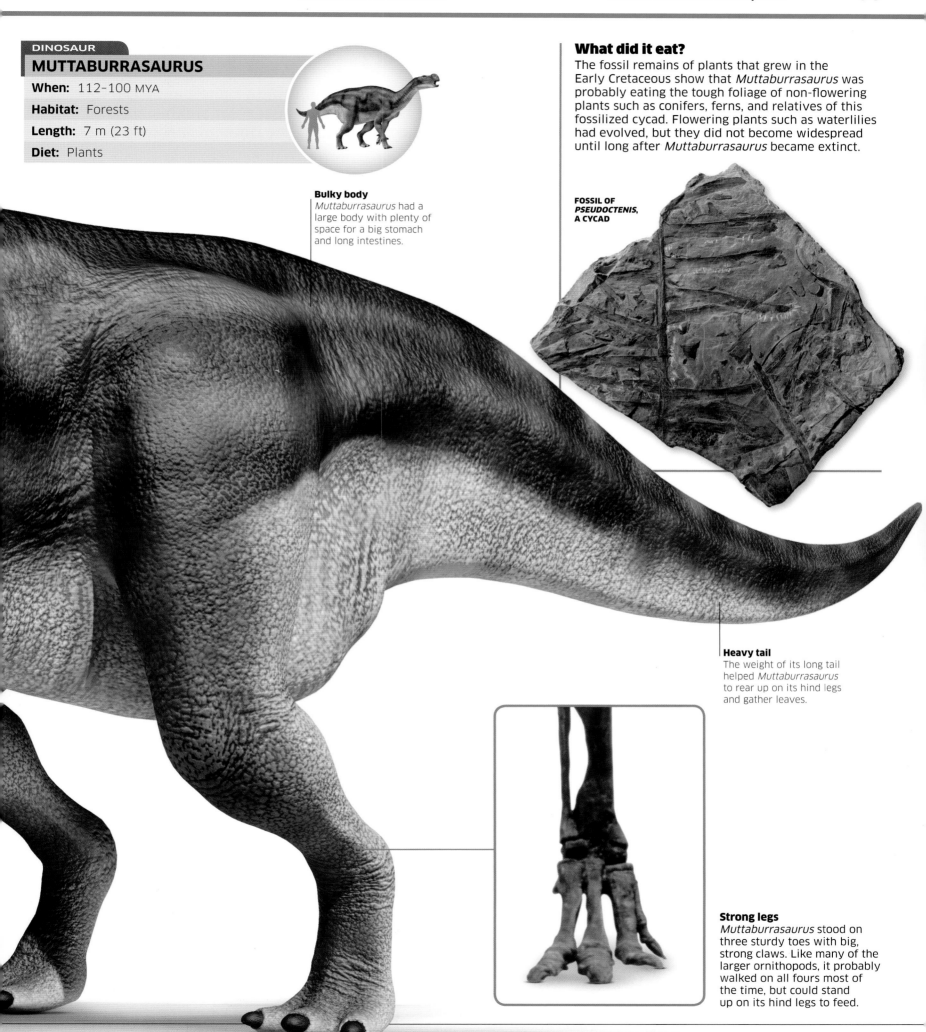

DINOSAUR

MUTTABURRASAURUS

When: 112–100 MYA

Habitat: Forests

Length: 7 m (23 ft)

Diet: Plants

Bulky body
Muttaburrasaurus had a large body with plenty of space for a big stomach and long intestines.

What did it eat?

The fossil remains of plants that grew in the Early Cretaceous show that *Muttaburrasaurus* was probably eating the tough foliage of non-flowering plants such as conifers, ferns, and relatives of this fossilized cycad. Flowering plants such as waterlilies had evolved, but they did not become widespread until long after *Muttaburrasaurus* became extinct.

FOSSIL OF *PSEUDOCTENIS*, A CYCAD

Heavy tail
The weight of its long tail helped *Muttaburrasaurus* to rear up on its hind legs and gather leaves.

Strong legs
Muttaburrasaurus stood on three sturdy toes with big, strong claws. Like many of the larger ornithopods, it probably walked on all fours most of the time, but could stand up on its hind legs to feed.

TRIASSIC	JURASSIC	CRETACEOUS	CENOZOIC
252 MYA	201 MYA	145 MYA	66 MYA 0

Pterodaustro

This strange animal was one of the oddest and most specialized of the pterosaurs, with an amazing set of teeth adapted for sifting small creatures from the water of shallow lagoons.

A relative of *Pterodactylus* (pages 68–69), and equipped with similar, but even bigger, webbed feet, *Pterodaustro* lived in the same types of coastal, shallow-water habitats. But instead of feeding normally, it strained the water through hundreds of long, slender teeth that were more like bristles. These trapped tiny aquatic animals, which *Pterodaustro* then mashed up and swallowed. Whole flocks of these pterosaurs seem to have fed together, like flocks of shorebirds.

Folded wings
On the ground, the outer wings were folded up above the animal's back.

Furry body
Pterodaustro's body was covered with hair-like fibres that would have looked like fur.

Long neck
Its long, flexible neck allowed *Pterodaustro* to reach down below the water surface to feed.

Big feet
The very big, webbed feet were ideal for walking on soft mud, and even swimming.

Clawed hands
Pterodaustro's clawed hands were used for walking.

750 The number of **fossil specimens found** so far **in Argentina and Chile**.

The **bristle-like teeth** of *Pterodaustro* are the **most specialized that have ever evolved**.

1,000 The total number of **teeth** in the jaws of *Pterodaustro*.

97

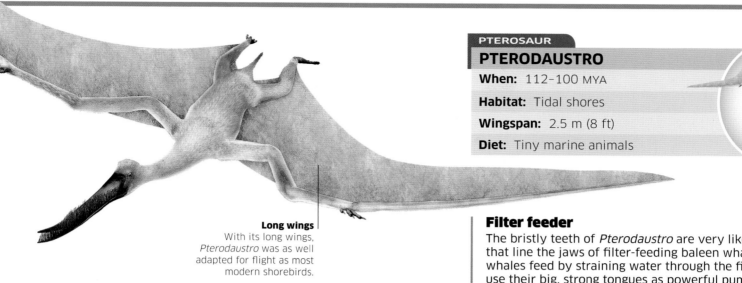

PTEROSAUR
PTERODAUSTRO

When: 112–100 MYA

Habitat: Tidal shores

Wingspan: 2.5 m (8 ft)

Diet: Tiny marine animals

Long wings
With its long wings, *Pterodaustro* was as well adapted for flight as most modern shorebirds.

Extraordinary teeth
The lower teeth were up to 30 mm (1.2 in) long, and shaped like flattened bristles, forming a comb-like row on each side. There were also hundreds of tiny teeth in the upper jaw, probably used to crush prey.

Filter feeder
The bristly teeth of *Pterodaustro* are very like the fibres that line the jaws of filter-feeding baleen whales. These whales feed by straining water through the fibres. Many use their big, strong tongues as powerful pumps, and it is likely that *Pterodaustro* used the same technique.

Social animal
The upcurved shape of this pterosaur's jaws is like the beak of an avocet – a bird that gathers food from the water surface by sweeping its beak from side to side. These birds live and feed in flocks, and hundreds of *Pterodaustro* fossils found together at one site indicate that it did the same.

Jaw muscles
There are traces of strong jaw muscles, used to force water out through the sieve-like teeth.

Some scientists suggest that, like flamingos with the same diet, the tiny animals eaten by this pterosaur may **have tinted it pink**.

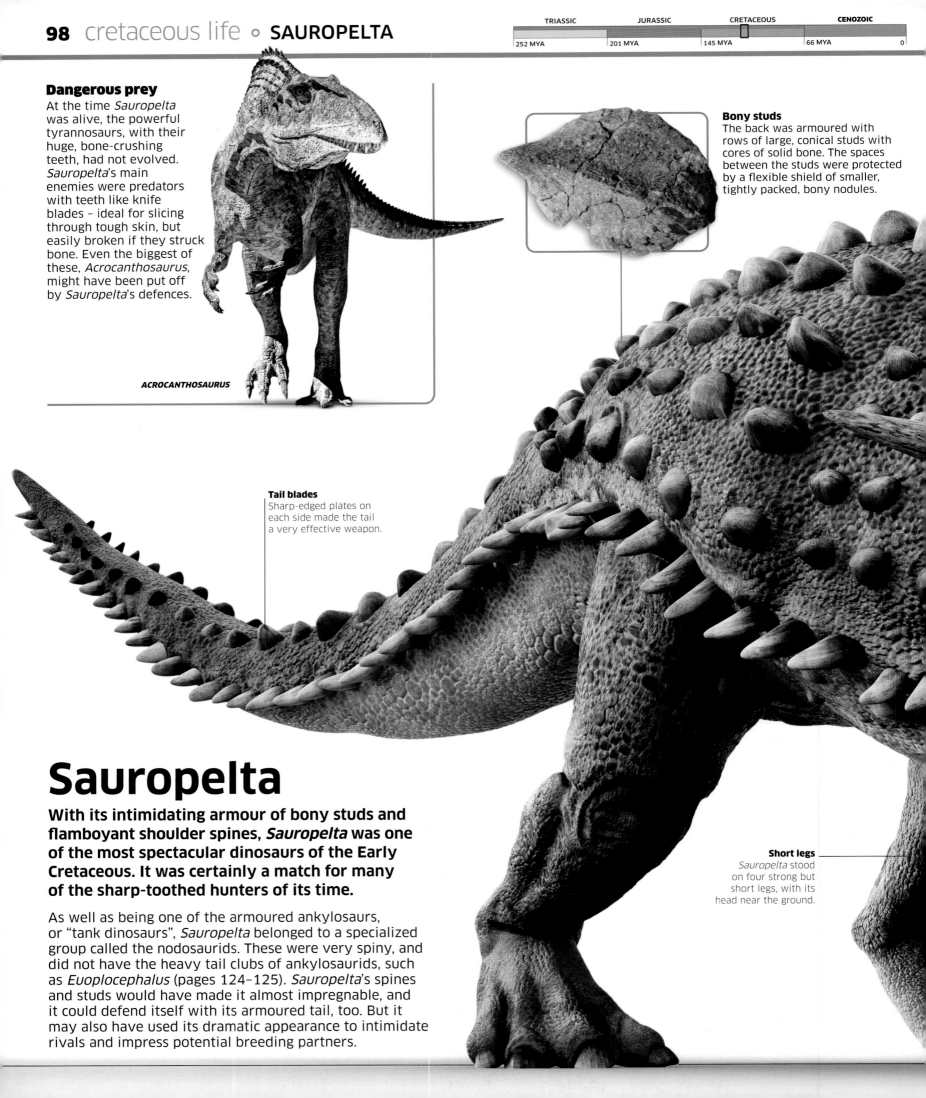

TRIASSIC	JURASSIC	CRETACEOUS	CENOZOIC
252 MYA	201 MYA	145 MYA	66 MYA	0

Dangerous prey

At the time *Sauropelta* was alive, the powerful tyrannosaurs, with their huge, bone-crushing teeth, had not evolved. *Sauropelta*'s main enemies were predators with teeth like knife blades – ideal for slicing through tough skin, but easily broken if they struck bone. Even the biggest of these, *Acrocanthosaurus*, might have been put off by *Sauropelta*'s defences.

ACROCANTHOSAURUS

Bony studs

The back was armoured with rows of large, conical studs with cores of solid bone. The spaces between the studs were protected by a flexible shield of smaller, tightly packed, bony nodules.

Tail blades

Sharp-edged plates on each side made the tail a very effective weapon.

Sauropelta

With its intimidating armour of bony studs and flamboyant shoulder spines, *Sauropelta* was one of the most spectacular dinosaurs of the Early Cretaceous. It was certainly a match for many of the sharp-toothed hunters of its time.

As well as being one of the armoured ankylosaurs, or "tank dinosaurs", *Sauropelta* belonged to a specialized group called the nodosaurids. These were very spiny, and did not have the heavy tail clubs of ankylosaurids, such as *Euoplocephalus* (pages 124–125). *Sauropelta*'s spines and studs would have made it almost impregnable, and it could defend itself with its armoured tail, too. But it may also have used its dramatic appearance to intimidate rivals and impress potential breeding partners.

Short legs

Sauropelta stood on four strong but short legs, with its head near the ground.

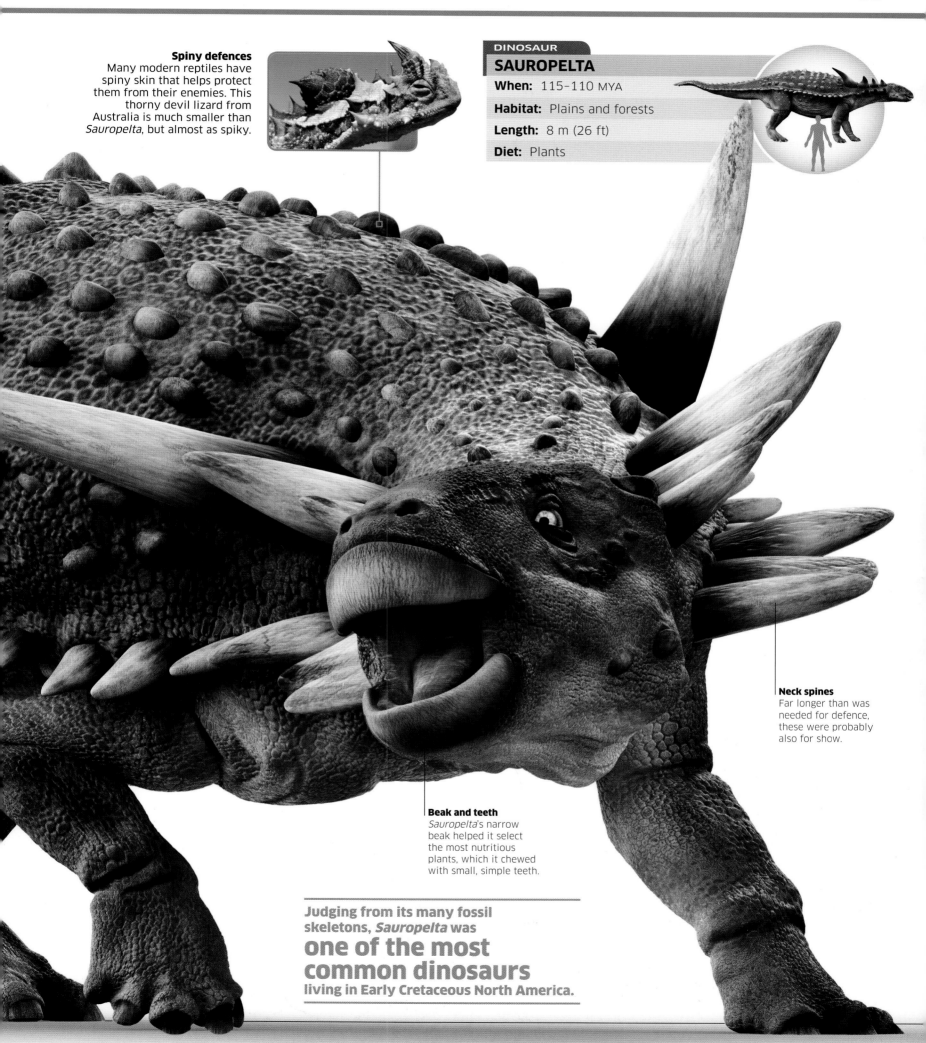

38 cm (15 in) – the length of the **bony cores** of the longest neck spines.

The name *Sauropelta* means **"shield lizard"**.

These dinosaurs probably lived in **herds** for **mutual defence**.

99

Spiny defences
Many modern reptiles have spiny skin that helps protect them from their enemies. This thorny devil lizard from Australia is much smaller than *Sauropelta*, but almost as spiky.

DINOSAUR
SAUROPELTA

When: 115–110 MYA

Habitat: Plains and forests

Length: 8 m (26 ft)

Diet: Plants

Neck spines
Far longer than was needed for defence, these were probably also for show.

Beak and teeth
Sauropelta's narrow beak helped it select the most nutritious plants, which it chewed with small, simple teeth.

Judging from its many fossil skeletons, *Sauropelta* was

one of the most common dinosaurs living in Early Cretaceous North America.

ALARM CALLS

On a late afternoon in early autumn, a group of *Psittacosaurus* search a forest lake for juicy plants that they can pluck from the shallow water with their sharp beaks.

A sudden commotion makes them look up as the first of many *Confuciusornis* fly out of the trees with harsh cries of alarm. They swoop low over the lake and dive into cover on the other side. But whatever scared them so badly is clearly no threat to the bigger dinosaurs, which soon get back to their business.

Spinosaurus

Longer and probably heavier than the mighty *Tyrannosaurus rex* (pages 140–141), this gigantic theropod dinosaur may have been the largest land predator that the world has ever seen.

This is one of the most exciting dinosaurs ever discovered, but also one of the most mysterious because only a few of its bones have been found. These show that it was a giant, with a spectacular "sail" on its back supported by specially extended vertebrae (the bones of its spine). Remains of the skull show that it had long jaws with sharp-pointed teeth, just like a crocodile, and it is thought likely that *Spinosaurus* largely preyed on fish in shallow waters.

Bony crest
The short, fan-like, bony crest in front of its eyes was a display feature.

Mobile neck
Its long, flexible neck allowed *Spinosaurus* to strike fast with its specialized jaws.

Fish-catching jaws
The upper jaw was like a crocodile's, with a crown-like array of long teeth at the front – ideal for seizing big, slippery fish. Small pores in the snout may have held pressure sensors for detecting prey in murky water.

Curved claws
It had strong arms with three-fingered hands and very big, curved claws, especially on the thumb. It could have used these to hook fish from the water.

Webbed toes
The toes were long and had flat undersides to the claws. They may have been webbed.

Some researchers think that the **"sail"** of *Spinosaurus* extended **down much of its tail.**

Most of the **best fossil remains** of this dinosaur were **destroyed** in bombing raids during **World War II.**

Spectacular sail
The tall "sail" rising from the dinosaur's back made it look even bigger.

Flexible tail
Fossil bones show that *Spinosaurus* had a long, flexible tail.

Spinosaurus most likely hunted the various giant fish that swam in the rivers and estuaries, such as
giant sawfishes and coelacanths.

Scaly skin
The skin was probably scaly, like that of most other large theropod dinosaurs.

DINOSAUR
SPINOSAURUS
When: 112–97 MYA

Habitat: Tropical swamps

Length: 16 m (52 ft)

Diet: Fish

Spinosaurus reimagined
Dinosaur experts once assumed that *Spinosaurus* was much like other big predatory dinosaurs, with long back legs suited for walking and running on land. However, in a 2014 study, some scientists argued that *Spinosaurus* actually had short legs and was adapted for swimming and fishing in large rivers and estuaries. The study was promptly challenged and the debate continues. It seems probable that while *Spinosaurus* may not have been specialized for an aquatic lifestyle, it was a fish-eating, shoreline predator.

Argentinosaurus

Many dinosaurs were giants, but this colossal titanosaur was of a size that almost defies belief. It is one of the largest dinosaurs ever found, and perhaps the biggest that ever lived.

The titanosaurs were a group of long-necked sauropod dinosaurs that flourished from the Late Jurassic until the great extinction. Some were relatively small, but *Argentinosaurus* was truly titanic. Only parts of its skeleton survive as fossils, but comparing these with the bones of better-known titanosaurs shows that it could have been heavier than any land animal that has lived before or since. Like most sauropods, it was specialized for stripping the foliage from the upper branches of tall trees, but *Argentinosaurus* probably ate almost any plant material it could find to satisfy its enormous appetite.

Everything that we know about *Argentinosaurus* has been deduced from **a few ribs, some bones from the spine, and two leg bones.** This is why we are still not sure how big it was.

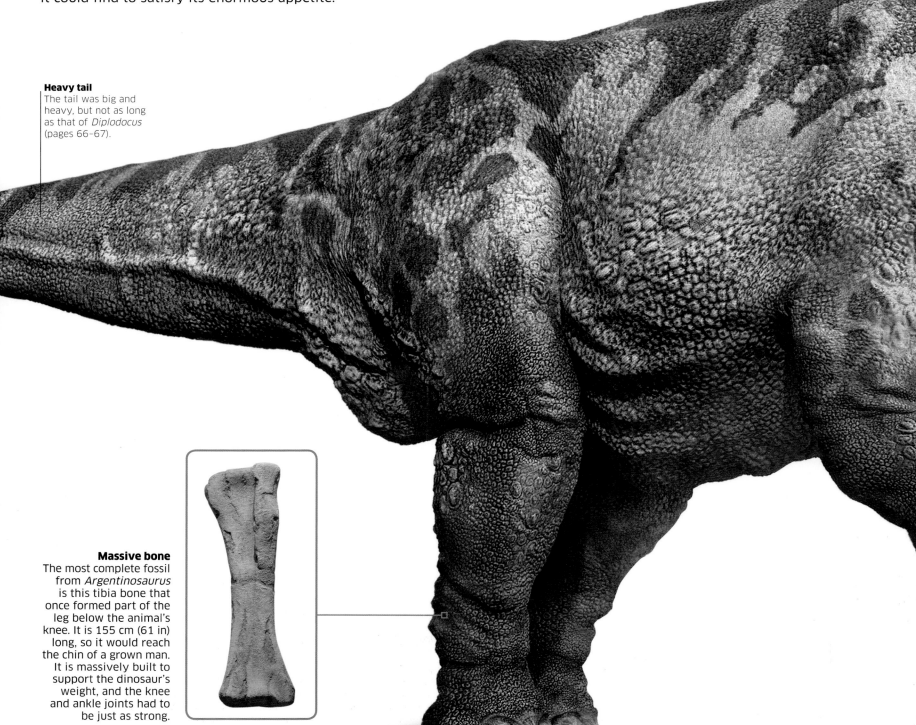

Scaly skin
Its skin would have had an outer layer of tough protective scales.

Heavy tail
The tail was big and heavy, but not as long as that of *Diplodocus* (pages 66–67).

Massive bone
The most complete fossil from *Argentinosaurus* is this tibia bone that once formed part of the leg below the animal's knee. It is 155 cm (61 in) long, so it would reach the chin of a grown man. It is massively built to support the dinosaur's weight, and the knee and ankle joints had to be just as strong.

The **only animal that has weighed more** than *Argentinosaurus* is the **gigantic blue whale**.

24 kph (15 mph) – the **likely top speed** of an *Argentinosaurus* on the move.

105

ARGENTINOSAURUS

When: 96–94 MYA

Habitat: Forests

Length: 35 m (115 ft)

Diet: Plants

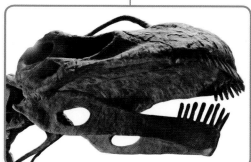

Skull
A skull of this dinosaur has still not been found, but scientists think it would have had a broad, short snout with large pencil-shaped teeth at the front of its jaws, and no chewing teeth. Shown here is a reconstruction.

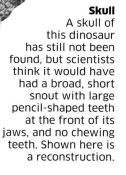

Long neck
Like other titanosaurs, it had a long neck for feeding from treetops.

Colossal dinosaur
Although not the longest dinosaur that has been found, *Argentinosaurus* was probably the largest, and therefore the heaviest. However, we will not know for sure until fossil hunters find a more complete skeleton of this enormous sauropod.

ARGENTINOSAURUS   **SIX FIRE ENGINES**

Stumpy feet
Titanosaurs had very odd front feet. They were modified hands, but they had no fingers. This means that the titanosaurs stood on their metacarpals – the same bones that form the palms of the hands in humans.

Titanic weight
Argentinosaurus was clearly a very heavy dinosaur. Scientists analysing the few surviving bones have worked out that it could have weighed anywhere between 60 and 100 tonnes. This means it could have been as heavy as six or more fire engines – a colossal weight to support on four legs.

ARGENTINOSAURUS
35 m (115 ft)

GIRAFFE
6 m (19.6 ft)

AFRICAN ELEPHANT
3.1 m (10 ft)

HUMAN
1.83 M (6 FT)

Stupendous size
As one of the biggest of the giant sauropods, *Argentinosaurus* would have dwarfed most of the dinosaurs that lived in its native South America at the same time. It would certainly tower over the biggest land animals living today, such as giraffes and African elephants.

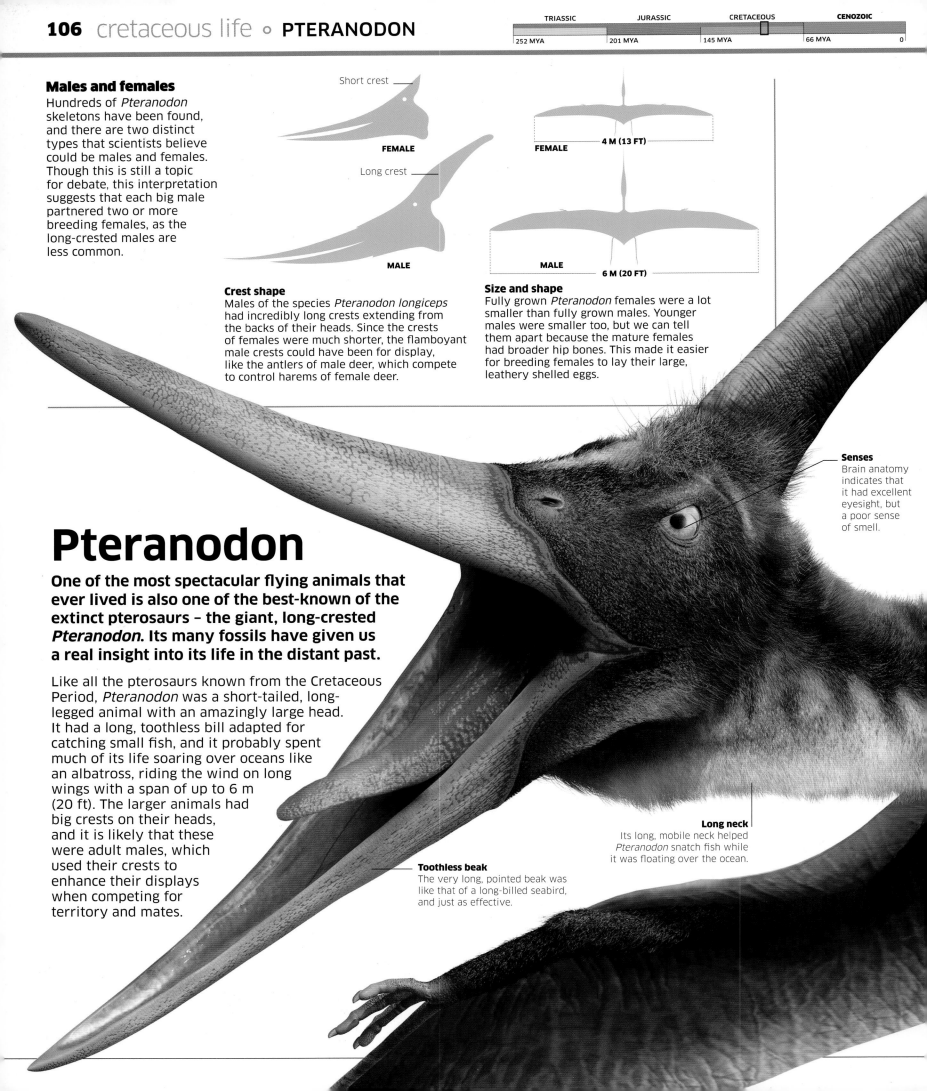

Males and females

Hundreds of *Pteranodon* skeletons have been found, and there are two distinct types that scientists believe could be males and females. Though this is still a topic for debate, this interpretation suggests that each big male partnered two or more breeding females, as the long-crested males are less common.

Short crest

FEMALE

Long crest

MALE

FEMALE

4 M (13 FT)

MALE

6 M (20 FT)

Crest shape

Males of the species *Pteranodon longiceps* had incredibly long crests extending from the backs of their heads. Since the crests of females were much shorter, the flamboyant male crests could have been for display, like the antlers of male deer, which compete to control harems of female deer.

Size and shape

Fully grown *Pteranodon* females were a lot smaller than fully grown males. Younger males were smaller too, but we can tell them apart because the mature females had broader hip bones. This made it easier for breeding females to lay their large, leathery shelled eggs.

Pteranodon

One of the most spectacular flying animals that ever lived is also one of the best-known of the extinct pterosaurs – the giant, long-crested *Pteranodon*. Its many fossils have given us a real insight into its life in the distant past.

Like all the pterosaurs known from the Cretaceous Period, *Pteranodon* was a short-tailed, long-legged animal with an amazingly large head. It had a long, toothless bill adapted for catching small fish, and it probably spent much of its life soaring over oceans like an albatross, riding the wind on long wings with a span of up to 6 m (20 ft). The larger animals had big crests on their heads, and it is likely that these were adult males, which used their crests to enhance their displays when competing for territory and mates.

Senses
Brain anatomy indicates that it had excellent eyesight, but a poor sense of smell.

Long neck
Its long, mobile neck helped *Pteranodon* snatch fish while it was floating over the ocean.

Toothless beak
The very long, pointed beak was like that of a long-billed seabird, and just as effective.

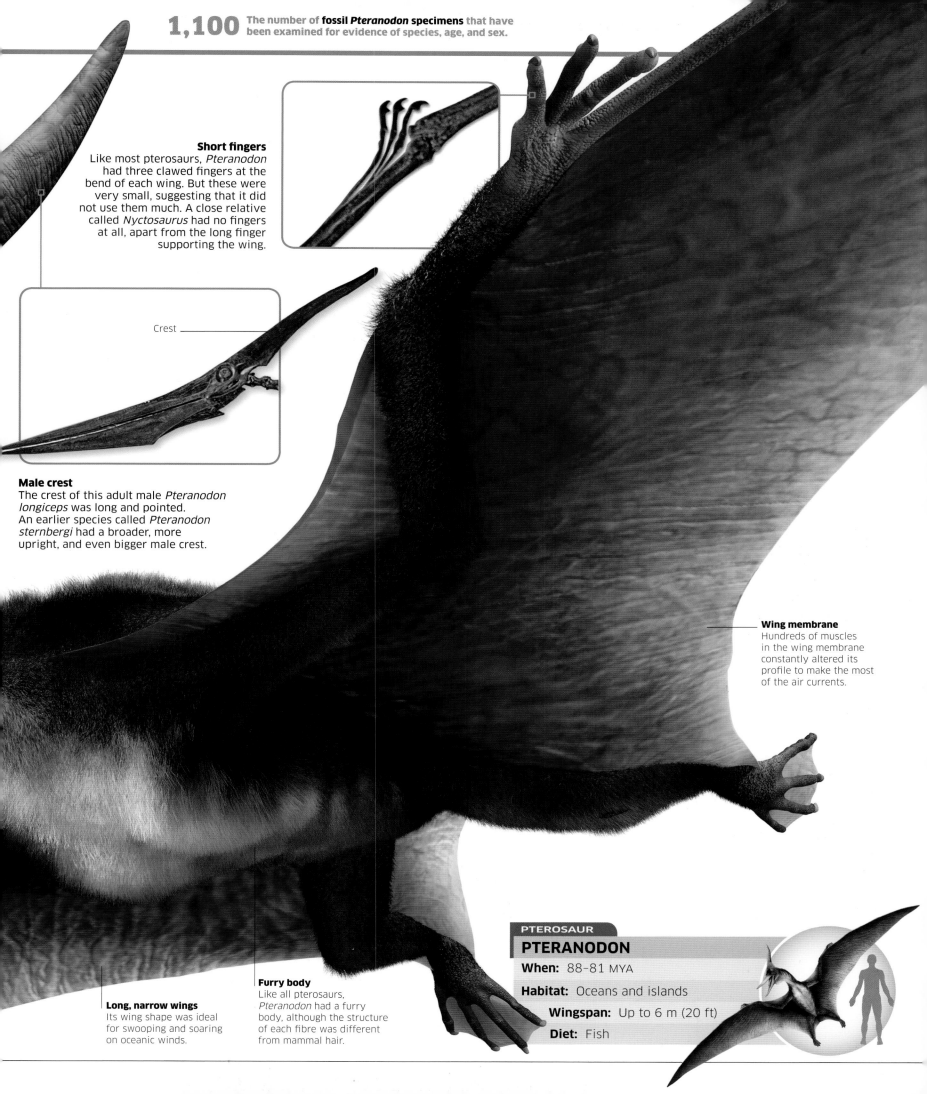

Short fingers
Like most pterosaurs, *Pteranodon* had three clawed fingers at the bend of each wing. But these were very small, suggesting that it did not use them much. A close relative called *Nyctosaurus* had no fingers at all, apart from the long finger supporting the wing.

Crest

Male crest
The crest of this adult male *Pteranodon longiceps* was long and pointed. An earlier species called *Pteranodon sternbergi* had a broader, more upright, and even bigger male crest.

Wing membrane
Hundreds of muscles in the wing membrane constantly altered its profile to make the most of the air currents.

Long, narrow wings
Its wing shape was ideal for swooping and soaring on oceanic winds.

Furry body
Like all pterosaurs, *Pteranodon* had a furry body, although the structure of each fibre was different from mammal hair.

PTEROSAUR
PTERANODON

When: 88–81 MYA

Habitat: Oceans and islands

Wingspan: Up to 6 m (20 ft)

Diet: Fish

Athletic build
Its lean, lightweight body was built for agility rather than sheer strength.

Razor teeth
The long, low, upturned snout was equipped with up to 56 teeth. Each tooth was a back-curved blade with serrated razor edges, ideal for carving meat from bones.

Velociraptor

Light, fast, and very agile, this was one of the smaller dromaeosaurids – bird-like hunters that were armed with special, lethally sharp "killer claws" on each foot.

Now known to have been covered with dense feathers, including long, vaned feathers on its powerful arms, *Velociraptor* was a close relative of the earliest bird-like dinosaurs such as *Archaeopteryx* (pages 76–77). *Velociraptor* could not fly, but in most other respects it would have looked and even behaved very like an eagle, ripping into a prey animal with specialized claws before pinning it down and using curved, meat-slicing teeth to tear it apart.

Clawed hands
Velociraptor had big, grasping hands, with three very strong, sharp claws.

Velociraptor's large eyes may have helped it to see small prey better, or to hunt at night to avoid the **desert's scorching daytime heat**.

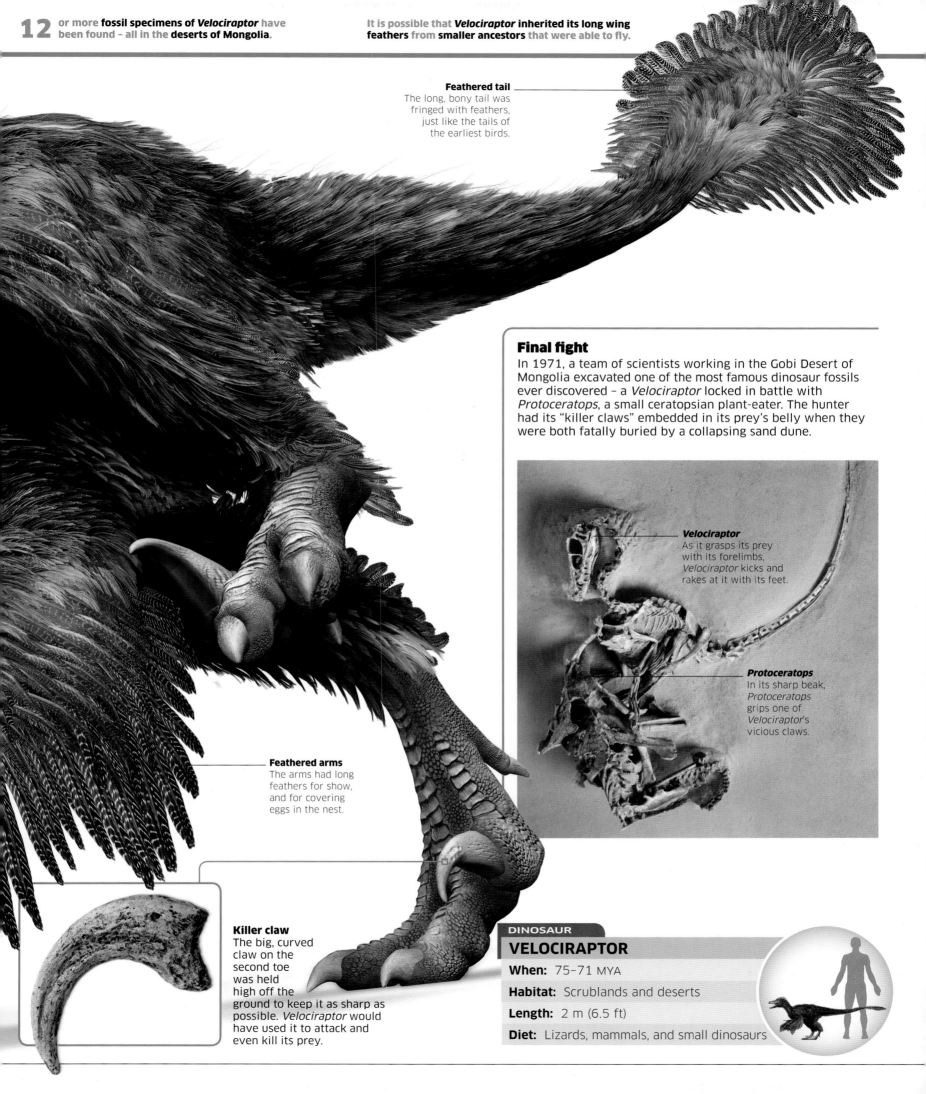

It is possible that ***Velociraptor*** inherited its long wing feathers from smaller ancestors that were able to fly.

Feathered tail
The long, bony tail was fringed with feathers, just like the tails of the earliest birds.

Final fight

In 1971, a team of scientists working in the Gobi Desert of Mongolia excavated one of the most famous dinosaur fossils ever discovered – a *Velociraptor* locked in battle with *Protoceratops*, a small ceratopsian plant-eater. The hunter had its "killer claws" embedded in its prey's belly when they were both fatally buried by a collapsing sand dune.

Velociraptor
As it grasps its prey with its forelimbs, *Velociraptor* kicks and rakes at it with its feet.

Protoceratops
In its sharp beak, *Protoceratops* grips one of *Velociraptor*'s vicious claws.

Feathered arms
The arms had long feathers for show, and for covering eggs in the nest.

Killer claw
The big, curved claw on the second toe was held high off the ground to keep it as sharp as possible. *Velociraptor* would have used it to attack and even kill its prey.

DINOSAUR
VELOCIRAPTOR

When: 75–71 MYA

Habitat: Scrublands and deserts

Length: 2 m (6.5 ft)

Diet: Lizards, mammals, and small dinosaurs

Albertonectes

The neck of this astonishing marine reptile was longer than the rest of its body, and it had more neck bones than any other animal known to us. Quite why it needed such an incredibly long neck is still not certain.

Some of the most spectacular marine reptiles of the Mesozoic Era were the plesiosaurs – big-bodied creatures that drove themselves through the water with four long flippers. Some, usually known as pliosaurs, had big heads and short necks. Others, including *Albertonectes*, had small heads and very long necks. This seems to have been an adaptation for picking shellfish and similar animals off the sea bed as the creature swam slowly forwards, but it probably also captured fish, squid, and other prey.

76 The record-breaking number of bones in the neck of this massive plesiosaur.

Small scales
The skin was protected by small, smooth scales, which streamlined its body.

Long neck
This animal has the longest neck of any plesiosaur discovered so far, although its relative *Elasmosaurus* comes close.

Front flipper
Each front flipper was a modified arm with the bones of five "fingers" supporting the broad paddle blade.

Small head
The small head and jaws were typical of long-necked plesiosaurs.

Short tail
This reptile's tail was much shorter than its neck. The structure of its fossil tail vertebrae suggests that *Albertonectes* may have had a tail fin to help it manoeuvre in the water.

Back flipper
The back flippers had the same basic form as the front flippers.

Swimming style
Albertonectes swam by sweeping its flippers up and down in the water like wings.

TRIASSIC	JURASSIC	CRETACEOUS	CENOZOIC
252 MYA	201 MYA	145 MYA	66 MYA	0

Albertonectes swallowed stones
to help grind up food in its **stomach**.

111

Extravagant coils

When long-necked plesiosaurs were first found, people thought these animals could twist their necks into serpentine coils to snatch passing fish, as in this old print. But careful study of their neck bones shows that this was impossible. The neck of *Albertonectes* was probably no more flexible than that of a long-necked dinosaur.

***ELASMOSAURUS* AS DEPICTED IN 1897**

LIOPLEURODON

ALBERTONECTES

Plesiosaurs and pliosaurs

Plesiosaurs such as *Albertonectes* had amazingly long necks and small jaws. Pliosaurs, such as *Liopleurodon* (pages 56–57), had the same body form, but their short necks carried massive heads with huge jaws used for seizing and eating other marine reptiles.

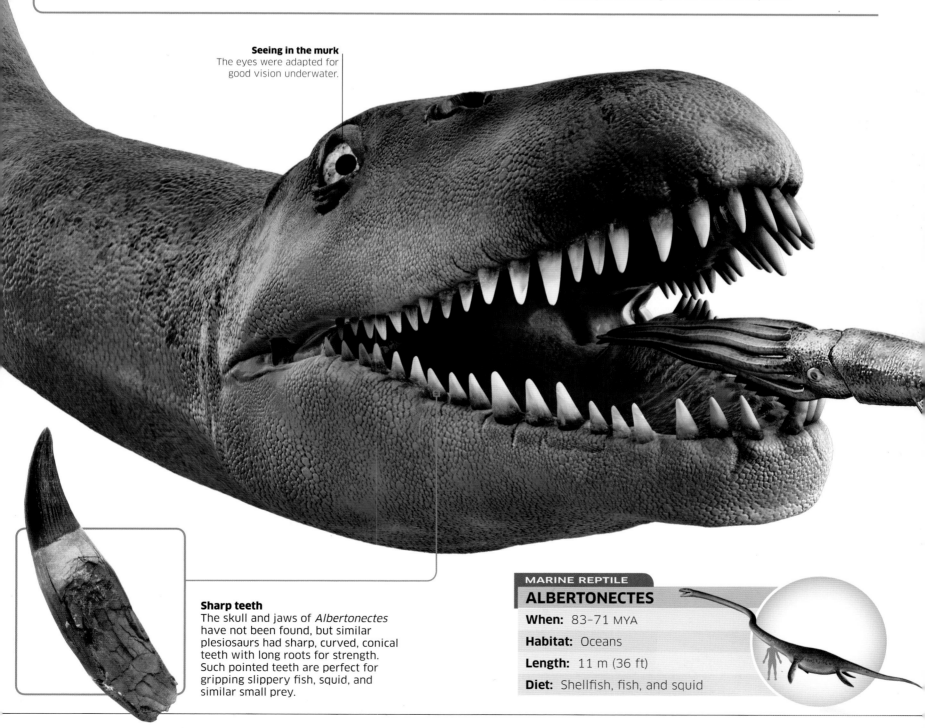

Seeing in the murk
The eyes were adapted for good vision underwater.

Sharp teeth

The skull and jaws of *Albertonectes* have not been found, but similar plesiosaurs had sharp, curved, conical teeth with long roots for strength. Such pointed teeth are perfect for gripping slippery fish, squid, and similar small prey.

MARINE REPTILE
ALBERTONECTES

When: 83–71 MYA

Habitat: Oceans

Length: 11 m (36 ft)

Diet: Shellfish, fish, and squid

Small skull

The small skull had a long snout with toothless jaws. The bones of the snout probably supported a beak made from keratin – the same material that forms bird beaks and our own fingernails. The large eye sockets contained big eyes.

Nostril

Eye socket

Grappling fingers

Each long arm had three long fingers equipped with sharp, curved claws. The second and third fingers may have been bound together by soft tissue, and used like a grappling hook to pull fruit within reach of the animal's mouth.

Ostrich mimic

The name *Struthiomimus* means "ostrich mimic", which describes this dinosaur well. Its long neck, beaky head, and powerful legs were very like those of a modern ostrich, and it may have ran just as fast. Ostriches can hit 70 kph (43 mph), and it is possible that *Struthiomimus* could match that. It also had a similar mixed diet, so its name suits it perfectly.

Long neck

Its long, slender, flexible neck helped *Struthiomimus* reach food on the ground.

Struthiomimus

With its long legs and sleek, streamlined body, this agile theropod was built for speed. *Struthiomimus* lived alongside some powerful killer dinosaurs, and probably needed its speed to survive.

The ornithomimosaurs were theropods that evolved at the same time as the tyrannosaurs, but they were very different. Unlike their massive-jawed relatives, they were slender, speedy animals with small heads, and specialized ones such as *Struthiomimus* had a beak instead of teeth. *Struthiomimus* would have eaten a mixed diet of small animals, seeds, and fruits. Its long legs gave it the speed it needed to help catch small prey, but they probably evolved to help the animal escape being eaten by predators.

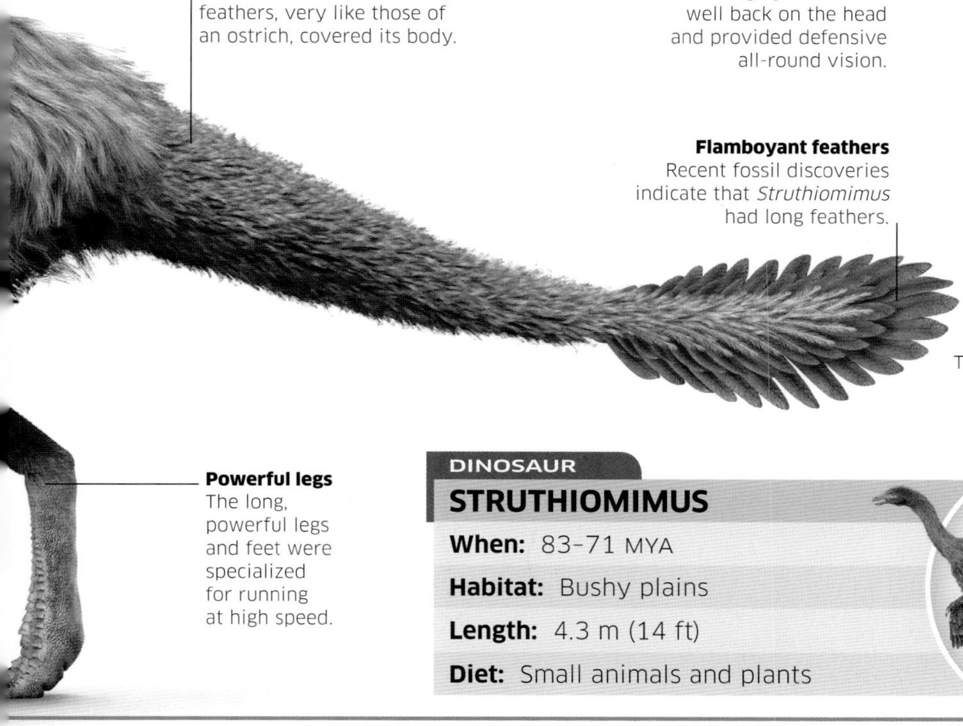

Feathery body
A warm coat of soft, downy feathers, very like those of an ostrich, covered its body.

Big eyes
The big eyes were set well back on the head and provided defensive all-round vision.

Flamboyant feathers
Recent fossil discoveries indicate that *Struthiomimus* had long feathers.

Toothless beak
The beak was toothless, exactly like that of a modern bird.

Powerful legs
The long, powerful legs and feet were specialized for running at high speed.

DINOSAUR
STRUTHIOMIMUS

When: 83–71 MYA

Habitat: Bushy plains

Length: 4.3 m (14 ft)

Diet: Small animals and plants

Fossil skeleton
Discovered in Alberta, Canada, in 1914, this *Struthiomimus* skeleton is one of the most complete dinosaur fossils ever found. Its strange posture may indicate that the animal died by drowning.

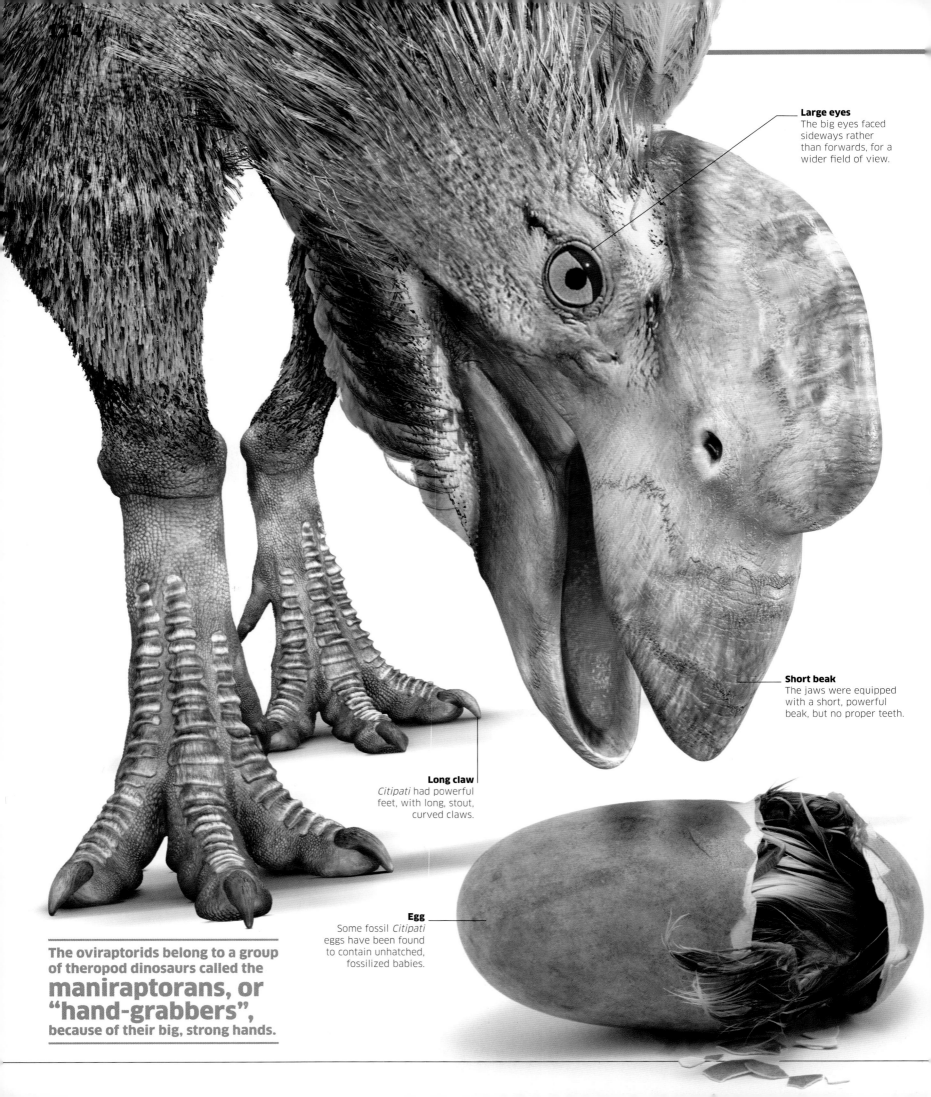

Large eyes
The big eyes faced sideways rather than forwards, for a wider field of view.

Short beak
The jaws were equipped with a short, powerful beak, but no proper teeth.

Long claw
Citipati had powerful feet, with long, stout, curved claws.

Egg
Some fossil *Citipati* eggs have been found to contain unhatched, fossilized babies.

The oviraptorids belong to a group of theropod dinosaurs called the **maniraptorans, or "hand-grabbers",** because of their big, strong hands.

Citipati's oval-shaped eggs were huge – even bigger than **a man's hand**.

DINOSAUR
CITIPATI

When: 83–71 MYA

Habitat: Plains and deserts

Length: 3 m (10 ft)

Diet: Small animals, eggs, seeds, and leaves

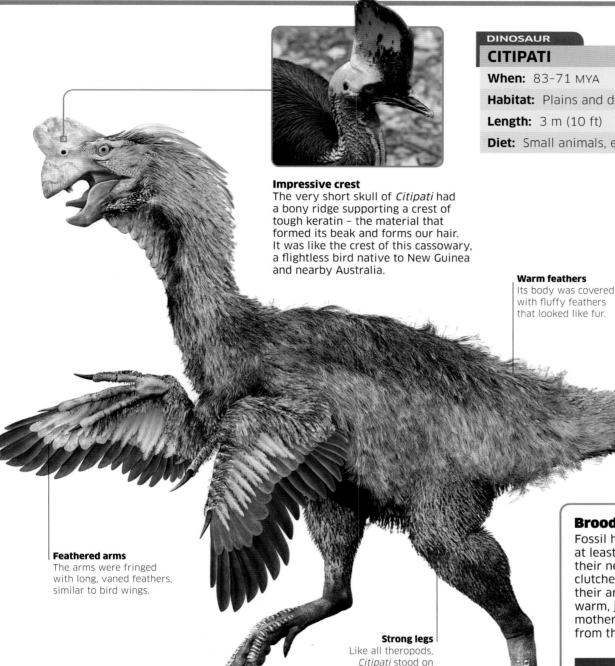

Impressive crest
The very short skull of *Citipati* had a bony ridge supporting a crest of tough keratin – the material that formed its beak and forms our hair. It was like the crest of this cassowary, a flightless bird native to New Guinea and nearby Australia.

Warm feathers
Its body was covered with fluffy feathers that looked like fur.

Tail plumes
The long tail may have been adorned with feathery plumes.

Feathered arms
The arms were fringed with long, vaned feathers, similar to bird wings.

Strong legs
Like all theropods, *Citipati* stood on its strong hind legs, balanced by its tail.

Brooding mother
Fossil hunters in the Gobi Desert have found at least four specimens of *Citipati* sitting on their nests, with their arms outspread over clutches of oval eggs. The long feathers on their arms covered the eggs and kept them warm, just as the wings of birds do. But this mother could not save herself or her eggs from the sandstorm that killed them.

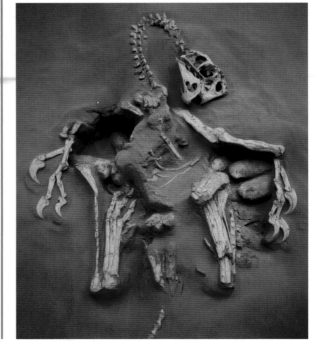

Citipati

This odd-looking dinosaur was an oviraptorid – a toothless, beaked theropod adapted to live on a broad diet of small animals, eggs, fruits, seeds, and other foods. It was closely related to birds and fierce predators such as *Velociraptor* (pages 108–109).

The oviraptorids are named after a similar animal called *Oviraptor*, or "egg-thief", which was given this name because its fossil was found near a nest of dinosaur eggs, and its discoverers thought it was stealing them when it died. In fact, they were its own eggs, but both *Oviraptor* and *Citipati* have a pair of bony knobs in the roof of the mouth that would be ideal for cracking eggs. Modern crows steal the eggs of other birds, and it is likely that *Citipati* behaved in the same way. But we also know that it took great care of its own eggs, brooding them in the nest until they hatched.

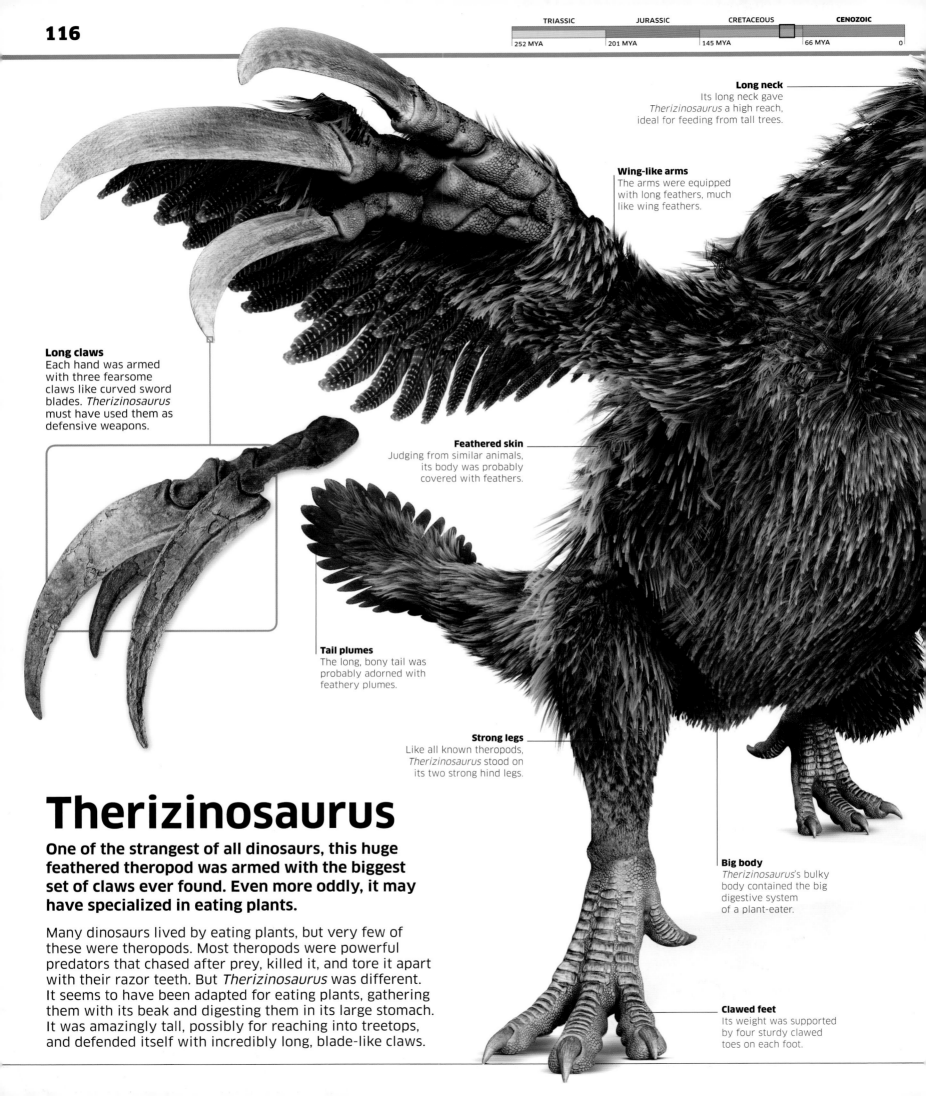

Long neck
Its long neck gave
Therizinosaurus a high reach,
ideal for feeding from tall trees.

Wing-like arms
The arms were equipped
with long feathers, much
like wing feathers.

Long claws
Each hand was armed
with three fearsome
claws like curved sword
blades. *Therizinosaurus*
must have used them as
defensive weapons.

Feathered skin
Judging from similar animals,
its body was probably
covered with feathers.

Tail plumes
The long, bony tail was
probably adorned with
feathery plumes.

Strong legs
Like all known theropods,
Therizinosaurus stood on
its two strong hind legs.

Big body
Therizinosaurus's bulky
body contained the big
digestive system
of a plant-eater.

Therizinosaurus

One of the strangest of all dinosaurs, this huge feathered theropod was armed with the biggest set of claws ever found. Even more oddly, it may have specialized in eating plants.

Many dinosaurs lived by eating plants, but very few of these were theropods. Most theropods were powerful predators that chased after prey, killed it, and tore it apart with their razor teeth. But *Therizinosaurus* was different. It seems to have been adapted for eating plants, gathering them with its beak and digesting them in its large stomach. It was amazingly tall, possibly for reaching into treetops, and defended itself with incredibly long, blade-like claws.

Clawed feet
Its weight was supported
by four sturdy clawed
toes on each foot.

Small head
The head was small, and probably had side-facing eyes for a wide view.

Although plants made up most of its diet, *Therizinosaurus* **probably ate a few small animals too.**

Beaky jaws
The jaws were tipped with a tough, sharp-edged beak, ideal for cropping leaves.

DINOSAUR
THERIZINOSAURUS

When: 83–71 MYA

Habitat: Forests

Length: 8–11 m (26–36 ft)

Diet: Plants and small animals

Teeth for the job
The teeth of *Therizinosaurus* have not been found, but its close relatives had leaf-shaped teeth, like those of many plant-eating dinosaurs.

Amazing claws
The claw bones were up to 76 cm (30 in) long – a lot longer than a Roman sword. In life each claw had a horny sheath, making it longer still!

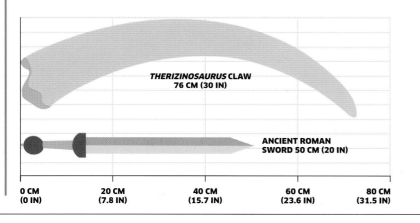

THERIZINOSAURUS CLAW
76 CM (30 IN)

ANCIENT ROMAN
SWORD 50 CM (20 IN)

0 CM (0 IN)	20 CM (7.8 IN)	40 CM (15.7 IN)	60 CM (23.6 IN)	80 CM (31.5 IN)

Panda bear
If *Therizinosaurus* really was adapted for eating plants, then it resembled a very well-known modern animal. The giant panda is a bear that specializes in eating bamboo shoots. Bears are usually carnivores, but pandas only rarely eat meat.

GIANT PANDA

Ambush tactics

Modern alligators and crocodiles are specialized for hunting in the water. They can lie in wait with just their eyes and nostrils above the surface, then surge forwards, driven by their powerful tails, to seize prey in their jaws. Nile crocodiles often use this technique to prey on land animals such as this wildebeest. *Deinosuchus* may have used exactly the same tactics to hunt dinosaurs.

Giant crocodilian

Compared to modern alligators and crocodiles, *Deinosuchus* was a monster. It grew to at least 12 m (39 ft) long – almost twice the length of the saltwater crocodile, which is the largest living crocodilian. It may have weighed more than 8,000 kg (17,630 lb), which was a lot more than many of the dinosaurs that shared its North American habitat. In some parts of its range it was probably the most powerful predator, since no theropod dinosaurs of comparable size lived in its neighbourhood.

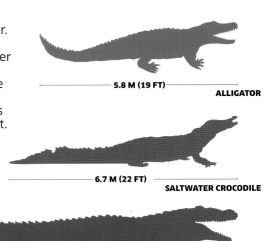

5.8 M (19 FT) ——— **ALLIGATOR**

6.7 M (22 FT) ——— **SALTWATER CROCODILE**

12 M (39 FT) ——— *DEINOSUCHUS*

Deinosuchus

This giant relative of the alligators was one of the most powerful predators of its era. Although it hunted in rivers, it could easily have ambushed and killed dinosaurs drinking in the shallows.

With its heavy body and very short legs, *Deinosuchus* would have been quite clumsy on land, and not as agile as modern alligators and crocodiles. Once in the water, however, it was transformed into a fast, deadly hunter. It probably preyed mainly on large fish and turtles, and was equipped with strong, shell-crushing teeth at the back of its jaws for dealing with armoured prey. But it would also have kept watch for any land animals wading into the water, and was quite strong enough to seize and drown a mid-sized dinosaur.

The fearsome jaws of *Deinosuchus* were immensely powerful, with a bite force that was comparable to that of *Tyrannosaurus rex.*

88 **teeth**, or more, armed the **jaws** of *Deinosuchus*.

Some dinosaur bones found in Texas, USA, show evidence of ***Deinosuchus* tooth marks**.

Although *Deinosuchus* was an ancestral alligator, its name means **"terror crocodile"**.

119

Reconstructed skull
Only fragments of the skull have been found, but were used to create this reconstruction. Scientists now think that *Deinosuchus* had a broader snout, like a modern alligator's.

CROCODILIAN
DEINOSUCHUS

When: 80–71 MYA

Habitat: Rivers and swamps

Length: 12 m (39 ft)

Diet: Fish, turtles, and dinosaurs

High-set eyes
These allowed *Deinosuchus* to lurk in ambush with its body hidden beneath the surface of the water.

Broad snout
The long, broadly U-shaped snout was well adapted for seizing prey underwater.

Spiky teeth
Sharp-pointed teeth in the front of the jaw ensured a good grip on slippery fish.

Stout claw

Small hands
The small, five-toed hands would have been partially webbed to stop them sinking into soft mud, and to make them more useful in the water.

Heavy armour
Its body was armoured and strengthened by very thick, heavy, bony plates.

Short legs
The legs were very short, which indicates that *Deinosuchus* probably lived mainly in the water.

Length
From head to tail, *Deinosuchus* was as long as *Tyrannosaurus rex*.

Long tail
The reptile used its long, muscular tail to propel itself through the water.

BREAKING OUT

After spending the cold, starry desert night keeping her nest of eggs warm, a mother *Citipati* takes advantage of the morning sun to look for something she can eat.

As she stands up, soft calls from inside the eggs tells her they are going to hatch. Within minutes the babies are chipping at the shells, and before long one of them is almost ready to emerge. Covered with fluffy feathers, they will soon be able to follow their mother into the desert scrub to look for their first meal.

Nemegtbaatar

This small furry mammal was one of many that scurried around the feet of Late Cretaceous dinosaurs. It looks like a rodent such as a mouse, but was actually a type of mammal that has been extinct for 35 million years.

Nemegtbaatar was one of a group of small mammals called the multituberculates. The group name refers to their specialized back teeth, which had many small bumps known as tubercles. It also had big, blade-like cheek teeth in its lower jaw, and it used these to slice through tough plant food. It probably had a broad diet, eating small animals as well.

Warm fur
A dense coat of fur kept *Nemegtbaatar*'s body warm, which was vital for such a small mammal.

Low profile
Nemegtbaatar may have held its body close to the ground, but some think it stood with its legs upright.

Slicing jaws
Like many of its relatives, *Nemegtbaatar* had a very big, sharp-edged, serrated tooth on each side of its lower jaw. It was able to pull its jaw backwards as it chewed, slicing each blade tooth through its food like a knife. This must have been very useful for cutting through tough plant stems or large seeds.

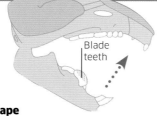

Gape
Sliding its jaw back, the animal could gape its mouth wide open, take a mouthful of food, and close it again to get a good grip.

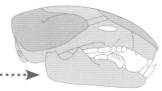

Snap
As *Nemegtbaatar* closed its mouth, its special jaw joint allowed the lower jaw to slide forwards. This ensured that the front teeth came together.

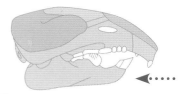

Slice
Specially adapted muscles pulled the jaw back, so the blade teeth could saw through its food, like a serrated kitchen knife.

Nemegtbaatar gets its name from the Nemegt rock formation of Mongolia, where its fossils were found.

Like many modern small mammals, *Nemegtbaatar* probably foraged at night to avoid its enemies.

123

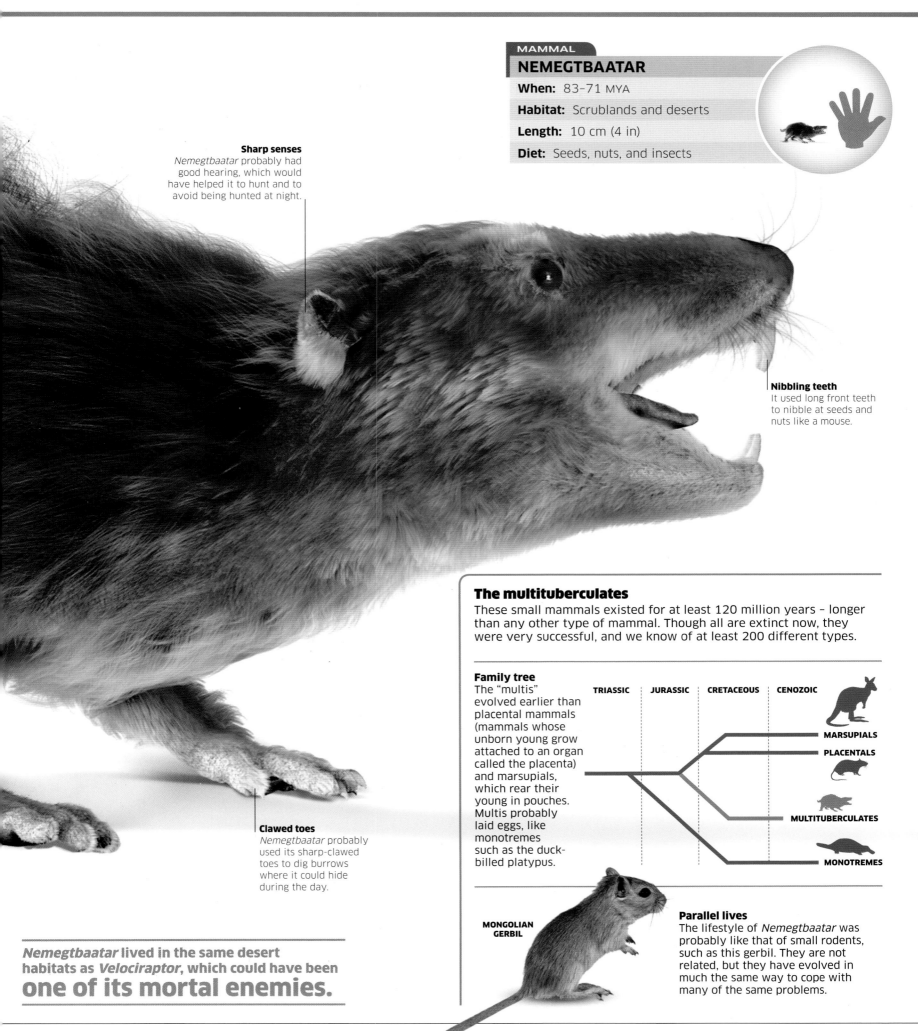

MAMMAL

NEMEGTBAATAR

When: 83–71 MYA

Habitat: Scrublands and deserts

Length: 10 cm (4 in)

Diet: Seeds, nuts, and insects

Sharp senses
Nemegtbaatar probably had good hearing, which would have helped it to hunt and to avoid being hunted at night.

Nibbling teeth
It used long front teeth to nibble at seeds and nuts like a mouse.

Clawed toes
Nemegtbaatar probably used its sharp-clawed toes to dig burrows where it could hide during the day.

The multituberculates
These small mammals existed for at least 120 million years – longer than any other type of mammal. Though all are extinct now, they were very successful, and we know of at least 200 different types.

Family tree
The "multis" evolved earlier than placental mammals (mammals whose unborn young grow attached to an organ called the placenta) and marsupials, which rear their young in pouches. Multis probably laid eggs, like monotremes such as the duck-billed platypus.

TRIASSIC | JURASSIC | CRETACEOUS | CENOZOIC

MARSUPIALS

PLACENTALS

MULTITUBERCULATES

MONOTREMES

MONGOLIAN GERBIL

Parallel lives
The lifestyle of *Nemegtbaatar* was probably like that of small rodents, such as this gerbil. They are not related, but they have evolved in much the same way to cope with many of the same problems.

Nemegtbaatar lived in the same desert habitats as *Velociraptor*, which could have been **one of its mortal enemies.**

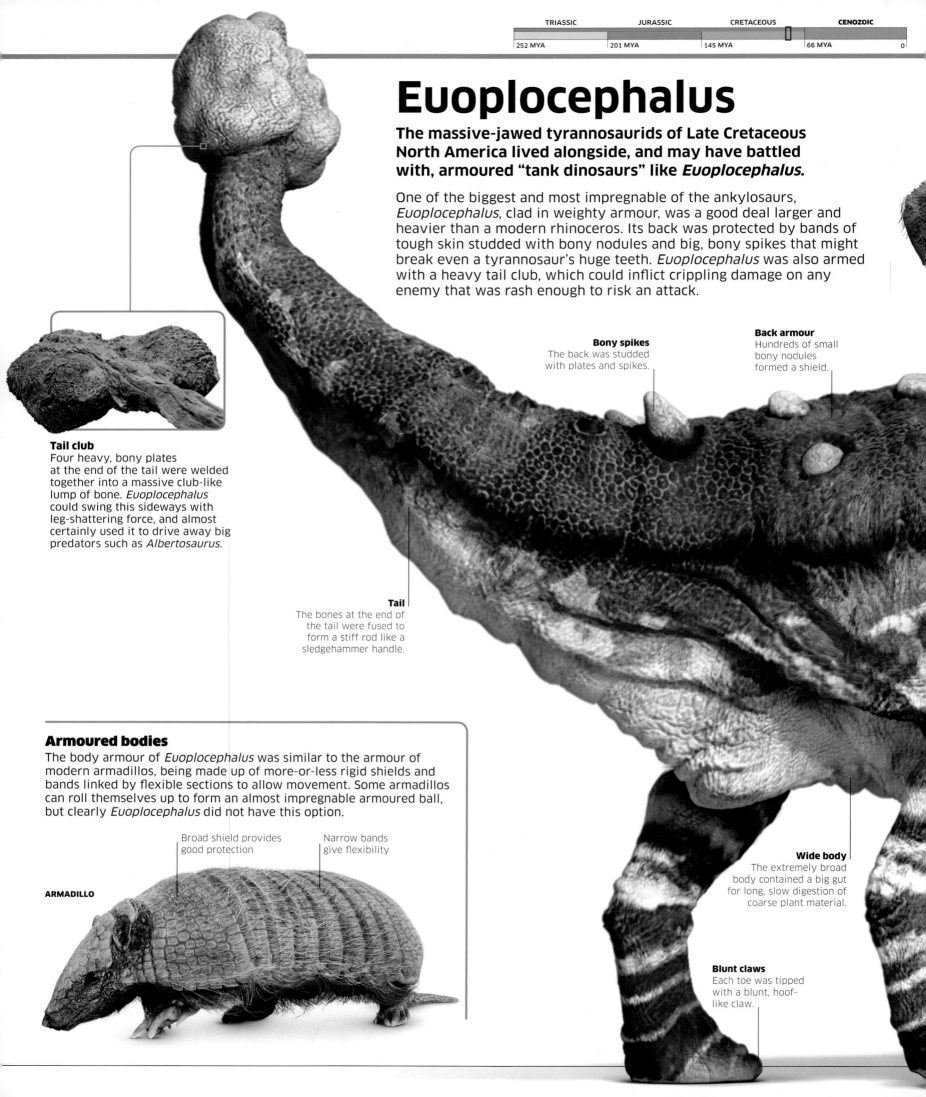

Euoplocephalus

The massive-jawed tyrannosaurids of Late Cretaceous North America lived alongside, and may have battled with, armoured "tank dinosaurs" like *Euoplocephalus*.

One of the biggest and most impregnable of the ankylosaurs, *Euoplocephalus*, clad in weighty armour, was a good deal larger and heavier than a modern rhinoceros. Its back was protected by bands of tough skin studded with bony nodules and big, bony spikes that might break even a tyrannosaur's huge teeth. *Euoplocephalus* was also armed with a heavy tail club, which could inflict crippling damage on any enemy that was rash enough to risk an attack.

Bony spikes
The back was studded with plates and spikes.

Back armour
Hundreds of small bony nodules formed a shield.

Tail club
Four heavy, bony plates at the end of the tail were welded together into a massive club-like lump of bone. *Euoplocephalus* could swing this sideways with leg-shattering force, and almost certainly used it to drive away big predators such as *Albertosaurus*.

Tail
The bones at the end of the tail were fused to form a stiff rod like a sledgehammer handle.

Armoured bodies

The body armour of *Euoplocephalus* was similar to the armour of modern armadillos, being made up of more-or-less rigid shields and bands linked by flexible sections to allow movement. Some armadillos can roll themselves up to form an almost impregnable armoured ball, but clearly *Euoplocephalus* did not have this option.

Broad shield provides good protection

Narrow bands give flexibility

ARMADILLO

Wide body
The extremely broad body contained a big gut for long, slow digestion of coarse plant material.

Blunt claws
Each toe was tipped with a blunt, hoof-like claw.

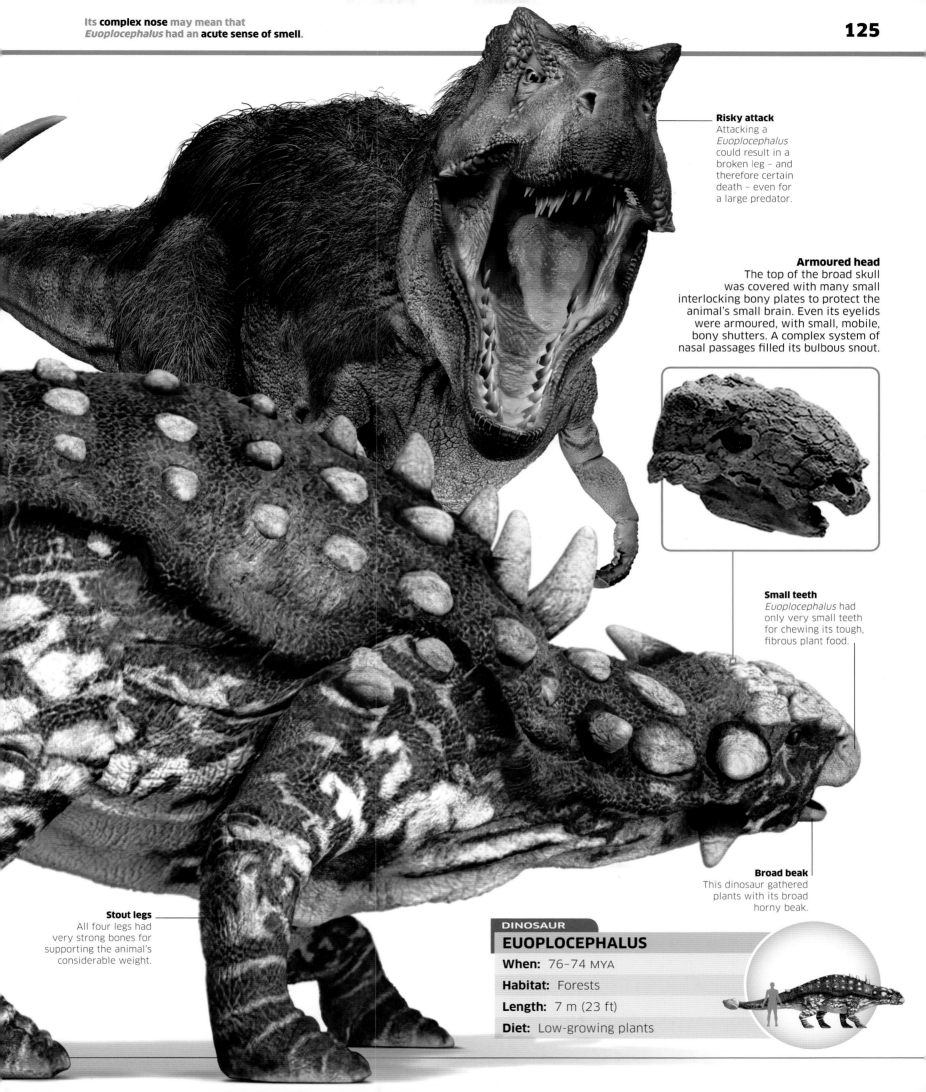

Its **complex nose** may mean that *Euoplocephalus* had an **acute sense of smell**.

Risky attack
Attacking a *Euoplocephalus* could result in a broken leg – and therefore certain death – even for a large predator.

Armoured head
The top of the broad skull was covered with many small interlocking bony plates to protect the animal's small brain. Even its eyelids were armoured, with small, mobile, bony shutters. A complex system of nasal passages filled its bulbous snout.

Small teeth
Euoplocephalus had only very small teeth for chewing its tough, fibrous plant food.

Broad beak
This dinosaur gathered plants with its broad horny beak.

Stout legs
All four legs had very strong bones for supporting the animal's considerable weight.

DINOSAUR

EUOPLOCEPHALUS

When: 76–74 MYA

Habitat: Forests

Length: 7 m (23 ft)

Diet: Low-growing plants

In the 1930s, at least one scientist believed that *Parasaurolophus* searched for food underwater, using its crest as a snorkle.

Broad beak
The tough, sharp-edged beak was perfect for gathering plant food.

High back
Tall extensions of the spine bones made its back much higher than usual.

Heavy tail
A long, heavy tail helped the dinosaur balance on its hind legs.

All fours
Strong arms allowed *Parasaurolophus* to walk on all fours when looking for food.

Strong legs
The legs had powerful muscles attached to big, strongly built hip bones.

Small scales
Fossilized impressions of *Parasaurolophus* skin show small, rounded scales.

Parasaurolophus

The impressive bony crest of this elegant plant-eater contained a network of tubes that must have had a special function. It is likely that the tubes worked like a trumpet to generate very loud, booming calls.

Towards the end of the Mesozoic, a branch of the ornithopod line related to *Iguanodon* (pages 82–83) evolved into a group of broad-beaked herbivores called hadrosaurs. Also known as duckbills, they had highly specialized grinding teeth for mashing their fibrous plant food to make it easier to digest. Some also had flamboyant crests extending from the tops of their skulls. *Parasaurolophus* had one of the longest, and almost certainly used it for display and even calling to other dinosaurs of its kind.

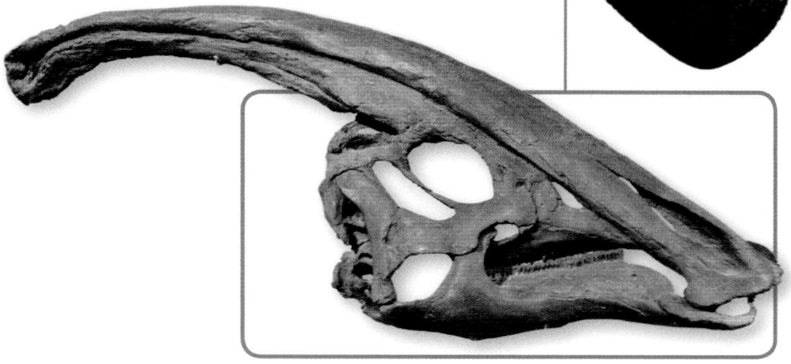

2 m (6.5 ft) – the length of the **longest** *Parasaurolophus* **skull**, including its crest.

127

Skull and crest

The long, bony crest was part of the skull, and in the species *Parasaurolophus walkeri*, shown here, it was as long as the skull itself. It was covered with skin, and may have had a web of skin between the crest and neck.

DINOSAUR

PARASAUROLOPHUS

When: 83–71 MYA

Habitat: Dense forests

Length: 9.5 m (31 ft)

Diet: Leaves

Bony trumpet

The hollow crest of *Parasaurolophus* contained tubes that extended the passages in its nose, rather like a bony version of an elephant's trunk. It may have used its crest to make similar trumpeting calls, which would have helped the animals stay in contact in dense forests. The crest of each species was different, so their calls would have varied too.

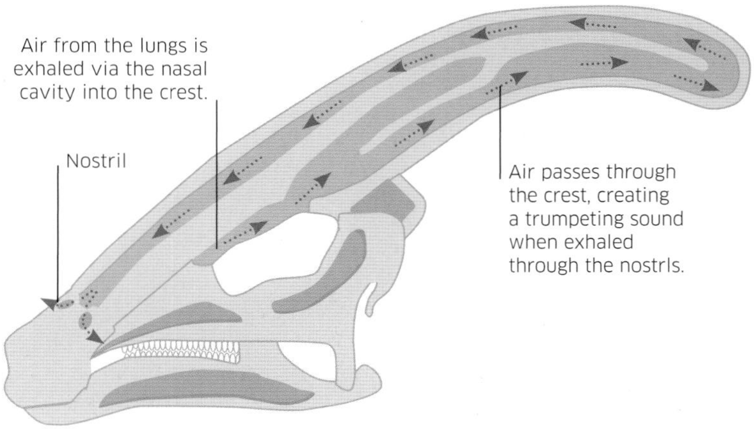

Air from the lungs is exhaled via the nasal cavity into the crest.

Nostril

Air passes through the crest, creating a trumpeting sound when exhaled through the nostrls.

PARASAUROLOPHUS SKULL

Saltasaurus's **main enemy** was a ferocious meat-eating theropod called *Abelisaurus*.

25 The number of **eggs** in a typical *Saltasaurus* nest.

All-round vision
Eyes on the sides of its head gave *Saltasaurus* good all-round vision.

Like all titanosaurs, this animal is odd because **its front feet have no toes.** It didn't need front toes (fingers) to support its weight, so over millions of years of evolution they gradually vanished.

Nostrils
Nasal openings high in the skull led to nostrils at the tip of the snout.

Mobile neck
Like all sauropods, *Saltasaurus* had a long, mobile neck supporting a small head.

Jaws
Its jaws had no cheek teeth, so *Saltasaurus* swallowed its leafy food without chewing.

Rounded jaws
The skull of *Saltasaurus* has not been found, but it would have been very like this *Nemegtosaurus* skull, with broad, rounded jaws and short, peg-like front teeth suitable for combing leaves from the twigs of trees.

Broad snout
The snout was broader near the tip, making it slightly spoon-shaped.

Spherical eggs
The reconstructed *Saltasaurus* eggs are almost perfectly round, and the size of grapefruits or small melons. They were enormous compared to a chicken's egg, but they were tiny compared to the fully grown adult dinosaurs. They were probably buried in heaps of plant material that heated up as it decayed, keeping the eggs warm.

SALTASAURUS EGG RECONSTRUCTION

Nesting ground
A huge *Saltasaurus* nesting ground was discovered in 1997 near Auca Mahuevo in Argentina. It contained the remains of thousands of eggs laid some 80 million years ago – there were so many that the ground is littered with broken fragments of their shells. They were probably laid in a traditional nesting site by several hundred females.

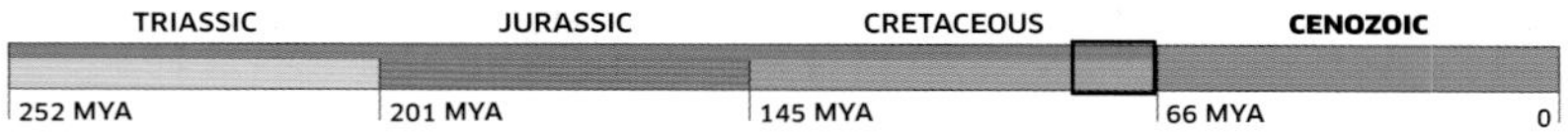

TRIASSIC
JURASSIC
CRETACEOUS
CENOZOIC
252 MYA
201 MYA
145 MYA
66 MYA
0

Some *Saltasaurus* eggs contained **fossilized embryos**, complete **with tiny, bead-like armour plates.**

DINOSAUR

SALTASAURUS

When: 80–66 MYA

Habitat: Forests and open plains

Length: 12 m (39 ft)

Diet: Leaves

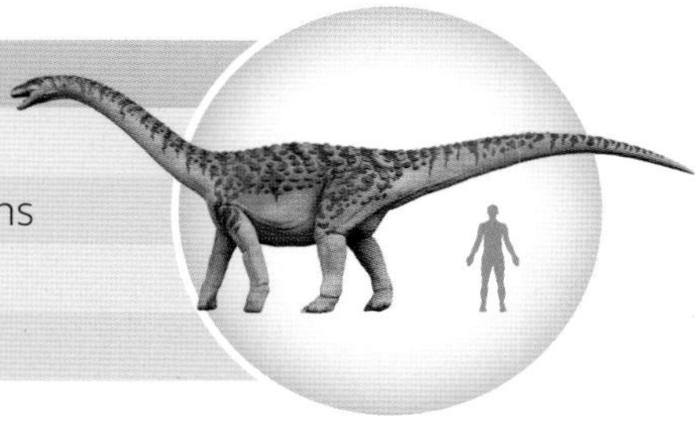

Saltasaurus

Although quite small compared to some of its giant relatives, this sauropod is intriguing because it was studded with armoured scutes that protected it from hungry predators.

Saltasaurus was a titanosaur – one of a group of sauropods that evolved quite late in the Mesozoic and flourished until the very end of the era. It lived in South America, where the titanosaurs were among the most common Late Cretaceous dinosaurs. They had broad hips and wide-spaced legs, giving them a very stable stance that helped them reach high leaves by rearing up on their hind legs. *Saltasaurus* was armoured, and it is likely that many other titanosaurs were too.

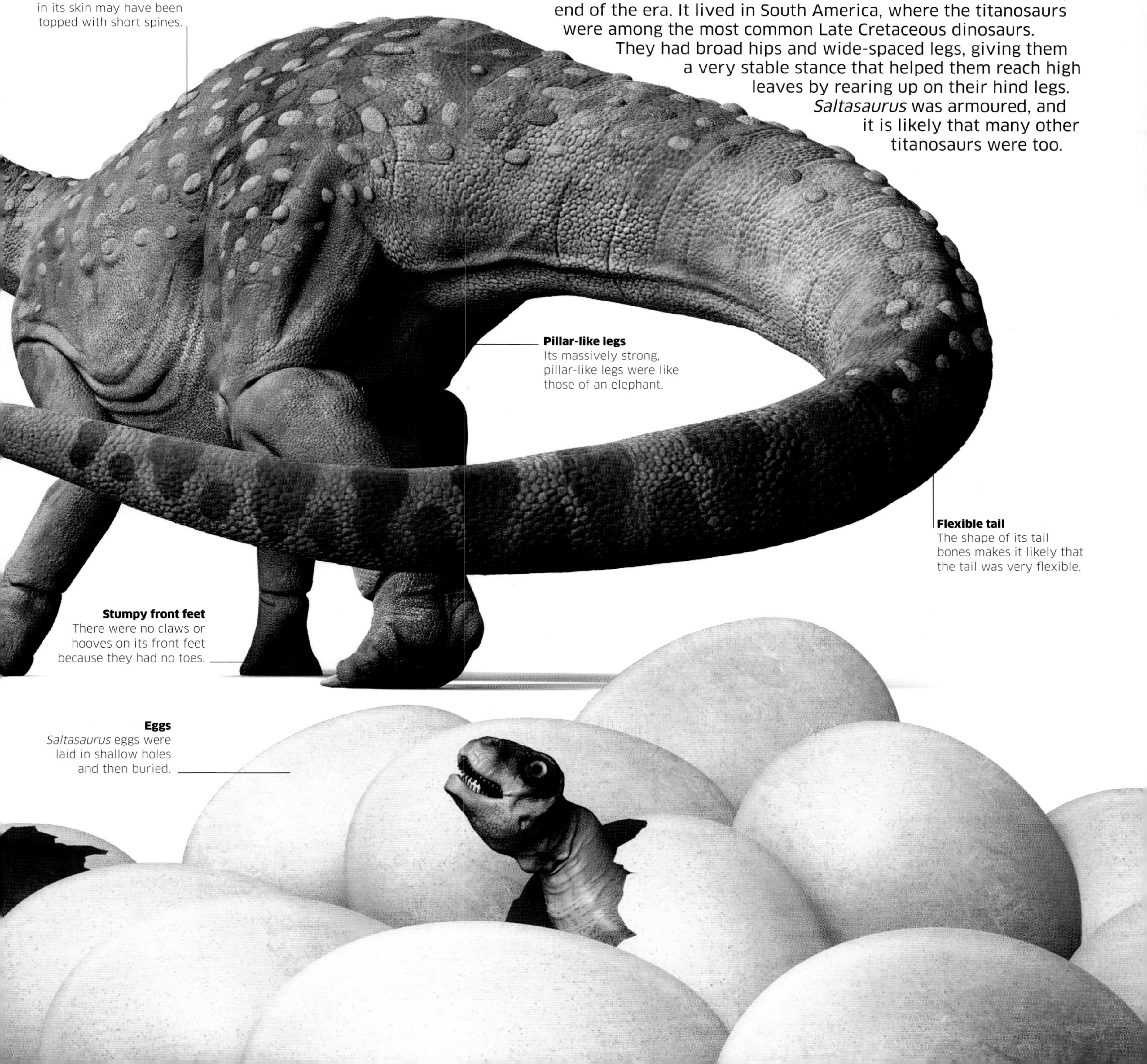

Body armour
Oval bony plates embedded in its skin may have been topped with short spines.
Pillar-like legs
Its massively strong, pillar-like legs were like those of an elephant.
Flexible tail
The shape of its tail bones makes it likely that the tail was very flexible.
Stumpy front feet
There were no claws or hooves on its front feet because they had no toes.
Eggs
Saltasaurus eggs were laid in shallow holes and then buried.

Mosasaurus

Armed with long jaws full of big, sharp-pointed teeth like those of a crocodile, this powerful oceanic hunter was one of the last of the giant marine reptiles.

The mosasaurs evolved towards the end of the Mesozoic Era, and went on to become the top marine predators of the Late Cretaceous, taking over from heavy-jawed pliosaurs such as *Liopleurodon* (pages 56–57). *Mosasaurus* was one of the biggest, growing to some 15 m (49 ft) long. It had massive jaws, like a pliosaur, but a much more streamlined, flexible body and a long tail with a vertical fin that it used to drive itself through the water. It preyed on other marine reptiles, fish, and free-swimming shellfish.

Large eyes
Mosasaurus's big eyes were well adapted for seeing in dim underwater light.

Pointed teeth
All of its teeth were sharp spikes, adapted for seizing and gripping its prey.

Shellfish prey
Ammonites – relatives of squid – were a favourite target. They ranged in size from the size of your palm to 2 m (6 ft) in diameter.

Strong skull
The skull and jaws of *Mosasaurus* were more strongly built than those of most other mosasaurs. This makes it likely that *Mosasaurus* often attacked and killed big, powerful prey.

1.8 m (6 ft) – the **length of the skulls** of the **biggest mosaurs**.

Giant turtle shells have been found with marks that match the teeth of *Mosasaurus*.

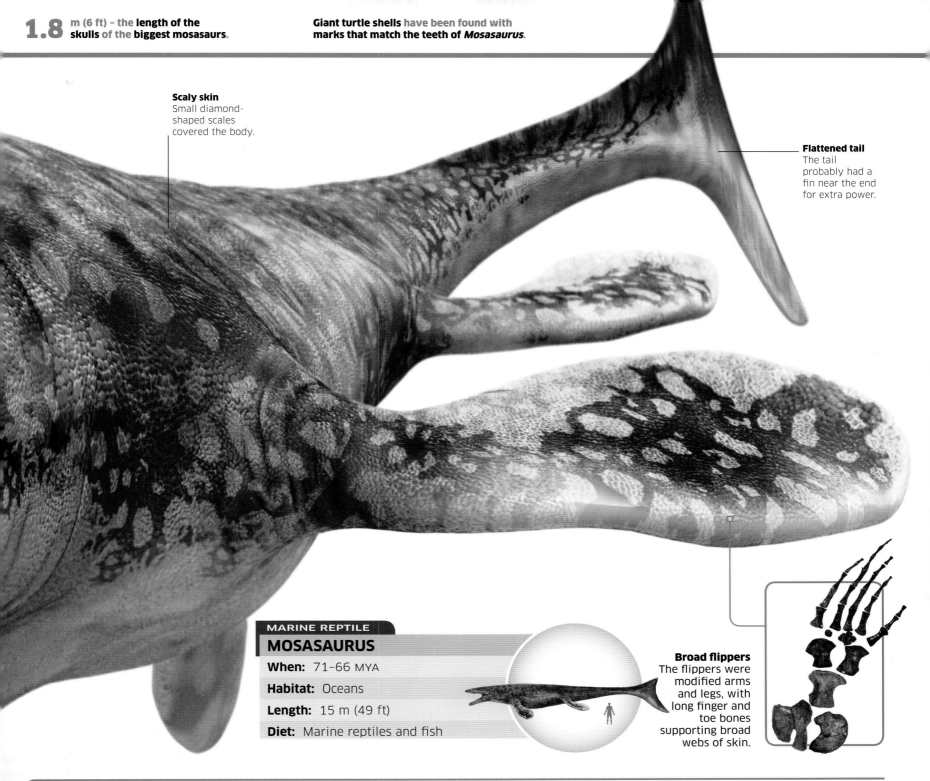

Scaly skin
Small diamond-shaped scales covered the body.

Flattened tail
The tail probably had a fin near the end for extra power.

Broad flippers
The flippers were modified arms and legs, with long finger and toe bones supporting broad webs of skin.

MARINE REPTILE

MOSASAURUS

When: 71–66 MYA

Habitat: Oceans

Length: 15 m (49 ft)

Diet: Marine reptiles and fish

Dutch discovery

Mosasaurus was one of the first prehistoric animals to be recognized for what it was. Its fossil skull was found in a chalk quarry in Holland in 1764, as shown in this 18th-century engraving. At first it was thought to be a whale or crocodile, but was named *Mosasaurus* in 1822.

Living relatives

The mosasaurs were oceanic relatives of the powerful monitor lizards that prey on other animals in the tropics. They include the Komodo dragon, one of the largest living reptiles. Monitor lizards are closely related to snakes, and have forked tongues. It is possible that *Mosasaurus* had a forked tongue too, but it would not have been so sensitive to tastes and scents.

MONITOR LIZARD

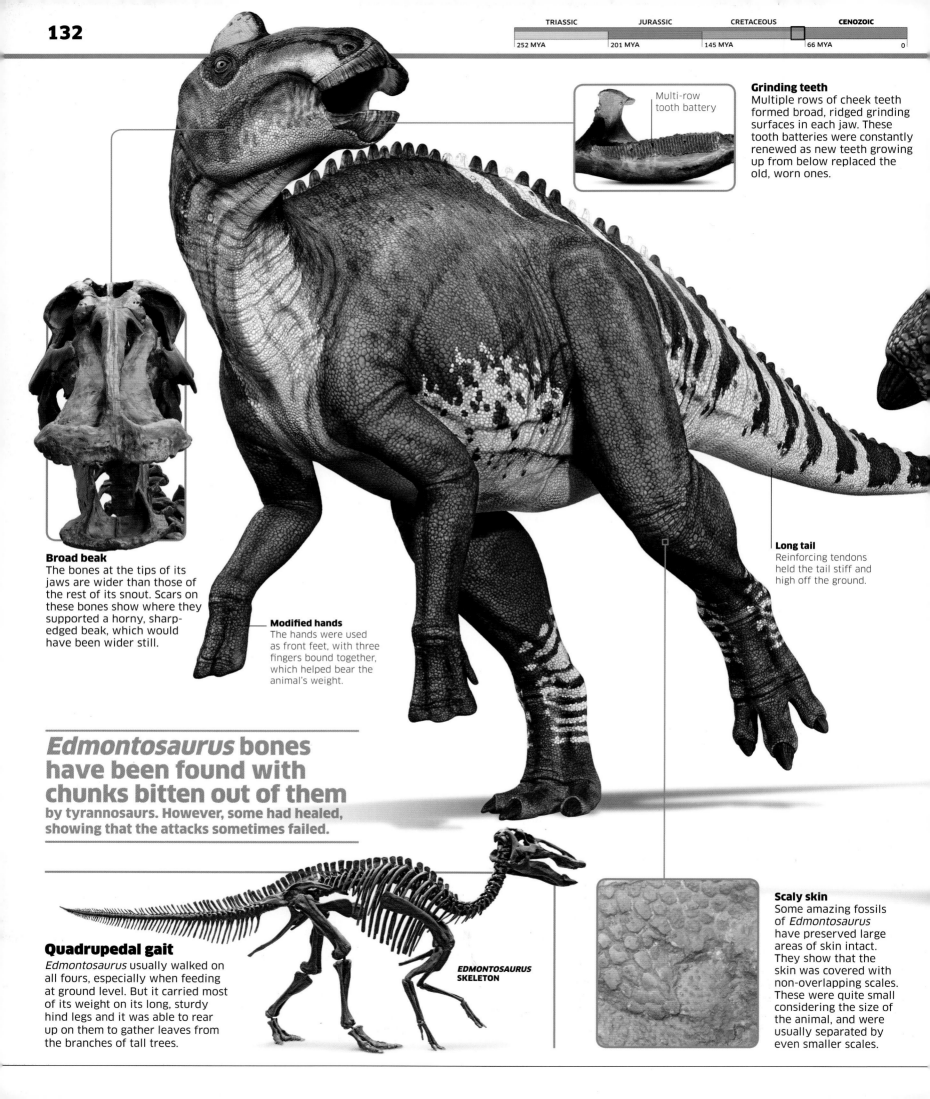

Grinding teeth
Multiple rows of cheek teeth formed broad, ridged grinding surfaces in each jaw. These tooth batteries were constantly renewed as new teeth growing up from below replaced the old, worn ones.

Multi-row tooth battery

Broad beak
The bones at the tips of its jaws are wider than those of the rest of its snout. Scars on these bones show where they supported a horny, sharp-edged beak, which would have been wider still.

Modified hands
The hands were used as front feet, with three fingers bound together, which helped bear the animal's weight.

Long tail
Reinforcing tendons held the tail stiff and high off the ground.

Edmontosaurus bones have been found with chunks bitten out of them by tyrannosaurs. However, some had healed, showing that the attacks sometimes failed.

Quadrupedal gait
Edmontosaurus usually walked on all fours, especially when feeding at ground level. But it carried most of its weight on its long, sturdy hind legs and it was able to rear up on them to gather leaves from the branches of tall trees.

EDMONTOSAURUS SKELETON

Scaly skin
Some amazing fossils of *Edmontosaurus* have preserved large areas of skin intact. They show that the skin was covered with non-overlapping scales. These were quite small considering the size of the animal, and were usually separated by even smaller scales.

Long hind legs
The hind legs were much longer than the arms, with stout, strong bones.

Tyrannosaurus
The deadly enemy of so many animals, *Tyrannosaurus* was also a voracious predator of *Edmontosaurus*.

Strong toes
Each hind foot had three massively built toes with blunt, rounded hooves.

Edmontosaurus

Equipped with a sharp beak and some of the most efficient chewing teeth that have ever evolved, *Edmontosaurus* was one of the most successful plant-eaters of the Late Cretaceous. Yet it was also one a common victim of the most notorious killer alive at the time – *Tyrannosaurus* (pages 140–141).

The hadrosaurs, or duckbilled dinosaurs, were among the most specialized of the ornithopods. They are named for their rather duck-like beaks, which varied in shape depending on their diet. *Edmontosaurus* was one of the biggest, and had an unusually broad beak suitable for gathering a lot of food at once without stopping to pick and choose. Its bulky body contained a large digestive system that could deal with anything it ate, especially when the food had been chewed to a pulp by millstone-like teeth. *Edmontosaurus* shared its North American habitat with *Tyrannosaurus rex* – as the evidence on some of its fossil bones testifies.

DINOSAUR
EDMONTOSAURUS

When: 71–66 MYA

Habitat: Plains and swamps

Length: 13 m (43 ft)

Diet: Leaves and fruits

Scaly skin
The skin was probably scaly and protected the animal from thorns and biting insects.

Short arms
Their short arms show that they walked on their hind legs.

Pachycephalosaurus

Some of the most puzzling dinosaurs evolved at the very end of the Mesozoic – the pachycephalosaurs, with their immensely thick skulls. We still do not know why their skulls were so thick.

Also known as "boneheads", these dinosaurs were relatives of the horned and frilled ceratopsians. Very few fossils have been found, but they include a complete skull of the largest known type, *Pachycephalosaurus*. The bone protecting its brain is at least 20 times thicker than regular dinosaur skulls, and some scientists think that this was an adaptation, allowing rival males to fight for status and territory by ramming their heads together.

Some **small pachycephalosaur** "species" may just be
examples of **half-grown** *Pachycephalosaurus* adults.

The name *Pachycephalosaurus*
means "thick-headed lizard".

135

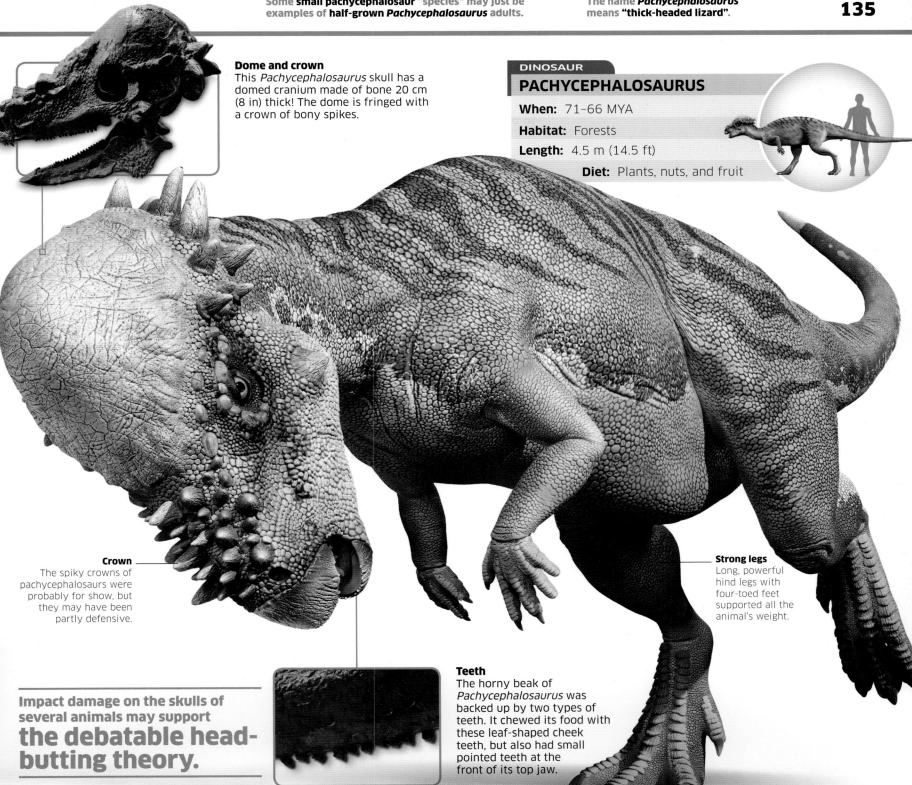

Dome and crown
This *Pachycephalosaurus* skull has a
domed cranium made of bone 20 cm
(8 in) thick! The dome is fringed with
a crown of bony spikes.

DINOSAUR

PACHYCEPHALOSAURUS

When: 71–66 MYA

Habitat: Forests

Length: 4.5 m (14.5 ft)

Diet: Plants, nuts, and fruit

Crown
The spiky crowns of
pachycephalosaurs were
probably for show, but
they may have been
partly defensive.

Strong legs
Long, powerful
hind legs with
four-toed feet
supported all the
animal's weight.

Impact damage on the skulls of
several animals may support
the debatable head-butting theory.

Teeth
The horny beak of
Pachycephalosaurus was
backed up by two types of
teeth. It chewed its food with
these leaf-shaped cheek
teeth, but also had small
pointed teeth at the
front of its top jaw.

Butting heads

Head-butting might seem like
a dangerous way for two rivals
to settle a dispute, and many
scientists think that the thick skull
of *Pachycephalosaurus* had some
other use. However, some modern
animals, such as these American
bighorn rams, fight by ramming
their heads together. The impact
is absorbed by their horns, which
protect their brains from damage.
A reinforced skull could provide
the same protection.

Broad diet

A typical dinosaur has teeth
that are all much the same
shape. But a pachycephalosaur
had different types of teeth,
which may mean that it ate
several different types of
food. Though it may have
eaten nuts and fruits,
Pachycephalosaurus was
basically a leaf-eater,
and likely ate leaves
similar to this one, from
an *Araliopsoides* tree.

ARALIOPSOIDES
LEAF

Quetzalcoatlus

The height of a giraffe, and with a wingspan as big as a small aircraft, this colossal pterosaur was one of the biggest flying animals that has ever lived.

Discovered in the USA in the 1970s, *Quetzalcoatlus* was probably the largest of the Late Cretaceous azhdarchids – the giants of the pterosaur world. It could clearly fly well, and probably covered vast distances with little effort. But it would have hunted on the ground, stalking prey such as small dinosaurs, seizing them in its long, toothless beak, and probably swallowing them whole.

Thanks to the great muscular power of its wings, *Quetzalcoatlus* could probably **fly at speeds of 90 kph (56 mph)**.

All fours
Like all known later pterosaurs, *Quetzalcoatlus* had long limbs, and was probably very agile.

Small feet
Quetzalcoatlus had compact, padded feet, well suited to fast movement over firm ground.

Broad wings
Quetzalcoatlus had broad wings that were perfect for soaring on rising air currents, similar to modern-day vultures.

Bony crest
A bony crest on top of the skull was sheathed in keratin – the material that forms claws. It may have been brightly coloured, and it is possible that males had larger crests than females.

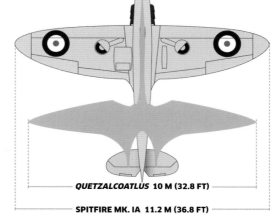

PTEROSAUR

QUETZALCOATLUS

When: 71–66 MYA

Habitat: Plains and woodlands

Wingspan: 10 m (33 ft)

Diet: Small dinosaurs

Toothless beak
Its long, sharp beak had no teeth, so the pterosaur could not chew its prey.

QUETZALCOATLUS **10 M (32.8 FT)**

SPITFIRE MK. IA 11.2 M (36.8 FT)

Folded wings
It folded its wings up out of the way when hunting on the ground.

Huge wingspan
Measuring 10 m (33 ft) or more, the wingspan of this spectacular animal was almost as broad as that of the famous Spitfire fighter aircraft from World War II. With its neck extended, it was almost as long too. However, its small body and light build meant that it weighed less than 250 kg (550 lb). This is a lot compared to the biggest modern birds, but it is certain that *Quetzalcoatlus* was well able to fly.

Small prey
Small dinosaurs and similar animals would have been easy prey for *Quetzalcoatlus*.

Taking off
Giant pterosaurs such as *Quetzalcoatlus* had the same wing anatomy and flight muscles as smaller ones. They launched themselves into the air by vaulting upwards on their clawed hands, swiftly extending their long outer wings to power themselves into the sky.

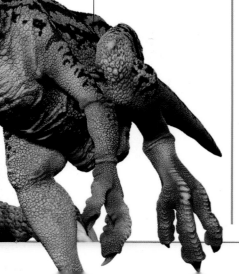

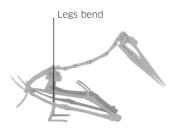

Legs bend

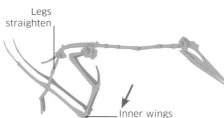

Legs straighten

Inner wings pushed down

Outer wings unfold

Body pushed upwards

CROUCH
Preparing for take-off, the pterosaur crouches down with its wings swung forwards. It gets a good grip on the ground with its hands.

VAULT
Pushing up with all four limbs, it leaps up and forwards, using its long inner wings like the poles of a skier to vault into the air.

LAUNCH
As it launches itself off the ground, it spreads its outer wings and sweeps them down, to propel itself into the air and start flying.

Triceratops

The three-horned *Triceratops* was one of the last and biggest of the ceratopsians – a group of plant-eaters famous for their spectacular horns and neck frills.

Although the size of an elephant, *Triceratops* was built more like a rhinoceros, with its low-slung head and intimidating horns. Like other ceratopsians, it also had a big, bony frill extending from the back of its skull and covering its neck. This was a useful defensive shield for an animal that shared its North American habitat with the fearsome *Tyrannosaurus* (pages 140–41). With its spiky fringe, the neck frill also looked dramatic, and it could have played an important role in the displays of rivals competing for territory or breeding partners.

Neck frill
The frill was made of solid bone, covered with scaly skin.

Bony spikes
A fringe of spikes around the frill made it look more impressive.

Long horns
The two brow horns were up to 1.3 m (4 ft) long, with sharp tips and strong, bony cores.

Scaly skin
Fossilized skin fragments show that it was covered with scales.

Slicing teeth
Closely packed rows of cheek teeth sliced through plant food like scissors.

Some *Triceratops* bones show damage inflicted by tyrannosaur teeth, but there is also evidence of a *Triceratops* surviving an attack – and maybe killing a tyrannosaur.

Triceratops and *Torosaurus*

Triceratops lived in the same time and place as another ceratopsian with a bigger neck frill, known as *Torosaurus*. Some researchers think that *Triceratops* was a younger version of the same animal, and that it turned into "*Torosaurus*" when it became fully mature. However, the evidence is not conclusive, and most scientists disagree.

Longer neck frill

TOROSAURUS

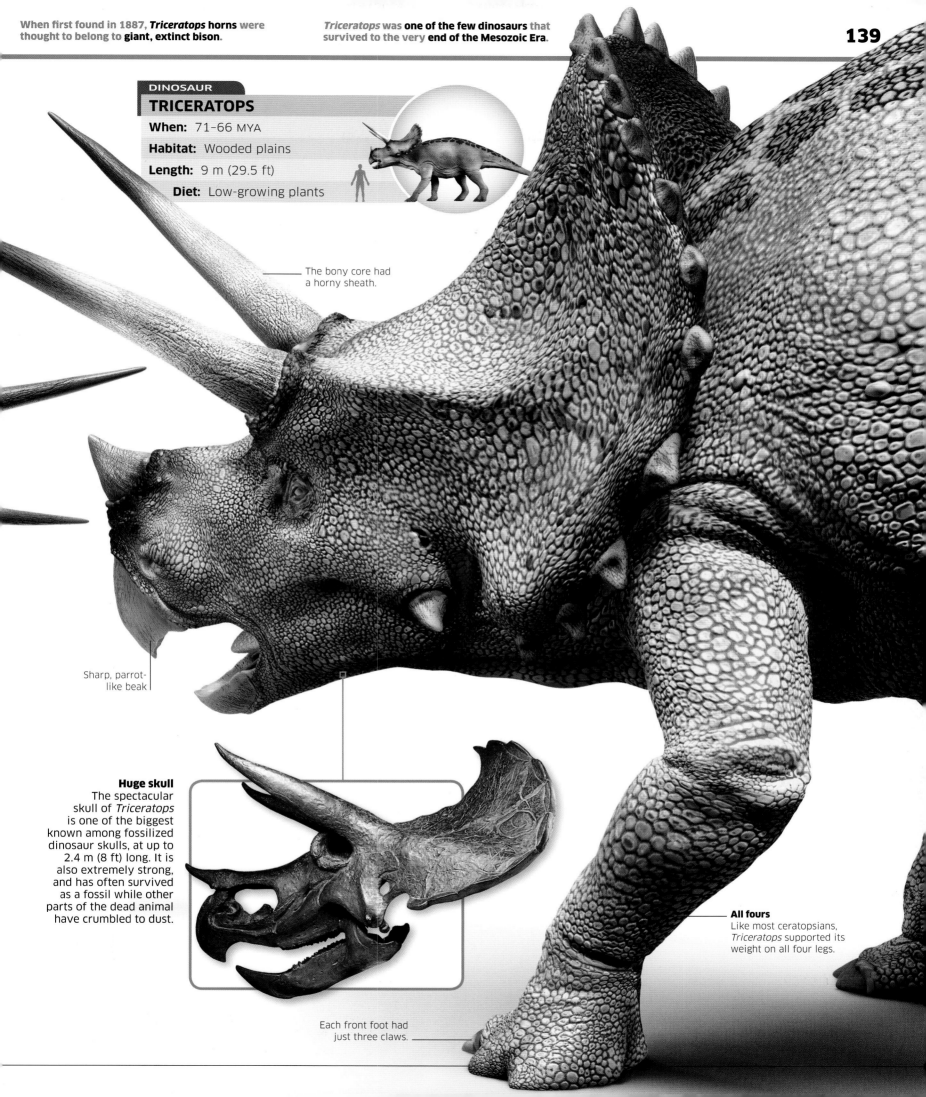

When first found in 1887, *Triceratops* horns were thought to belong to **giant, extinct bison**.

Triceratops was **one of the few dinosaurs that** survived to the very **end of the Mesozoic Era**.

DINOSAUR

TRICERATOPS

When: 71–66 MYA

Habitat: Wooded plains

Length: 9 m (29.5 ft)

Diet: Low-growing plants

The bony core had a horny sheath.

Sharp, parrot-like beak

Huge skull
The spectacular skull of *Triceratops* is one of the biggest known among fossilized dinosaur skulls, at up to 2.4 m (8 ft) long. It is also extremely strong, and has often survived as a fossil while other parts of the dead animal have crumbled to dust.

All fours
Like most ceratopsians, *Triceratops* supported its weight on all four legs.

Each front foot had just three claws.

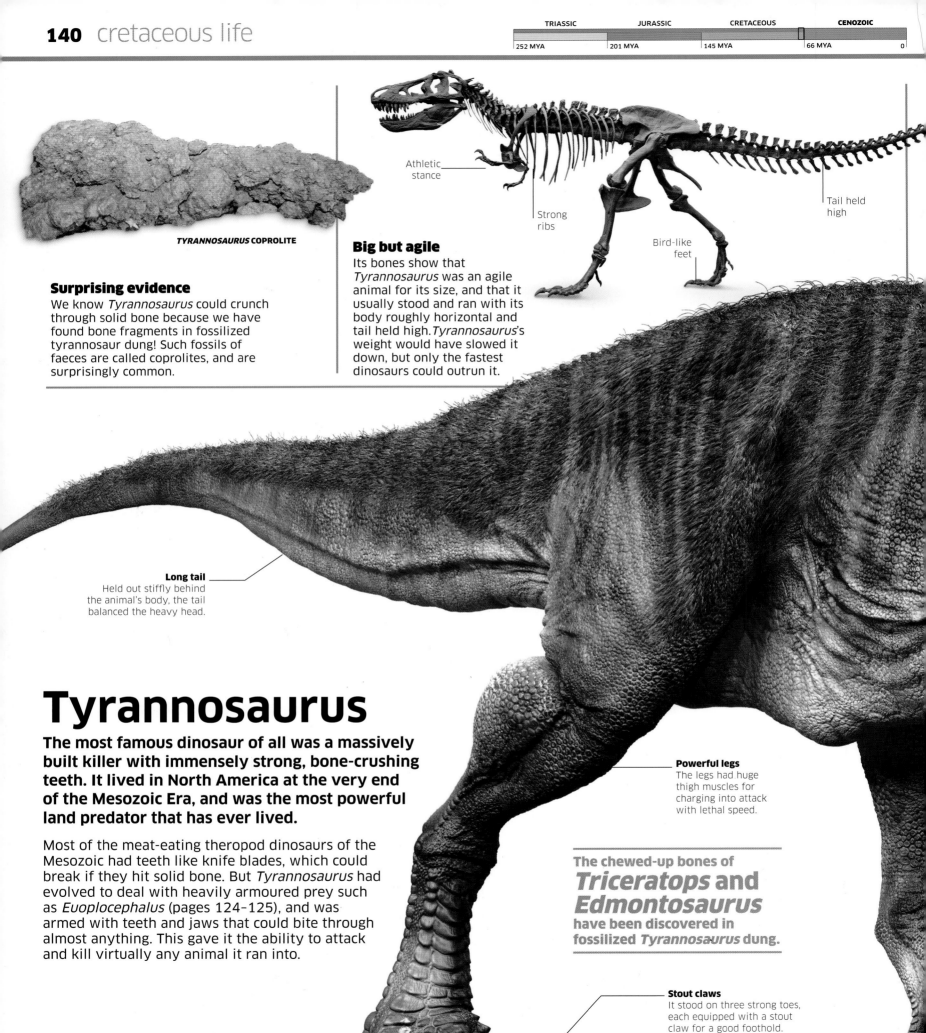

TRIASSIC	JURASSIC	CRETACEOUS	CENOZOIC
252 MYA	201 MYA	145 MYA	66 MYA	0

TYRANNOSAURUS COPROLITE

Athletic stance

Strong ribs

Tail held high

Bird-like feet

Surprising evidence

We know *Tyrannosaurus* could crunch through solid bone because we have found bone fragments in fossilized tyrannosaur dung! Such fossils of faeces are called coprolites, and are surprisingly common.

Big but agile

Its bones show that *Tyrannosaurus* was an agile animal for its size, and that it usually stood and ran with its body roughly horizontal and tail held high. *Tyrannosaurus*'s weight would have slowed it down, but only the fastest dinosaurs could outrun it.

Long tail
Held out stiffly behind the animal's body, the tail balanced the heavy head.

Tyrannosaurus

The most famous dinosaur of all was a massively built killer with immensely strong, bone-crushing teeth. It lived in North America at the very end of the Mesozoic Era, and was the most powerful land predator that has ever lived.

Most of the meat-eating theropod dinosaurs of the Mesozoic had teeth like knife blades, which could break if they hit solid bone. But *Tyrannosaurus* had evolved to deal with heavily armoured prey such as *Euoplocephalus* (pages 124–125), and was armed with teeth and jaws that could bite through almost anything. This gave it the ability to attack and kill virtually any animal it ran into.

Powerful legs
The legs had huge thigh muscles for charging into attack with lethal speed.

The chewed-up bones of
Triceratops and Edmontosaurus
have been discovered in fossilized *Tyrannosaurus* dung.

Stout claws
It stood on three strong toes, each equipped with a stout claw for a good foothold.

A *Tyrannosaurus rex* fossil, nicknamed "Sue", became the **most expensive fossil** when it was auctioned in 1997.

141

DINOSAUR

TYRANNOSAURUS

When: 67–66 MYA

Habitat: Forests and swamps

Length: 12 m (39 ft)

Diet: Large dinosaurs

Terrifying teeth
Its sharp-pointed teeth were strong enough to crunch through the heavy armour of its prey.

Scales and feathers
Tyrannosaurus is likely to have had a largely scaly skin with possibly some feathers on its back.

Deadly rivals
Rival tyrannosaurs may have fought to the death over territory and food.

Slim ankles
Its slender lower legs and ankles suggest that *Tyrannosaurus* could run quite fast.

Small arms
Tyrannosaurus's arms were tiny compared to its body, but had strong muscles for gripping prey.

Sharp claw

Fingers to grasp struggling prey

A NEW ERA

The Cretaceous world was destroyed by a global catastrophe that changed the nature of life on Earth. The Mesozoic had been dominated by the giant dinosaurs, but the new Cenozoic Era was to see the rise of the mammals. And unlike all the other dinosaurs, the birds survived and flourished.

THE CENOZOIC WORLD

The Mesozoic Era had ended in a mass extinction that eliminated most of the dominant animals on land and in the oceans – the big dinosaurs, the winged pterosaurs, and most of the marine reptiles. As the world recovered from the catastrophe, the surviving animals started evolving new forms that took the place of animals that had disappeared. They included the first large mammals, which replaced the dinosaurs as the main land animals. The new era also saw the appearance of humans.

PACIFIC OCEAN

NORTH AMERICA

NORTH ATLANTIC OCEAN

In the early Cenozoic there was clear blue water between the two American continents. Volcanic activity created a narrow bridge of land just 4 million years ago.

SOUTH AMERICA

By this time Antarctica had split away from Australia and drifted over the South Pole. Meanwhile Australia and New Guinea were moving north into the tropics.

SOUTH ATLANTIC OCEAN

CONTINENTS AND OCEANS IN THE EARLY CENOZOIC ERA

OCEANS AND CONTINENTS

By the early Cenozoic, 50 million years ago, the world's continents had broken up into the ones we know today, but their shapes and positions were different. Large areas of southwest Asia were still flooded by shallow seas, India was adrift in the ocean, and South America was not linked to North America. But the ensuing 50 million years saw the gradual creation of the modern world.

ENVIRONMENT

In contrast with the warm, relatively stable Mesozoic Era, the Cenozoic has been a time of dramatic change. Some periods have been very hot, others bitterly cold. But conditions on the separate continents have always been very different, providing havens for a wide variety of plants, animals, and other life.

Climate

The era started with a cool period, but then global temperatures soared dramatically 56 million years ago. After 7 million years the world started cooling until it entered the ice ages 2.5 million years ago. We are now living in a warmer phase of one of these ice ages.

CURRENT AVERAGE GLOBAL TEMPERATURE

°F	°C
140	60
104	40
68	20
32	0

14.5 °C (58 °F)

Grasslands
Early in the Cenozoic, the warmth and high rainfall created vast rainforests. As the climate became cooler and drier, large areas turned to grassland.

Ice age
During the ice ages at the end of the Cenozoic, large areas of the polar regions were covered by ice sheets. These still exist on Greenland and Antarctica.

ERA			MESOZOIC ERA	
PERIOD	TRIASSIC PERIOD		JURASSIC PERIOD	
MILLIONS OF YEARS AGO	252		201	145

ANIMALS

The disappearance of the giant dinosaurs had a dramatic effect on animal life, and especially on the mammals that took their place. But the birds had also survived and went on to be hugely successful. Insects and similar animals evolved in many new ways to make the most of new habitats.

India had moved north and soon collided with Asia, pushing up the rocky Himalayas and the high plateau of Tibet.

EUROPE

ASIA

AFRICA

AUSTRALIA

ANTARCTICA

Land Invertebrates
Pollinating insects such as butterflies flourished in the flower-rich forests. The wide grasslands were colonized by huge numbers of grasshoppers and beetles.

BEETLE FOSSIL

TERATORNIS

Birds
Most of the modern types of birds had evolved by the mid-Cenozoic. Some were giants, such as the flightless *Gastornis* and the later, condor-like *Teratornis*.

THYLACOSMILUS

Mammals
The mammals increased dramatically in variety and size, with big plant-eaters hunted by predators such as this sabre-toothed marsupial, *Thylacosmilus*. But small mammals also became much more successful.

KEY

■ ANCIENT LANDMASS
〰 OUTLINE OF MODERN LANDMASS

Plants

During the Cenozoic the flowering plants and grasses that evolved late in the previous era have become the dominant plants over much of the world. Ice-age glaciations destroyed a lot of plant life in the far north, but it has recovered since.

Deciduous trees
The new forms of plants flourishing in the Cenozoic included many more trees, with broad leaves that fall in winter.

Ferns
The success of new types of forest tree created many different habitats for ferns, which evolved new forms in response.

Fragrant flowers
Flowers evolved rapidly to attract insects and other pollinating animals, with colourful petals and sweet, fragrant nectar.

Grasses
One significant change in plant life was the spread of grasses, which became a major source of food for some animals.

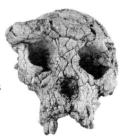

Human origins
This may be the fossil skull of one of our earliest ancestors. *Sahelanthropus* lived 6 million years ago, which is 2 million years before the first known people to walk upright. Modern humans evolved about 350,000 years ago.

Forked tongue
Like modern snakes, *Titanoboa* would have detected and tracked prey using its forked tongue. It would flick this out to pick up scent traces, then flick it back in to transfer the scent to a sensory organ in the roof of its mouth.

Titanoboa

Found in the rocks of Colombia in South America, the fossils of this gigantic snake show that it was one of the biggest, longest, and heaviest snakes that has ever lived. It probably weighed as much as a small car!

The earliest snakes evolved from lizards during the Cretaceous Period, and survived the mass extinction that ended the Mesozoic. During the warm period that followed, some, such as *Titanoboa*, were able to grow to epic proportions. This giant constrictor killed prey by coiling tightly around its victims to stop them from breathing, just as modern boas do. *Titanoboa* lived in swamps where it preyed on fish and other reptiles.

Reptile prey
Its main prey were fish, but *Titanoboa* could easily have eaten small crocodilians.

Muscular body
Titanoboa's body was 15 m (49 ft) of almost solid muscle.

This giant snake lived in **tropical rainforests just like the modern-day Amazon rainforest.**

Engineers in Canada have built a **life-sized robotic *Titanaboa*** to study how it moved.

Titanoboa bones are so big that, at first, scientists thought they belonged to **extinct crocodiles.**

147

Gaping jaws

Just like all snakes, *Titanoboa* would have swallowed its prey whole. A snake's flexible lower jaw and stretchy skin have evolved to allow the snake to swallow food several times larger than its own diameter. After feeding, *Titanoboa* would not have needed to eat for several days.

Big mouthful

This African egg-eating snake just about manages to stretch its jaws around this bird egg. Next, it will crush the egg, extract the liquid, and regurgitate the crushed shell.

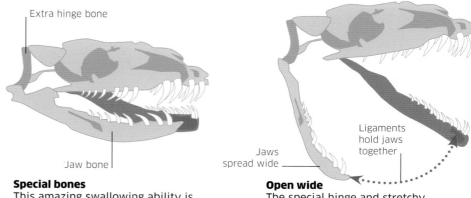

Extra hinge bone

Jaw bone

Jaws spread wide

Ligaments hold jaws together

Special bones

This amazing swallowing ability is possible because snake jaw bones are joined at the front by an elastic ligament, and loosely hinged to the skull.

Open wide

The special hinge and stretchy ligament allow the jaw bones to open incredibly wide, and the jaws pull back to draw prey into the mouth.

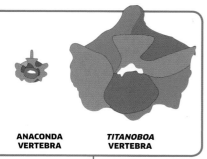

ANACONDA VERTEBRA

TITANOBOA VERTEBRA

Super-sized bones

The anaconda is the largest living snake, but the bones of its spine – its vertebrae – are dwarfed by the fossil vertebrae of *Titanoboa*.

Titanoboa was as long as

a school bus,

and its back was a full 1 m (3 ft) off the ground.

SNAKE

TITANOBOA

When: 60-58 MYA

Habitat: Tropical swamps

Length: 15 m (49 ft)

Diet: Fish and reptiles

Patterned skin

The scaly skin was probably patterned like an anaconda's.

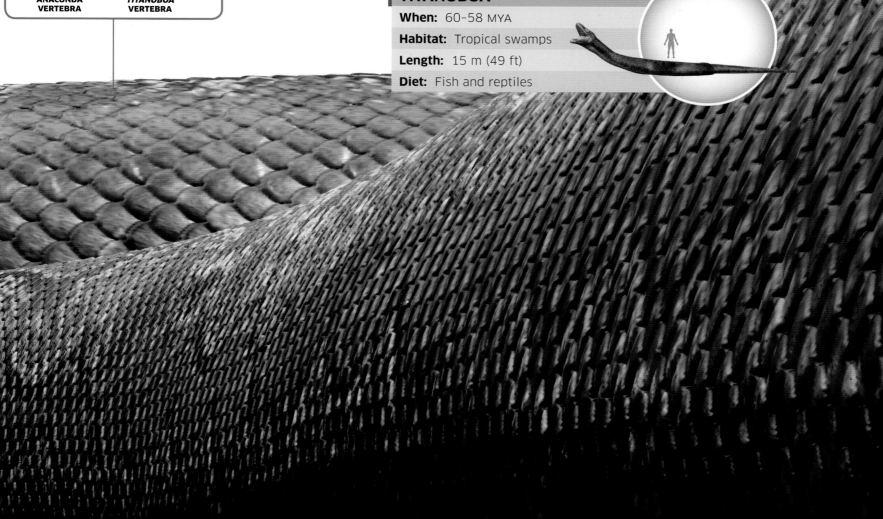

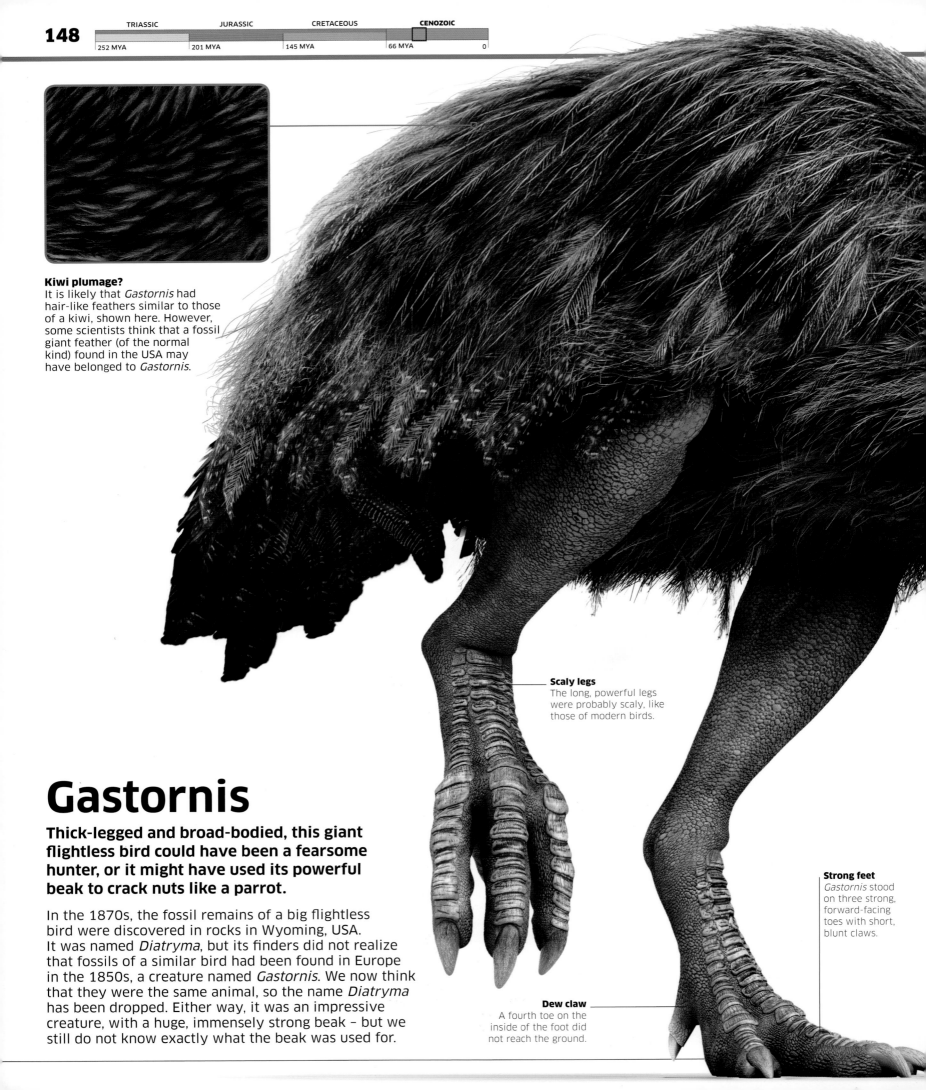

Kiwi plumage?
It is likely that *Gastornis* had hair-like feathers similar to those of a kiwi, shown here. However, some scientists think that a fossil giant feather (of the normal kind) found in the USA may have belonged to *Gastornis*.

Scaly legs
The long, powerful legs were probably scaly, like those of modern birds.

Gastornis

Thick-legged and broad-bodied, this giant flightless bird could have been a fearsome hunter, or it might have used its powerful beak to crack nuts like a parrot.

In the 1870s, the fossil remains of a big flightless bird were discovered in rocks in Wyoming, USA. It was named *Diatryma*, but its finders did not realize that fossils of a similar bird had been found in Europe in the 1850s, a creature named *Gastornis*. We now think that they were the same animal, so the name *Diatryma* has been dropped. Either way, it was an impressive creature, with a huge, immensely strong beak – but we still do not know exactly what the beak was used for.

Strong feet
Gastornis stood on three strong, forward-facing toes with short, blunt claws.

Dew claw
A fourth toe on the inside of the foot did not reach the ground.

2009 The year a landslide near **Seattle, USA**, exposed a **row of footprints** probably made by *Gastornis*.

149

Apart from its beak and short tail, *Gastornis* looks just like a
theropod dinosaur.

Hooked beak
Gastornis may have used its slightly hooked beak to seize prey.

Nuts
Gastornis would have eaten ancient relatives of hazelnuts and walnuts, alongside many other edible plants.

Long neck
The long, flexible neck enabled *Gastornis* to move its big head in any direction.

Massive skull
The skull and lower jaw were immensely strong, and their anatomy shows that the jaw muscles were massively powerful. Such strength must have been needed to do some special job, but we don't know what that was.

BIRD
GASTORNIS
When: 56–40 MYA

Habitat: Dense tropical forests

Height: 2 m (6.5 ft)

Diet: Not known

Gigantic eggs
Fragments of fossil eggs have been found that may belong to *Gastornis*. When reconstructed they measure more than 23 cm (9 in) long but just 10 cm (4 in) across, and are more elongated than the eggs of modern birds such as ostriches or chickens. In fact, they look more like the eggs of its Mesozoic ancestors – theropod dinosaurs such as *Citipati* (pages 114–15).

GASTORNIS EGG   **OSTRICH EGG**   **CHICKEN EGG**

Nutcracker beak
In the tropical forests of South America, big parrots such as hyacinth macaws use their heavy beaks to crack the tough-shelled nuts that form their main diet. Nuts are very nutritious, and it is quite possible that the evolution of a massive beak helped *Gastornis* to break into even bigger nuts growing in the forests. But *Gastornis* may have used its beak to crack the bones of dead animals to get at the marrow, to kill and eat live prey, or even to do all of these things.

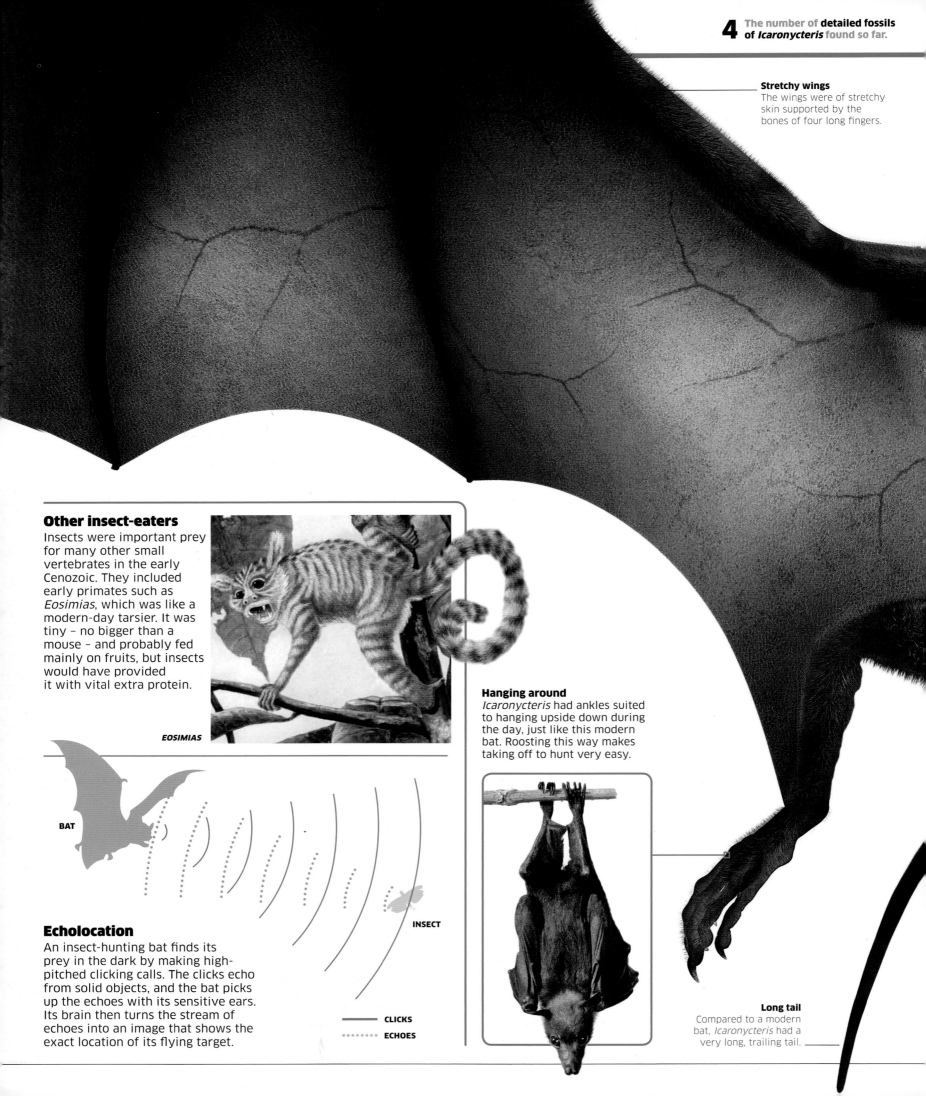

Stretchy wings
The wings were of stretchy skin supported by the bones of four long fingers.

Other insect-eaters

Insects were important prey for many other small vertebrates in the early Cenozoic. They included early primates such as *Eosimias*, which was like a modern-day tarsier. It was tiny – no bigger than a mouse – and probably fed mainly on fruits, but insects would have provided it with vital extra protein.

EOSIMIAS

BAT

INSECT

Echolocation

An insect-hunting bat finds its prey in the dark by making high-pitched clicking calls. The clicks echo from solid objects, and the bat picks up the echoes with its sensitive ears. Its brain then turns the stream of echoes into an image that shows the exact location of its flying target.

—— CLICKS

•••••• ECHOES

Hanging around

Icaronycteris had ankles suited to hanging upside down during the day, just like this modern bat. Roosting this way makes taking off to hunt very easy.

Long tail
Compared to a modern bat, *Icaronycteris* had a very long, trailing tail.

TRIASSIC | JURASSIC | CRETACEOUS | CENOZOIC
252 MYA | 201 MYA | 145 MYA | 66 MYA | 0

This animal seems to have **lived in Europe as well as North America**.

151

MAMMAL

ICARONYCTERIS

When: 52 MYA

Habitat: Woodlands

Length: 14 cm (5.5 in)

Diet: Insects

Detailed fossil
Fossils of *Icaronycteris* found in Wyoming, USA, are amazingly well preserved. They show every tiny detail of the skeleton, and some fossils even have traces of the animal's soft tissues.

Shrew-like teeth
Its teeth were very like those of a modern shrew – also an insect-eater.

Insect prey
Some fossils of *Icaronycteris* have moth wing scales in their stomachs, showing that the moths were its prey.

Flap free
Unlike modern bats, *Icaronycteris* had no uropatagium – the flap of skin linking the body to the tail.

Icaronycteris

This looks so like a modern bat that it is hard to believe it lived more than 50 million years ago. *Icaronycteris* even shared a modern bat's ability to hunt flying insects at night.

Icaronycteris is named after the mythical Greek **boy Icarus,** who flew using feathers stuck to his arms.

Bat bones are so slender and fragile that very few have survived as fossils. *Icaronycteris* is one of the earliest bats found so far, but it is clear from its anatomy that it was fairly well adapted to flight. Its teeth show that it was an insect-eater, and the form of its inner ear bones suggest that it hunted insects at night using echolocation, just like its modern descendants.

Uintatherium

Massively built and probably with an appetite to match, this heavyweight plant-eater was one of the mammals that evolved to fill the gap left by the giant dinosaurs.

During the Mesozoic Era animal life on land was dominated by gigantic plant-eating dinosaurs. After these became extinct, small mammals started evolving into larger and larger forms that could live in the same way. Over many millions of years this process resulted in big plant-eaters such as *Uintatherium* – a super-sized "megaherbivore" specialized for gathering and digesting enormous quantities of plant food.

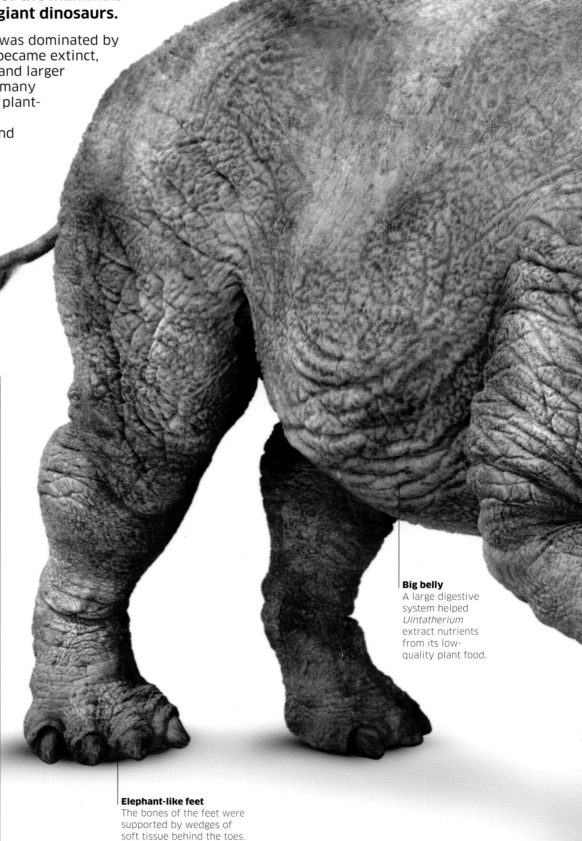

Thin tail
The slender, flexible tail would have helped the animal brush away bloodsucking flies.

Extinct megaherbivores

Uintatherium was one of many types of megaherbivore (giant plant-eater) that thrived from the mid-Cenozoic onwards. Today just a few survive, such as the elephants and rhinoceroses of Africa and Asia.

Paraceratherium
This 20-million-year-old relative of the rhinoceroses was the largest land mammal that has ever lived. Standing 5.5 m (18 ft) tall at the shoulder, it could reach into the treetops to feed like a giraffe.

Deinotherium
A relative of elephants, but larger than any living today, this had strange tusks that curved down from its lower jaw. It became extinct about a million years ago.

Elephant-like feet
The bones of the feet were supported by wedges of soft tissue behind the toes.

Big belly
A large digestive system helped *Uintatherium* extract nutrients from its low-quality plant food.

Uintatherium **fossils** have been found as far apart as **North America and China**.

1 m (3 ft) – the **length of** *Uintatherium's* **skull**.

Some skulls have **bigger horns**. These may belong to males that **used the horns to fight** each other.

153

Thick hide
Uintatherium probably had a thick hide, like a rhinoceros, to protect it from predators.

MAMMAL

UINTATHERIUM

When: 45–37 MYA

Habitat: Forests

Length: 4 m (13 ft)

Diet: Plants

Skull and horns
The skull was a strange shape, with big bony flanges and three pairs of knobbly horns. It had an unusually thick cranium, with air pockets to reduce its weight and a very small brain.

Sturdy legs
It stood on huge, heavy, pillar-like legs.

Stout tusks
The upper canine teeth were extended into long tusks. These may have been bigger in males.

The horns of *Uintatherium* were
covered in skin,
like those of a giraffe.

Jagged teeth

The flattened skull and jaw contain both milk teeth – like the first teeth of human children – and permanent teeth that had not yet appeared when the animal died. The jagged shape of the back teeth would have been ideal for slicing leaves and crushing seeds and fruits.

Furry body

The fossil preserves clear evidence of thick fur covering the skin.

Found in 1983, the fossil was **hidden away in a private collection for 24 years** until it was sold in 2007.

The **fossil has been nicknamed "Ida"** by the scientist who bought it from its finder.

Darwinius was **named in honour of the great naturalist Charles Darwin**, 200 years after his birth.

155

Darwinius

Some 47 million years ago, the trees of Europe were inhabited by small mammals that were clearly primates – the group that includes lemurs, monkeys, apes, and humans.

Found in a slab of oily rock dug from a German quarry in 1983, the amazingly detailed fossil of *Darwinius* preserves almost every bone in its skeleton, as well as outlines of its skin and fur. It can be identified as a female, just nine months old and still with her milk teeth. The shape of these teeth indicates that she was a plant-eater – and indeed the fossil even preserves her last meal of fruits and leaves. She would have gathered them by climbing into the trees, just like many modern primates.

Grasping hands
Darwinius had grasping hands with opposable thumbs – thumbs that can move across (oppose) the palm to touch the tips of other fingers – just like ours. This enabled it to get a good grip on branches while climbing in the trees. It had long fingernails rather than sharp claws.

Long tail
As with many modern primates, its tail was a lot longer than its body.

Binocular vision
Forward-facing eyes helped *Darwinius* to judge distances accurately when leaping from branch to branch.

Handy feet
Like the thumbs, its big toes were opposable, so *Darwinius* used its feet like hands.

Exquisite detail
When this fossilized animal died, it was visiting a lake in a region of volcanic activity. It is likely that it was suffocated by poisonous volcanic gas, tumbled into the lake, and was buried in oily, airless mud that stopped its body decaying. Eventually the mud turned to rock, sealing up its remains and preserving them in exquisite detail.

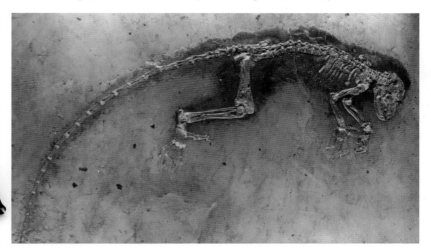

Distant ancestor?
In 2009 *Darwinius* made the news headlines as a "missing link" between human species and the rest of the animal kingdom. It was claimed that the fossil was the earliest to show features typical of monkeys, apes, and humans. If so, then *Darwinius* was related to our distant ancestors. But other scientists have noted features that show it was an ancestor of animals like this lemur, and this means that it was not on our branch of the family tree.

MAMAMAL
DARWINIUS

When:	47 MYA
Habitat:	Forests
Length:	58 cm (23 in)
Diet:	Leaves, fruits, and seeds

FOREST THREAT

About 65 million years after the last dinosaur walked the Earth, a giant *Megatherium* feeds among the redwood trees. But danger lurks in the undergrowth, as a fearsome, sabre-toothed *Smilodon* steps silently towards it.

The *Megatherium* is no killer, but it is armed with massively long claws backed up with big, powerful muscles. It could inflict serious damage on the sabre-toothed cat if it had to defend itself. *Smilodon* crouches nervously, judging its attack, for it knows that, despite its enormous, stabbing canine teeth, it is no match for the giant sloth.

TRIASSIC	JURASSIC	CRETACEOUS	CENOZOIC	
252 MYA	201 MYA	145 MYA	66 MYA	0

Andrewsarchus

Unearthed in the deserts of Mongolia, the giant skull of this formidable predator could belong to the largest meat-eating land mammal that has ever lived.

The long jaws and sharp front teeth of *Andrewsarchus* look like those of a giant hyena, and although it probably behaved like a hyena, its closest living relatives are hoofed animals such as pigs. It probably had broad hooves on each toe instead of claws, and it had blunt cheek teeth adapted for crushing rather than slicing. However, it may still have been a fearsome predator of other animals.

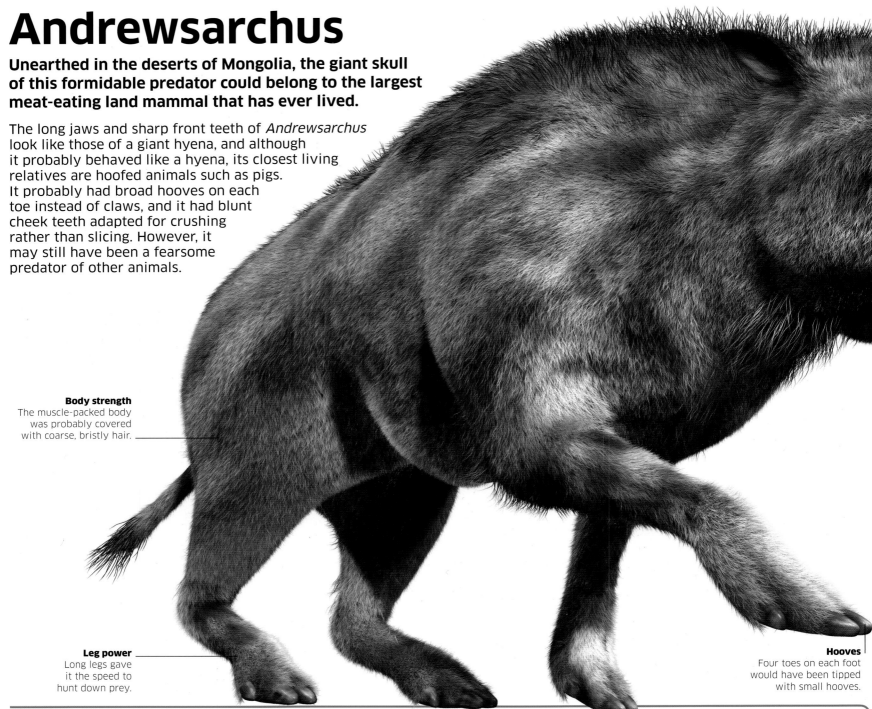

Body strength
The muscle-packed body was probably covered with coarse, bristly hair.

Leg power
Long legs gave it the speed to hunt down prey.

Hooves
Four toes on each foot would have been tipped with small hooves.

Roy Chapman Andrews

Andrewsarchus is named after the man who found it: American fossil hunter Roy Chapman Andrews. He led several expeditions to China and Mongolia in the 1920s, discovering fossils of many dinosaurs. Andrews started out as a humble lab assistant at the American Museum of Natural History in New York, but rose to become its president.

Meat-eating pigs

The closest relatives of *Andrewsarchus* were the entelodonts or "hell pigs" – hoofed predators and scavengers with massively strong jaws. The idea of a meat-eating pig might seem strange, but, in fact, wild pigs will eat almost anything. Wild boar such as this one can also be ferocious animals, as dangerous as any wolf.

The one surviving *Andrewsarchus* skull is twice the size of the skull of the **Alaskan brown bear,** the largest land predator alive today.

MAMMAL

ANDREWSARCHUS

When: 45–36 MYA

Habitat: Plains

Length: 4 m (13 ft)

Diet: Mainly meat

Skull and teeth
The skull had very broad cheekbones but narrow jaws. The pointed canine teeth were those of a hunter, but the back teeth were blunt.

Crushing jaws
Related animals have very deep, strong lower jaws that can crush bone.

TRIASSIC	JURASSIC	CRETACEOUS	CENOZOIC	
252 MYA	201 MYA	145 MYA	66 MYA	0

Otodus megalodon

A gigantic ancestor of the notorious great white shark, this enormous oceanic hunter was probably the most powerful and terrifying marine predator of its time.

Sharks have been prowling the world's oceans for at least 420 million years, since long before the evolution of the dinosaurs. By the late Cenozoic, 400 million years of evolution had refined them into some of the most efficient hunters on the planet. *Otodus megalodon* was one of the largest – a streamlined killer with huge jaws armed with row upon row of razor-edged teeth. Its highly tuned senses would have allowed it to track and target its prey in total darkness, and with lethal precision.

Tail fin
The shark surged through the water propelled by its powerful tail.

Solid muscle
Massively strong body muscles were used to power the shark through water.

Mega-shark

Otodus megalodon was probably related to the great white shark, but it was much bigger and far heavier. It would even have dwarfed the huge, plankton-eating whale shark, which is the world's largest living fish.

OTODUS MEGALODON 18 m (59 ft)

WHALE SHARK
RHINCODON TYPUS 10 m (33 ft)

GREAT WHITE SHARK
CARCHARODON CARCHARIUS 4 m (13 ft)

0 m (0 ft)	5 m (16.5 ft)	10 m (33 ft)	15 m (49 ft)	20 m (66 ft)

Pectoral fins
Long, wing-like pectoral fins created lift as the shark swam forwards.

Efficient gills
The gills gathered vital oxygen from the water. The faster the shark swam, the more oxygen its gills absorbed.

Super-sense

Like modern sharks, *Otodus megalodon* would have had very acute senses. At close range it could even detect faint electrical signals generated by the muscles of hidden prey. These were picked up through the ampullae of Lorenzini, special sensors named after the man who first described them in 1678.

The electrical sensors lay in a network of gel-filled pores on the shark's snout.

Overlapping scales
The skin was studded with tiny, tooth-like scales called dermal denticles. These acted as a form of armour, but also helped water flow over the shark's body, allowing it to swim all day without getting tired.

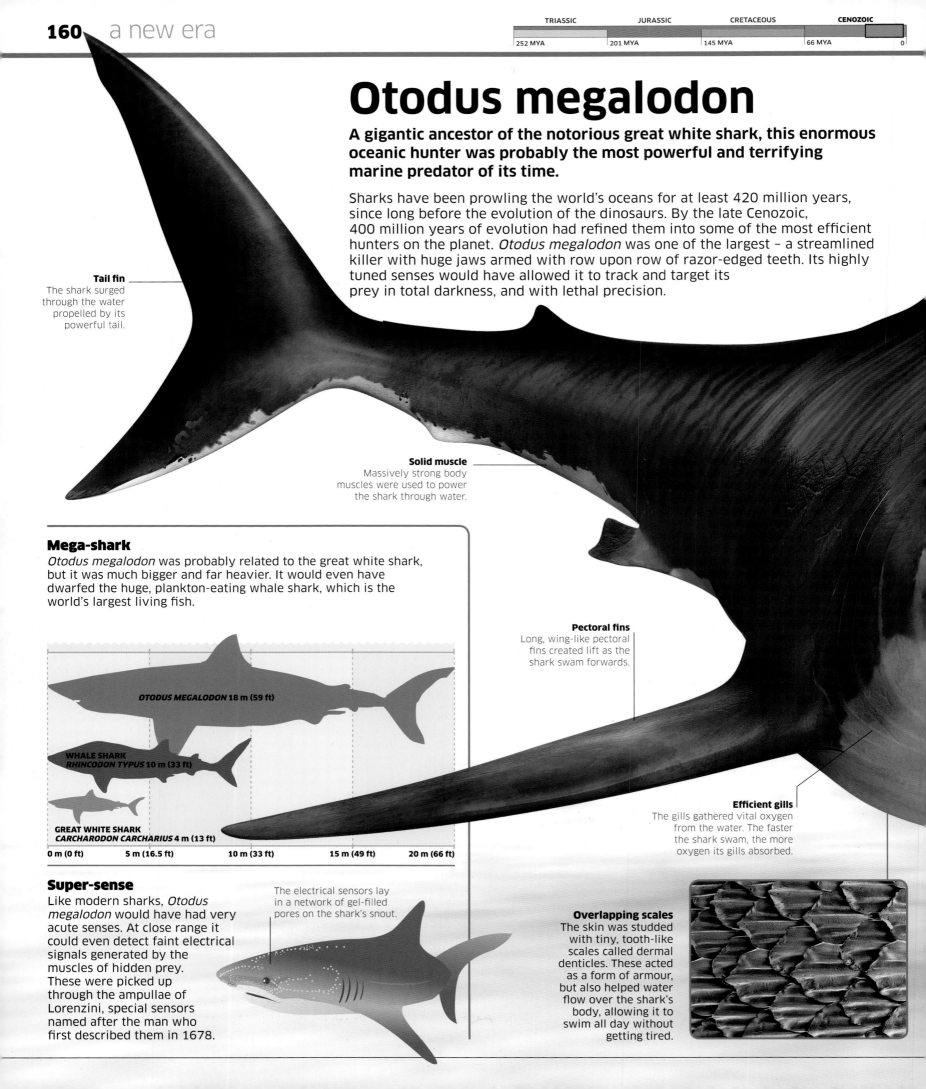

19 cm (7.4 in) – the **height** of the **largest** known *Otodus megalodon* tooth.

50 tonnes – the probable **maximum weight** of this **monster fish**.

276 The **number of teeth** in *Otodus megalodon*'s jaws at any one time.

161

SHARK

OTODUS MEGALODON

When: 28–2.6 MYA

Habitat: Oceans

Length: 18 m (59 ft)

Diet: Big marine animals

Dorsal fin
This helped to keep the shark on course as it swam.

Small prey
This sea turtle would be no more than a snack for the giant shark.

This monster had a bite at least
six times stronger
than that of the great white shark – the most powerful predatory shark alive today.

Renewable teeth
Rows of new, serrated teeth were constantly forming on the inside of the jaw, and rolling out to replace teeth that were losing their sharp edge. The older teeth were pushed to the outside of the jaw, and fell off before they got the chance to become blunt.

TRIASSIC
JURASSIC
CRETACEOUS
CENOZOIC
252 MYA
201 MYA
145 MYA
66 MYA
0

Megatherium

As big as an elephant, the giant ground sloth *Megatherium* was a super-sized relative of the leaf-eating tree sloths that still live in the rainforests of South America.

Modern sloths are specialized climbers that hang from high branches, but *Megatherium* was far too heavy to clamber into the trees. It lived on the ground, but it could feed from the treetops by rearing up on its hind legs, supported by its strong tail. It had enormously long claws, similar to those of a modern tree sloth, and it used these to pull high branches within reach of its mouth. However, its claws forced it to walk on the sides of its feet, despite its immense weight.

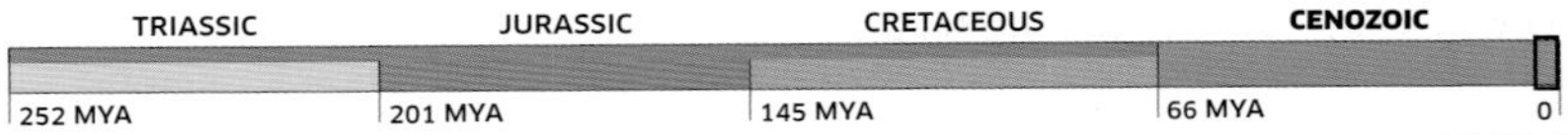

Slicing teeth
The sharp-edged teeth sliced vegetation instead of grinding it. They were very big, so they took a long time to wear down.
Twisted toes
Long claws made its toes twist inwards, so it stood on the side of each foot.

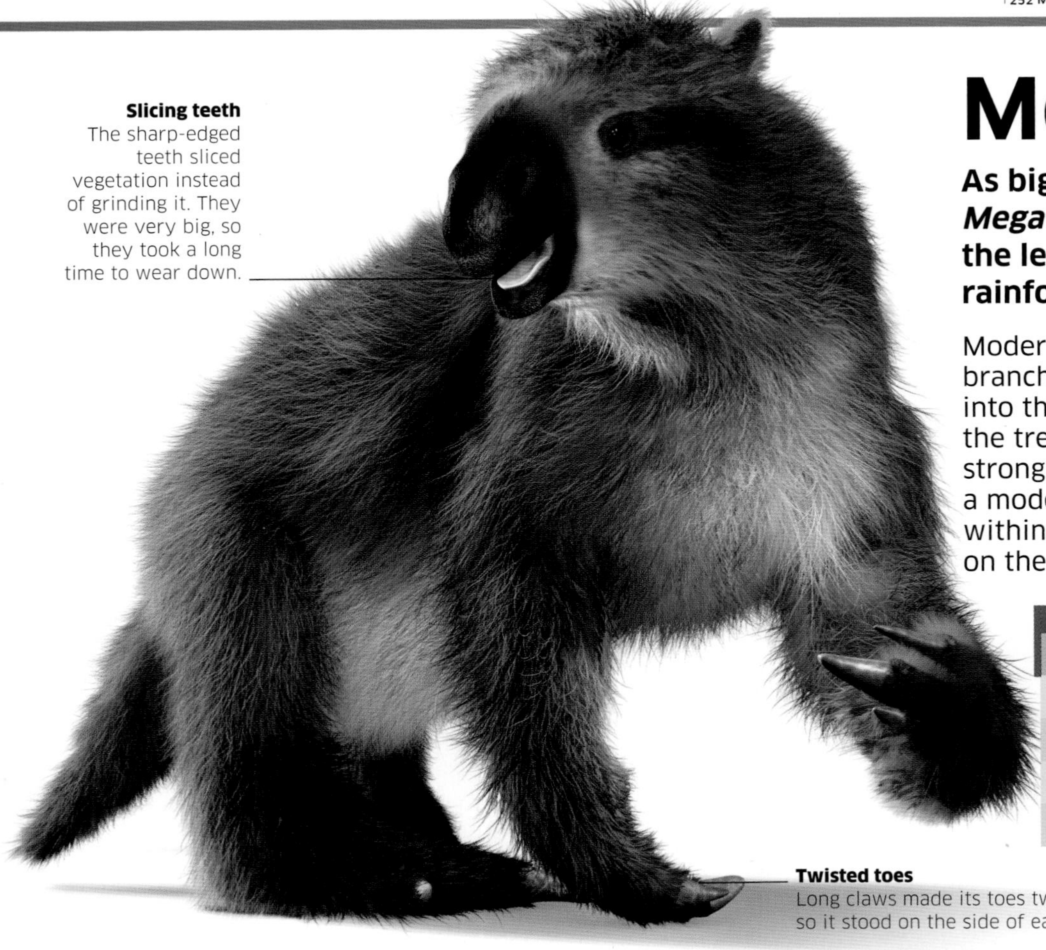

MAMMAL

MEGATHERIUM

When: 2 million–10,000 years ago

Habitat: Woodlands

Length: 6 m (20 ft)

Diet: Plants

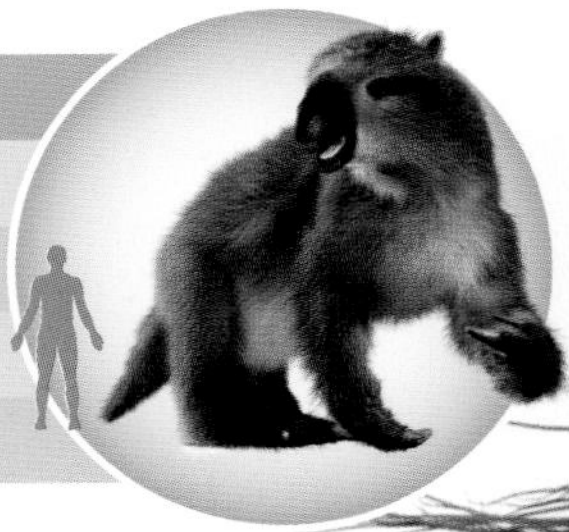

High reach

Its great size allowed *Megatherium* to reach high into the trees to gather the tender, nutritious leaves that were probably its main food. While standing up like this it could support some of its considerable weight with its strong tail, which acted like the third leg of a tripod.

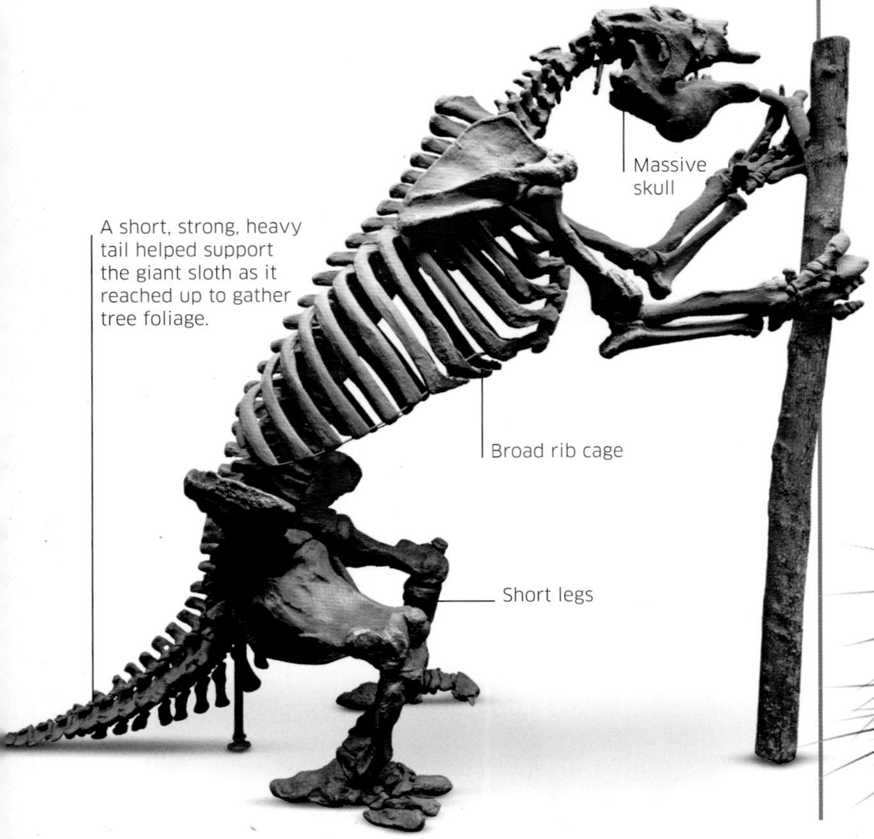

Massive skull
A short, strong, heavy tail helped support the giant sloth as it reached up to gather tree foliage.
Broad rib cage
Short legs

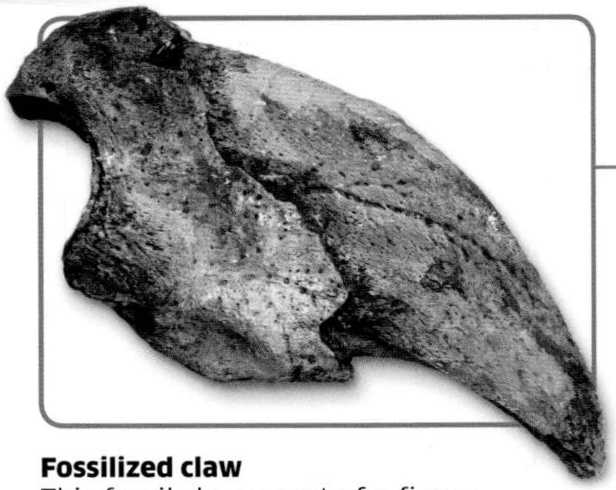

Fossilized claw
This fossil shows part of a finger and the bony core of a *Megatherium* claw. The horny sheaths of the claws would have been at least three times as long.

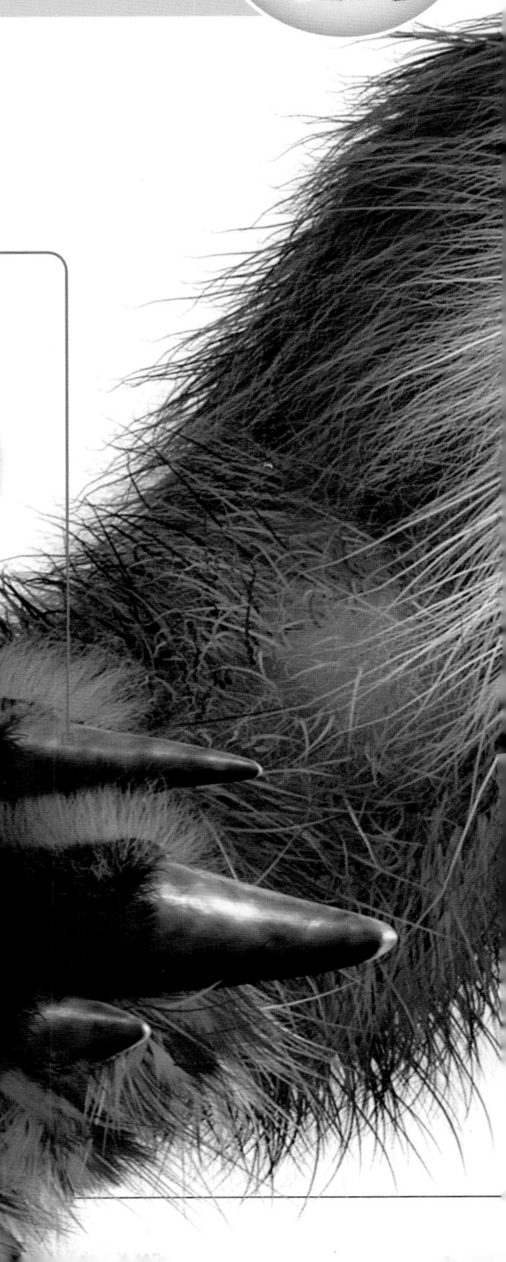

The naturalist **Charles Darwin** found fossils of **giant sloths** when visiting **South America** in 1832.

163

Big body
The bulky body contained a large stomach to cope with a big appetite.

Small eyes
Its relatively small eyes suggest that *Smilodon* usually hunted by day.

Powerful neck
The big neck muscles gave *Smilodon* the power to stab and slash at its victims.

Strong legs
The powerful front legs were adapted for grappling with prey and pinning it to the ground.

TRIASSIC	JURASSIC	CRETACEOUS	CENOZOIC	
252 MYA	201 MYA	145 MYA	66 MYA	0

2,000 The number of *Smilodon* skeletons found in the **La Brea Tar Pits**. **165**

Smilodon

Immensely strong and heavily armed, this was the biggest of the fearsome sabre-toothed cats that prowled the grasslands and woods at the end of the Cenozoic. *Smilodon* was an expert killer, mostly of plant-eating prey that was larger than itself.

Smilodon's main weapons were its powerful front legs and enormous canine teeth – so long that they were always exposed, even when it had its mouth closed. They were like curved, serrated knives, and were used to kill big animals by inflicting very deep wounds that severed vital blood vessels.

MAMMAL	
SMILODON	
When:	2.5 million–10,000 years ago
Habitat:	Open woods and plains
Length:	2 m (6.5 ft)
Diet:	Big plant-eating animals

Sabre teeth
The upper canine teeth were some 18 cm (7 in) long, not counting their deep roots. They had sharp, saw-toothed edges for slicing through soft tissue, but were quite narrow and might have snapped on impact with hard bone.

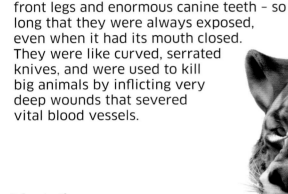

Huge gape
A sabre-toothed cat could open its jaws incredibly wide. A yawning tiger can open its jaw by about 70 degrees at full gape, but *Smilodon* could manage 90 or even 120 degrees. This moved its lower jaw out of the way, allowing it to drive its stabbing teeth deep into the belly or throat of its prey.

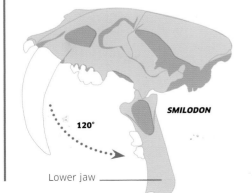
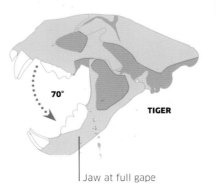

120°   *SMILODON*   70°   TIGER

Lower jaw   Jaw at full gape

Death trap
Thousands of *Smilodon* fossils have been found in California, USA, at a site called the La Brea Tar Pits, where black tar naturally oozes from the ground. The tar formed a sticky trap for animals and, attracted by the prospect of an easy meal, many sabre-toothed cats became stuck in the tar themselves. This picture shows part of a *Smilodon* skull, blackened by tar.

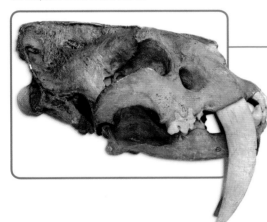

Woolly mammoth

During the last ice age, herds of magnificent woolly mammoths roamed the broad grasslands that fringed the vast ice sheets of the northern continents.

Mammoths were close relatives of modern Asian elephants that lived from about 5 million years ago in Africa, Europe, Asia, and North America. There were at least ten species, but the most famous is the woolly mammoth, which was adapted for life in the chill of the most recent ice age. It lived as far north as the Siberian shores of the Arctic Ocean, on the dry grassy plains we now call the mammoth steppe. Along with deer, bison, and wild horses, it was a favourite prey of ice-age human hunters.

Thick coat
This long-preserved strand of mammoth hair has acquired a reddish tinge. In life, mammoths were very dark brown, blonde, or even particoloured.

Fat layer
A thick layer of fat under the skin gave protection against the cold.

Curved tusks
Like elephants, they would have used their tusks to find food, perhaps even to scrape away snow and ice.

Short tail
The tail was shorter than an elephant's to reduce the risk of frostbite.

Handy trunk
It would have used its trunk for feeding and making trumpeting calls.

During the ice age, some people lived in small houses made of mammoth bones covered with animal skins.

Frozen remains

Amazingly, some mammoths that fell into bogs in the ice age have been deep-frozen and preserved intact for thousands of years. This baby, found in Siberia in 2007, was just a month old when she died 42,000 years ago. She has lost nearly all the hair that once covered her body, but she was so young that she still has traces of her mother's milk in her stomach.

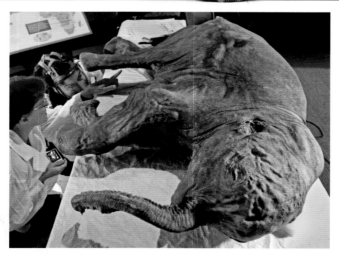

FROZEN WOOLLY MAMMOTH

Walking on tiptoe

Like modern elephants, the mammoth walked on the tips of its toes! But it didn't have to balance on them like a ballerina. The bones of each foot were supported by a wedge of spongy soft tissue, which acted as a shock absorber. It also spread the mammoth's great weight over broad, circular foot pads, so it could move across soft ground without sinking.

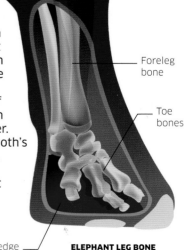

Foreleg bone

Toe bones

Spongy wedge

ELEPHANT LEG BONE

Mammoths may have been **driven to extinction** by **human hunters**.

4.2 m (13.7 ft) – the length of the longest-known mammoth tusk.

167

MAMMAL   NOT A DINOSAUR
WOOLLY MAMMOTH

When: 200,000–4,000 years ago

Habitat: Open plains

Height: 3.4 m (11 ft)

Diet: Grasses, herbs, and leaves

Multi-ridged teeth
The mammoth chewed its tough, fibrous plant food with four enormous, ridged cheek teeth. As they wore down they were pushed forwards and out of the jaws, and eventually replaced by a new set.

DINOSAUR SCIENCE

This is an exciting time for dinosaur science. At least 80 per cent of all known dinosaurs have been discovered since 1990. Astonishing fossils have been found, and they have been analysed in more detail than ever before, giving us new insights into these incredible creatures and how they lived.

Fossilization

The only reason that we know giant dinosaurs and other extinct animals existed is because their remains have been preserved as fossils. Usually, the bodies of animals and other living things are broken down and completely destroyed by decay. But sometimes the harder parts, such as bones and teeth, are buried in ways that slow or stop the decay process. Over time they may absorb minerals that turn them to stone, transforming them into typical fossils.

FOSSIL TYPES

Typical fossils are shells or bones that have been turned to stone. These are called body fossils. But a fossil can also preserve an impression or mould of an organism. Sub-fossils can form when animals or plants are preserved by natural chemicals, or smothered by fluids that harden over time.

In amber
Insects and other small animals can be trapped in sticky tree resin that hardens to become amber. This spider died in this way many millions of years ago, but every tiny detail of its body has been preserved.

A SLOW PROCESS

Fossilization is a gradual process that can take millions of years. Groundwater seeping into the buried bones of an animal such as a dinosaur contains dissolved stony minerals, which slowly replace the original animal material. The minerals harden, filling the spaces left by dead animal cells to create a stony fossil. The finest of these can reproduce the living tissue in microscopic detail.

Conifer trees
Pines and other conifer trees were common during the Mesozoic, and their needle-shaped leaves were the main food of many dinosaurs.

Tyrannosaurus rex
This famous dinosaur was the most powerful hunter that has ever lived on land; it prowled the land at the end of the Mesozoic Era.

Triceratops
This massively built plant-eater lived in the same places as Tyrannosaurus.

Flooded landscape
Long after the giant dinosaurs have died out, the land has been flooded by seawater.

Giant shark
Twenty million years ago, the colossal shark Carcharodon megalodon was the most powerful oceanic predator.

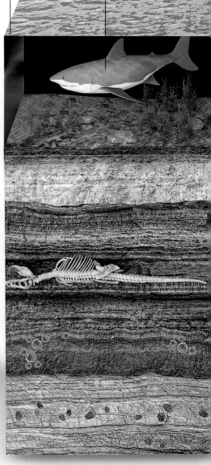

Drowned dinosaur

Rock layers
Rocks of different colours have formed from different types of soft mud and sand.

Ancient shells
The rock below the lake bed already contains fossils that formed millions of years earlier.

1 Doomed dinosaur
Crippled by a fight with heavily armed prey 67 million years ago, a Tyrannosaurus rex stumbles into a lake and drowns. Its body sinks and settles on the lake bed, where the soft tissues start to decay.

2 Buried in mud
The still conditions in the lake allow fine mud to settle around the body. The mud buries it and stops the bones being pulled apart by scavengers, so the skeleton stays joined together as it was in life.

3 Rising tide
Mud settling in the lake gradually turns it to dry land. Millions of years later, rising sea levels flood the area with ocean water, and the mud is covered with pale marine sediment.

Mould and cast
An ancient sea creature was buried in mud that turned to rock and preserved a mould of its shape. Later more mud filled the mould, and hardened to create a cast with the same shape as the animal.

Body fossils
These bones once supported the flipper of a marine reptile. They were buried and gradually absorbed minerals from the ground that have turned them to stone. Most dinosaur fossils are of this type.

Impression
More than 35 million years ago, a delicate poplar leaf fell into some mud in Colorado, USA. The leaf rotted away, but it left this impression in the mud, which then hardened into stone, preserving the impression as a fossil.

Trace fossil
Dinosaur footprints such as this trackway are often found in rocks that were once soft mud. This type of trace fossil can be very useful because it shows how an animal behaved when it was alive.

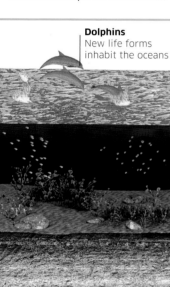

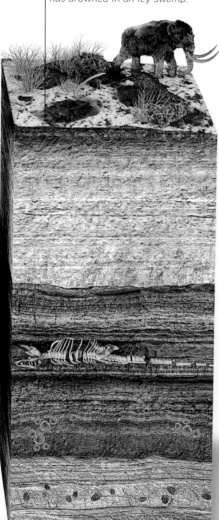

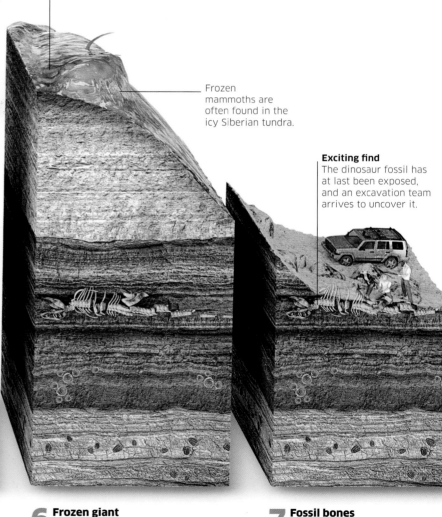

Dolphins
New life forms inhabit the oceans

Buried in ice
Woolly mammoths were adapted to cope with the bitter chill of the ice age, but this mammoth has drowned in an icy swamp.

Frozen fossil
The ice deep-freezes the mammoth's body, creating a type of fossil. It is called a sub-fossil because it has not been turned to stone.

THE OLDEST KNOWN FOSSILS HAVE BEEN FOUND IN ROCKS THAT ARE ALMOST 3.5 BILLION YEARS OLD.

Frozen mammoths are often found in the icy Siberian tundra.

Exciting find
The dinosaur fossil has at last been exposed, and an excavation team arrives to uncover it.

4 Seeping minerals
The sediments get deeper, and dissolved minerals turn them into solid rocks. The minerals also seep into the buried bones of the dinosaur, slowly turning them to stone.

5 Ice age
Much closer to our own time, sea levels fall when an ice age turns much of the world's fresh water to ice. Mammoths roaming the cold landscape sometimes fall into swamps, drown, and freeze solid.

6 Frozen giant
In the Middle Ages the frozen body of the mammoth is revealed when a river bank collapses during a flood. However, the fossilized skeleton of the *Tyrannosaurus* is still hidden deep below ground.

7 Fossil bones
Eventually a river carves away the rock and reveals part of the dinosaur skeleton. An excited fossil hunter calls in the scientists, who begin a slow, careful excavation.

Fossil hunters

The Ancient Greek philosopher Empedocles was the first to realize what fossils were. But at that time nobody understood how rocks formed or how old the world was, so they couldn't imagine how bones might be fossilized over millions of years. It was not until the 17th century that naturalists began to study fossils systematically, and only in the late 1700s did French scientist Georges Cuvier realize fossils were the remains of extinct living things. In the next century fossil hunters began to gather evidence that would help change our understanding of life on Earth.

THE FIRST PALEONTOLOGISTS

The early fossil hunters saw fossils as ornamental objects rather than evidence of life in the past. But as the true nature of fossils became clear, they became the subject of a new science called paleontology. The first scientists to work in this field struggled to make sense of the fossils they found, but gradually they came to conclusions that revolutionized our understanding of ancient life.

Georges Cuvier (1769–1832)
In 1796 Cuvier published the first descriptions of fossil bones that identified them as those of extinct animals. This marked the beginning of the science of paleontology.

FOSSIL FOLKLORE

Throughout history it has been obvious that fossils are not just normal pieces of rock. Some clearly looked like bones, teeth, or shells, but why were they made of stone? People came up with many different explanations. Most of these were fantastic, but a few were surprisingly close to the truth. The Ancient Chinese, for example, thought that dinosaur fossils were the bones of dragons.

Shell opening

Sharp point

Devil's toenails
Although they look very like modern seashells, people liked to think of these fossils as the ugly toenails of devils. They are actually fossilized Jurassic oysters, called *Gryphaea arcuata*.

Thunderbolts
These belemnites are the fossilized internal shells of animals related to cuttlefish. But they look more like bullets, and were once seen as "thunderbolts" from heaven.

Snakestone
You can see why someone might think this was a coiled snake turned to stone, and in fact the end of the coil has been carved to look like a head. It is actually an ammonite, a type of seashell.

Magic stone
In northern Europe, fossil sea urchins were known as thunderstones. People thought they fell during thunderstorms, and kept them as magic charms against being struck by lightning.

MARY ANNING (1799–1847)

In 1811, at the age of just 12, Mary found the intact fossil skeleton of an ichthyosaur near her home on the "Jurassic Coast" of southwest England. During the next 36 years she found many more important fossils, and became one of the most admired fossil experts of her time. Many discoveries by other scientists were based on her work, but she rarely received the recognition she deserved because she was a woman in a man's world.

Fossil hunter
Mary is shown here with her dog, Tray, on the coastal cliffs where she found her fossils.

Sea dragons
The fossils found by Mary Anning soon became famous. They inspired artists of her time to create scenes like this, showing *Ichthyosaurus* and *Plesiosaurus* as "sea dragons" near the surface. However, these depictions were often scientifically incorrect. For instance, both creatures lived almost entirely underwater.

William Smith (1769–1839)
While working as a surveyor in England, Smith realized that the relative ages of rock layers (strata) could be worked out by identifying the fossils in the rocks. He used this to make the first geological maps.

William Buckland (1784–1856)
In 1824 English scientist William Buckland wrote the world's first scientific description of a fossil dinosaur, which was named *Megalosaurus* in 1827. He was also the first to recognize fossil faeces, or coprolites.

Gideon Mantell (1790–1852)
Early 19th-century country doctor Gideon Mantell collected fossils in his spare time. In 1822 he discovered the dinosaur that he called *Iguanodon*, and began the first intensive scientific study of dinosaurs.

Richard Owen (1804–1892)
Owen was the paleontologist who invented the word "dinosaur". Famous in his time for his understanding of fossils, he also helped create the world-famous Natural History Museum in London, England.

BONE WARS

In 1860 just six types of dinosaur were known. But then people started finding spectacular dinosaur bones in America. In the 1870s, two American paleontologists, Edward Drinker Cope and Othniel Charles Marsh, started competing to find new fossils. This became known as the "bone wars". By 1892 they had discovered more than 120 new dinosaurs between them.

Dangerous work
The bearded O C Marsh (centre) is seen here with his crew, heavily armed for protection in the Native American Territories of the Midwest, where the best fossils were to be found.

DINOSAUR NAMES

All living things known to science have scientific names. A tiger's scientific name, for example, is *Panthera tigris*. Dinosaurs are named in exactly the same way. The names are based on Latin and Greek words that often describe some aspect of the animal.

Allo	strange
Brachio	arm
Brachy	short
Cera	horned
Coelo	hollow
Corytho	helmet
Di	two
Diplo	double
Hetero	different
Hypsi	high
Mega	huge
Micro	small
Pachy	thick
Plateo	flat
Poly	many
Ptero	winged
Quadri	four
Raptor	thief
Rhino	nose
Salto	jumping
Saurus	lizard, reptile
Stego	roofed
Thero	beast
Tops	head, face
Tri	three
Tyranno	tyrant
Veloci	fast

Back to front
Although Marsh and Cope found many important fossils, they were not always sure what they were. Notoriously, Cope reconstructed the skeleton of the plesiosaur *Elasmosaurus* with its head on the wrong end – much to the delight of his rival.

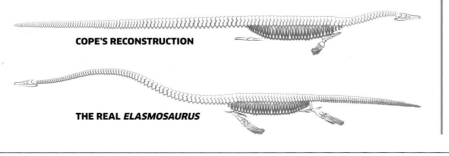

COPE'S RECONSTRUCTION

THE REAL *ELASMOSAURUS*

DINOSAUR PROVINCIAL PARK

Country: Canada

Famous fossil: *Euoplocephalus*

During the Late Cretaceous this area of land near the Red Deer River in Alberta, Canada, was a patchwork of marshes and warm, wet forest. Today it is dry and rocky, but the rocks contain the fossils of at least 40 different species of dinosaur.

MESSEL PIT

Country: Germany

Famous fossil: *Darwinius*

Poisonous gases rising from this volcanic site in the mid-Paleogene led to the death of thousands of animals. The toxic conditions prevented their rapid decay, and as a result the oily rock dug from the pit has preserved their fossils in spectacular detail.

DINOSAUR NATIONAL MONUMENT

Country: USA

Famous fossil: *Allosaurus*

The Morrison Formation of the North American Midwest is a mass of sedimentary rock that formed in the Late Jurassic. One section that was once a river floodplain is so rich in Jurassic dinosaur fossils that it has been named Dinosaur National Monument.

SOLNHOFEN

Country: Germany

Famous fossil: *Archaeopteryx*

The fine-grained limestones quarried at Solnhofen contain some of the most perfect Jurassic fossils ever found. They include the first-known dinosaur feathers, from *Archaeopteryx*, and detailed fossils of the pterosaurs *Rhamphorhynchus* and *Pterodactylus*.

HELL CREEK

Country: USA

Famous fossil: *Triceratops*

In the Late Cretaceous a broad sea covered what are now the American prairies. Hell Creek in Montana was a plain on its coast, inhabited by many dinosaurs whose fossils are now found in its sedimentary rocks.

GHOST RANCH

Country: USA

Famous fossil: *Coelophysis*

This site in New Mexico is famous for its fossils of just one dinosaur – the Late Triassic *Coelophysis*. But it was found in huge numbers, with remains of more than 1,000 individual animals. It is one of the largest dinosaur bonebeds ever discovered.

VALLEY OF THE MOON

Country: Argentina

Famous fossil: *Eoraptor*

Some of the earliest dinosaurs known to science have been discovered in the rocks of this region of South America. In the Late Triassic it was a desert, and it is now so desolate that the landscape looks like the surface of the Moon.

Fossil sites

Most fossils are found in fine-grained sedimentary rocks – the rocks that were once layers of soft mud or similar. These rocks occur worldwide, but some are especially rich in good fossils of dinosaurs and other organisms, and have become key sites for research. A lucky combination of local conditions prevented the remains being disturbed or decaying too rapidly, while the nature of the sediment has preserved the finest details.

AUCA MAHUEVO

Country: Argentina

Famous fossil: *Saltasaurus*

Once a river floodplain, this barren, rocky desert is littered with the broken shells of dinosaur eggs. Dating from the Late Cretaceous, they are probably the remains of a vast nesting site of the sauropod *Saltasaurus*.

BAHARIYA OASIS

Country: Egypt

Famous fossil: *Spinosaurus*

Although it is now mostly desert, Egypt was a region of coastal marshes and forest in the Late Cretaceous. It was the home of giant dinosaurs such as *Spinosaurus*, the remains of which were found at this Western Desert oasis early in the 20th century.

GOBI DESERT

Country: Mongolia

Famous fossil: *Velociraptor*

Even in the Late Cretaceous this part of Asia was a desert. Despite this, it was home to many dinosaurs, whose fossils have been amazingly well preserved in its rocks. Some of the best have been found in the red sandstones of the "Flaming Cliffs".

LIAONING

Country: China

Famous fossil: *Sinosauropteryx*

Liaoning has yielded some of the most exciting dinosaur fossils. Buried by volcanic ash settling in lakes in the Early Cretaceous, they show that many dinosaurs once thought to be scaly actually had feathers – radically changing our image of Mesozoic life.

KEY

TRIASSIC SITE

JURASSIC SITE

CRETACEOUS SITE

CENOZOIC SITE

TENDAGURU

Country: Tanzania

Famous fossil: *Kentrosaurus*

The Late Jurassic rocks of this East African site contained the fossils of spectacular dinosaurs such as the spiky stegosaur *Kentrosaurus* and the long-necked sauropod *Giraffatitan*. Taken to Germany, many of the fossils were destroyed during Word War II.

FROZEN FOSSILS

MOUNT KIRKPATRICK

Country: Antarctica

Famous fossil: *Cryolophosaurus*

Jurassic Antarctica was much warmer than it is now, with forests inhabited by dinosaurs and other life. Most fossils are hidden by deep ice sheets, and this rocky outcrop is one of the few places where scientists can get at them.

FOSSIL TRIANGLE

Country: Australia

Famous fossil: *Muttaburrasaurus*

This area of northeast Australia was a shallow sea in the Early Cretaceous. Its rocks preserve fossils of marine reptiles and even dinosaurs whose bodies were washed into the sea.

Dinosaur fossils

When we imagine dinosaur fossils we usually think of the mounted skeletons that tower over us in museums. The gigantic bones in them are certainly the most spectacular remains of these animals, but there are many other types of dinosaur fossils. Most are much smaller, but these fossils can often tell us a lot more about what dinosaurs were like, and how they may have lived. They show things like skin texture and feathers, and some fossils may even preserve evidence of colour.

TEETH

The hard enamel covering teeth makes them very durable, and teeth are often the only parts of an animal to survive as fossils. Their shape is very distinctive, so scientists can identify what type of animal they belonged to. Teeth can also tell us a lot about an animal's diet, and how it used them to gather and process its food.

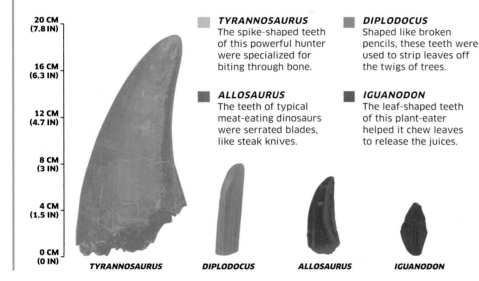

TYRANNOSAURUS
The spike-shaped teeth of this powerful hunter were specialized for biting through bone.

DIPLODOCUS
Shaped like broken pencils, these teeth were used to strip leaves off the twigs of trees.

ALLOSAURUS
The teeth of typical meat-eating dinosaurs were serrated blades, like steak knives.

IGUANODON
The leaf-shaped teeth of this plant-eater helped it chew leaves to release the juices.

20 CM (7.8 IN)
16 CM (6.3 IN)
12 CM (4.7 IN)
8 CM (3 IN)
4 CM (1.5 IN)
0 CM (0 IN)

TYRANNOSAURUS   DIPLODOCUS   ALLOSAURUS   IGUANODON

BONES

Apart from teeth, bones are the most likely parts of the body to form fossils. Some dinosaur bones are enormous, such as these being excavated at Dinosaur National Monument in Utah, USA, but others are surprisingly small and delicate. Fossil bones are usually broken and scattered, but the best fossils preserve complete skeletons.

TRACE FOSSILS

Some of the most interesting fossils do not actually preserve parts of dinosaurs. They are trace fossils that show where the dinosaurs have been and what the creatures were doing. These fossils help scientists work out how dinosaurs moved, what they ate, and even how they lived together.

Coprolites

Surprisingly common, these are fossilized dung, or faeces. They preserve bits of undigested food, so dedicated scientists can pull them apart and find out what the living dinosaurs were eating.

FOSSIL DUNG OF A PLANT-EATING DINOSAUR

Footprints

Dinosaur footprints are among the most useful trace fossils. These show how the animals walked or ran, and whether they were travelling in groups. Some may even show one dinosaur stalking another.

Theropod print
This three-toed footprint was made by a theropod dinosaur – a hunter, possibly searching for prey. The marks made by its toes and claws can be analysed to reveal how it moved.

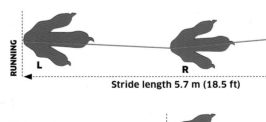

RUNNING
L   R   L
Stride length 5.7 m (18.5 ft)

Fast mover
A line of footprints can show how fast the animal was moving. This theropod started off by walking, but then broke into a run, increasing its speed from 7 kph (4 mph) to 29 kph (18 mph).

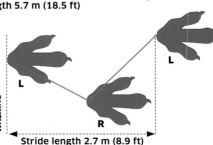

L
L
R
WALKING
Stride length 2.7 m (8.9 ft)

SOME FOSSILS EVEN PRESERVE THE REMAINS OF A DINOSAUR'S LAST MEAL, SO WE KNOW WHAT IT WAS EATING BEFORE IT DIED.

EGGS

Many dinosaur nesting sites have been found with fossilized eggs surviving in the nests. Some even contain fossilized embryos on the verge of hatching. The eggs were hard-shelled, like birds' eggs, and vary in shape from perfectly spherical to elongated, like these *Oviraptor* eggs. The spherical eggs of giant, long-necked sauropods are surprisingly small – each one no bigger than a grapefruit.

***OVIRAPTOR* EGGS**

SOFT TISSUES

Usually only the hard parts of an animal's body survive as fossils. This is because the soft tissues are eaten by other animals or destroyed by decay before they can be fossilized. But some fossil sites are formed in special conditions, such as airless lake beds with no oxygen to support scavengers and decay organisms. These sites contain amazing fossils that preserve skin, feathers, and even the outlines of muscles.

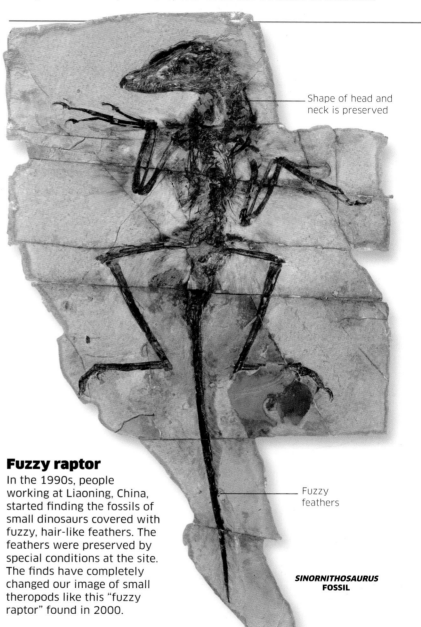

Shape of head and neck is preserved

Fuzzy feathers

***SINORNITHOSAURUS* FOSSIL**

Fuzzy raptor

In the 1990s, people working at Liaoning, China, started finding the fossils of small dinosaurs covered with fuzzy, hair-like feathers. The feathers were preserved by special conditions at the site. The finds have completely changed our image of small theropods like this "fuzzy raptor" found in 2000.

Scaly skin

Some fossils preserve impressions of dinosaur skin, or even actual skin remains. They show that many dinosaurs were scaly, as we would expect for reptiles. The scales formed a smooth, tough, protective surface like floor tiles, rather than overlapping each other like the scales of many fish.

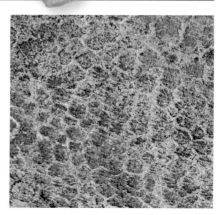

***Edmontosaurus* skin**
Some amazingly well-preserved fossils of this big hadrosaur include large areas of its skin, showing its scales.

Excavation and restoration

Many fossils are discovered by accident, or by amateur fossil hunters, but their excavation is a job for experts who know how to recover the fossils intact. These experts are also able to identify less obvious features such as traces of feathers, skin, and food remains that may be fossilized in the rock alongside the bones. The excavated fossils then have to be cleaned up, conserved to stop them falling apart, and scientifically described and identified. The best specimens are often used to make casts for display in museums.

RECOVERY

Despite being apparently made of stone, fossilized bones are fragile objects that need careful excavation. But first, the scientists must record their exact location. They must check any surrounding rock for other clues, such as traces of soft tissue, that might be destroyed when the fossil is extracted. Once all this is done, the rock can be chipped away to expose the fossils. If they are small enough they can be removed intact, but big bones are partly encased in plaster to reinforce them before they are cut out.

1 BEGINNING THE EXCAVATION
When a fossil is discovered, the team carefully expose it by removing any loose rock and soil. They check this carefully for fossil fragments, as well as evidence of the living animal's environment.

IDENTIFICATION

If the fossil is new to science it must be carefully described, with detailed scientific drawings such as this one, made by French paleontologist Georges Cuvier in the early 1800s, or photographs. The fossil will also be given a name, usually chosen by the scientist who describes it. Meanwhile if it is damaged, it will be repaired and strengthened with special glues and other materials. Sometimes fragments are missing, and are replaced with new material. If the fossil is of a type not found before, these restorations are based on fossils of similar animals.

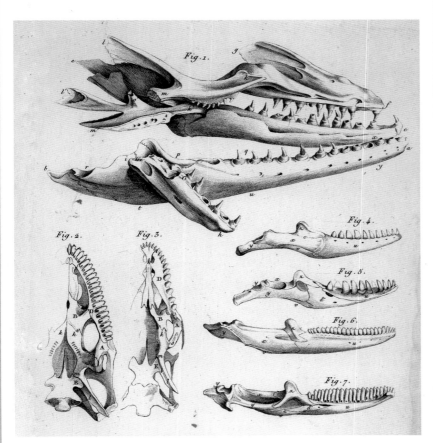

CUVIER'S DRAWING OF A FOSSIL OF *MOSASAUR HOFFMANNII*, A MARINE REPTILE

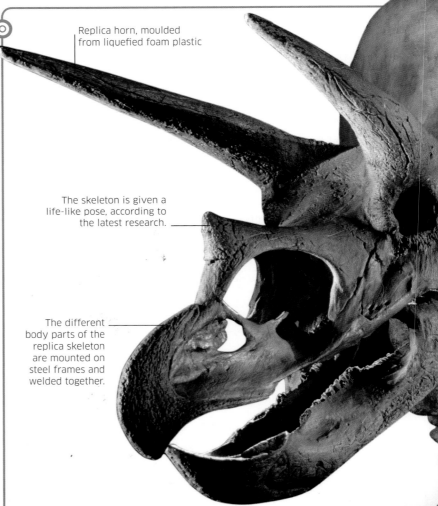

Replica horn, moulded from liquefied foam plastic

The skeleton is given a life-like pose, according to the latest research.

The different body parts of the replica skeleton are mounted on steel frames and welded together.

REBUILDING SKELETONS

Fossil bones are heavy, fragile, and scientifically valuable, so most of the mounted skeletons seen in museums are built from lightweight replicas of the real fossils, attached to steel frames. The replicas depict the bones in good condition, with missing parts or even entire missing bones restored. Clues on the bones indicate how they should be put together, but museum mounts are often rebuilt to match the results of new research.

2 EXPOSING THE FOSSIL
Once the fossil is exposed, the team can see what they are dealing with – its size, condition, and whether or not there are more fossils lying very close to it. At this point they can often work out what it is.

3 MAKING A SITE MAP
Before any part of the fossil is removed, the site is photographed and carefully mapped. The exact position of each visible object is marked on the map, in relation to a string or wire grid that is laid over the site.

4 WRAPPING IN PLASTER
Big, fragile specimens must be encased in plaster before they are dug out, to stop them falling apart. The fossil is protected with a coat of resin, then wrapped before being coated with wet plaster.

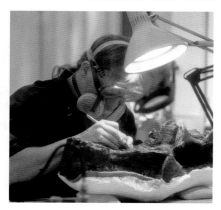

5 REMOVING PLASTER IN LAB
When the plaster sets, the scientists can dig the fossil out and take it back to the laboratory. Here they cut the plaster off and start work on the fossil, using fine tools to remove surrounding rock.

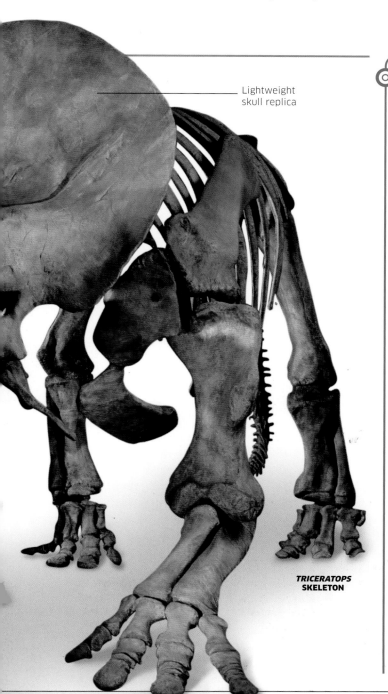

Lightweight skull replica

TRICERATOPS SKELETON

LIVING DINOSAURS

Fossil skeletons can look spectacular, but we want to know what the animals looked like when they were alive. We'll probably never know for sure, but careful study of the bones combined with a knowledge of anatomy can build up an image of the living dinosaur. Once we know what it looked like, artists can use computer software to create 3-D images of the animal that can be seen from different angles, and even moved into different poses.

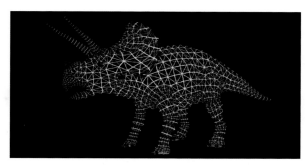

1 CONSTRUCTING THE FRAME
Using accurate drawings of the dinosaur's skeleton, the computer modeller creates an on-screen mesh, or framework, that will form the basis of the model. This starts off as a very coarse grid, but the computer divides this into much smaller units that the modeller can "mould" to shape.

2 ADDING TEXTURE AND OUTER FEATURES
Gradually the modeller can build up all the fine details, such as the scales and wrinkles of the animal's skin, and the exact form of its eyes and mouth. These are based on the latest research by paleontologists, often using fossils that reveal features that have never been seen before.

3 COLOURING AND FINAL POSE
A special digital technique allows the skin to be worked on as if it were laid out flat on the floor, to make sure the colours and textures are right. The computer wraps the skin around the animal, which then has its pose adjusted. Light and shadows are added to make it look real.

Modern dinosaur research

In the past most dinosaur science was based on what the fossil bones and teeth looked like, and how they seemed to fit together. Today we can probe deeper into the nature of fossils using microscopes, scanning technology, radiometric dating, and other techniques. Scientists can also use other types of technology to test their theories about dinosaurs – some build animated computer models of dinosaur bones and muscles to see how these animals might have moved.

ANIMAL STUDIES

One way that scientists can delve into the nature of extinct dinosaurs is by comparing them with modern, living animals. The Mesozoic Era was very different from our own, but the animals still had to find food, avoid being eaten, and compete for breeding partners so they could reproduce their kind. The adaptations and behaviour of living animals can give us clues about how dinosaurs might have lived.

Behaviour

Animals often behave in unpredictable ways. The big antlers of these rival stags look like weapons, but although they do use them for ritual combat, they also use them as status symbols to show who's boss. Many dinosaurs may have used their showy crests and horns in the same way.

Colour

We have almost no reliable information about dinosaur colour, but we can make guesses based on the colours of living animals. This chameleon has a "sail" on its back, like *Spinosaurus*, and this sail flushes with colour during courtship. Maybe the sail of *Spinosaurus* did too.

FOSSIL DATING

Until the 20th century scientists had no real idea how old fossils were. They knew which were older than others, but could not give them an absolute age in millions of years. But modern technology can give us this, and fossil dating is getting more accurate all the time.

How old?
Some fossils are easy to identify in general terms, but hard to date. This is a fossil fern, but how old is it? Scientists have two ways of working this out – stratigraphy and radiometric dating.

Stratigraphy

Fossils are found in rocks that were once soft sediments such as mud or sand. These were laid down in layers, which are preserved as rock strata. Normally older layers lie beneath more recent ones, so the fossils in each layer can be given a relative age. But this does not pinpoint their exact age.

VISIBLE ROCK STRATA IN THE PETRIFIED FOREST NATIONAL PARK, ARIZONA, USA

Radiometric dating

Some rocks contain radioactive elements that, over time, turn into different elements. For example, uranium in newly formed volcanic rock slowly turns into lead. This happens at a steady rate, so by measuring the proportions of uranium and lead in the rock, we can work out how long ago the rock formed. This is combined with stratigraphy to find the age of fossils.

Uranium atom   Lead atom

New rock
Molten rock from a volcano cools, forming crystals with radioactive uranium atoms.

700 million years
At 700 million years, half of the uranium atoms decay to form lead atoms.

1,400 million years
After another 700 million years, half the remaining uranium has turned to lead.

2,100 million years
There is a ratio of seven lead atoms to every uranium atom at 2,100 million years.

MODERN DISCOVERIES

Until recently everything we knew about dinosaurs was deduced from fossils of their bones and teeth. But the discovery of fossils preserving things such as skin and feathers has dramatically changed our view of these animals. Scientists have also made amazing breakthroughs using new analytic techniques.

SOME SCIENTISTS HAVE MADE ROBOTIC **DINOSAURS TO TRY TO TEST THEORIES** ABOUT STRENGTH, MOVEMENT, **AND EVEN THE MASSIVE** BITE POWER OF *TYRANNOSAURUS*.

Preserved feathers
These downy feathers sealed inside a lump of 100-million-year-old tree amber belonged to a Mesozoic dinosaur. Scientists have used high-powered X-rays to scan the feathers and create a 3-D image, allowing the scientists to analyse their form.

Soft tissue surprise
In 2004 a scientist placed a piece of *Tyrannosaurus rex* bone in acid to dissolve the hard minerals. She was left with this stretchy, brown material – soft protein tissue from the animal that had survived for 68 million years, giving us a greater insight into dinosaur tissue.

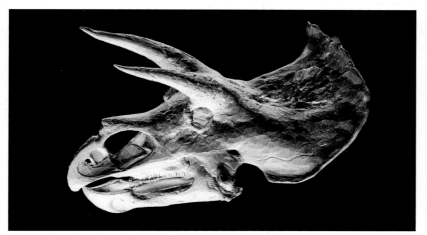

Fossil scanning
Most fossils are too fragile and valuable to be handled regularly for study. Instead scientists use sophisticated medical scanners to map every part of a fossil without leaving a scratch, leaving us with incredible computer models, such as this *Triceratops* skull.

Microfossils
We can now look at fossils in far more detail than ever before. This allows us to see their microscopic structure, and even fossilized cells that formed the living tissues, as this scientist is observing. We can also study the tiny fossils of extinct single-celled life.

COMPUTER MODELLING

Using data gathered from fossils, scientists can build computer models of dinosaur bones and muscles, and animate them to see how these bones and muscles worked. They do not always look very realistic, but they provide a valuable insight into the mechanics of these giant animals, which cannot be gained in any other way.

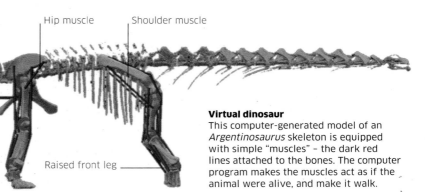

Hip muscle   Shoulder muscle

Tail muscle

Raised front leg

Virtual dinosaur
This computer-generated model of an *Argentinosaurus* skeleton is equipped with simple "muscles" – the dark red lines attached to the bones. The computer program makes the muscles act as if the animal were alive, and make it walk.

Dinosaur biology

The Mesozoic dinosaurs belonged to a group of animals called the archosaurs, which also includes crocodiles and birds. In the past we thought of dinosaurs as rather like crocodiles – cold-blooded, scaly monsters that must have spent a lot of their time doing very little. But over the years scientists have changed their views, and many now see dinosaurs as far more active, agile, and often feathered animals that were more like birds.

BONES AND MUSCLES

Big dinosaurs needed skeletons with big bones, and some of these bones were truly colossal. They contained air cavities that reduced their weight without drastically affecting their strength. The bones had to be strong because muscle attachment scars on fossil bones show that they had to withstand the stresses of powerful muscles.

All fours

Plant-eaters needed much larger, heavier digestive systems than meat-eaters, because plant foods take longer to digest. Many supported the extra weight on all four limbs. These quadrupeds developed stout front limb and shoulder bones, with big muscles. But although the large quadrupeds, such as *Iguanodon* must have been very strong, they were less agile than the bipeds.

HIGH AND MIGHTY

When dinosaurs were first discovered, people assumed that they walked like lizards, sprawling with legs outspread. Even though it soon became clear from their bones that they stood with their legs directly beneath their bodies, their fossil skeletons were still reconstructed with the tails trailing on the ground. We now know that even the giant dinosaurs had a far more agile stance.

Old idea

Many older pictures and models of big hunters such as *Tyrannosaurus rex* show them propped up on their tails like kangaroos. This "tripod" stance now seems very unlikely.

Trailing tail

Tail held straight

New look

Research into the way dinosaurs moved indicates that bipeds like *Tyrannosaurus rex* would have had a dynamic, athletic stance. They would have held their heads low and their tails high.

Heavy tail

Strong tail muscle

Large intestine

Walking tall

All the meat-eating theropods, and many plant-eaters, were bipeds that walked on two legs. Their full weight was supported by their massive hind legs and pelvic bones. The legs of big hunters, such as *Carnotaurus*, also had immensely strong muscles.

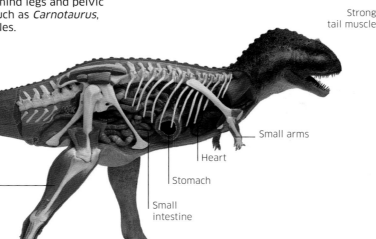

Small arms

Heart

Powerful legs

Stomach

Small intestine

Stout foot bones

CARNOTAURUS

FURRY FEATHERS

Most big dinosaurs had scaly, reptilian skin; we know this from preserved skin impressions. However, recently discovered fossils of small theropod dinosaurs show that many had feathers. Most of these feathers were very simple, hair-like structures that probably helped insulate the body, like fur. This suggests that these dinosaurs, at least, used the energy from food to generate heat within their bodies, and evolved insulating coats that retained heat and saved energy.

Stiff vanes

The flight feathers of modern birds have interlocking barbs that zip together to form vanes that fan the air. Some extinct, non-flying dinosaurs had these too, but they were mainly for insulation, for show, or used to protect young in the nest.

ON THE MOVE

Fossilized dinosaur trackways indicate that some dinosaurs could move quite fast. Although this is not verifiable fact, it is possible that the smaller ones that ran on two legs may have been capable of the same sort of speeds as a human sprinter. Bigger, heavier dinosaurs must have been slower, but even giants such as *Tyrannosaurus rex* would have moved fast as they charged into the attack. Exactly how fast is still the subject of fierce debate.

Possible running speeds

- *Stegosaurus* – 6 kph (3.7 mph)
- *Euoplocephalus* – 8 kph (4.9 mph)
- *Diplodocus* – 24 kph (14.9 mph)
- *Triceratops* – 26 kph (16.1 mph)
- *Spinosaurus* – 30 kph (18.6 mph)
- *Tyrannosaurus rex* – 32 kph (19.9 mph)
- *Velociraptor* – 39 kph (24.2 mph)
- Human – 40 kph (24.9 mph)

| 0 KPH (0 MPH) | 4 KPH (2.4 MPH) | 8 KPH (4.9 MPH) | 12 KPH (7.4 MPH) | 16 KPH (9.9 MPH) | 20 KPH (12.4 MPH) | 24 KPH (14.9 MPH) | 28 KPH (17.4 MPH) | 32 KPH (19.9 MPH) | 36 KPH (22.4 MPH) | 40 KPH (24.9 MPH) | 44 KPH (27.3 MPH) |

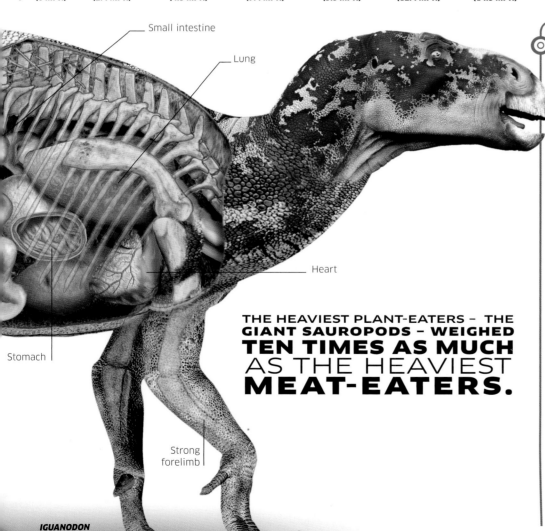

Small intestine

Lung

Heart

Stomach

Strong forelimb

IGUANODON

THE HEAVIEST PLANT-EATERS – THE GIANT SAUROPODS – WEIGHED **TEN TIMES AS MUCH** AS THE HEAVIEST **MEAT-EATERS.**

AIR POWER

The lungs of dinosaurs were similar to the lungs of birds, which is not surprising as birds inherited their lungs from their dinosaur ancestors. Dinosaurs had a complex one-way airflow system that was – and is – more efficient than the simple in-out airflow of mammal lungs. The airflow allowed dinosaurs to get more oxygen from each breath, and use it to generate more energy.

- Air sac
- Lung tissue
- ···▶ Exhalation

Bird

A bird's lungs have fine air tubes passing through them. Air is pumped through the tubes by many balloon-like air sacs.

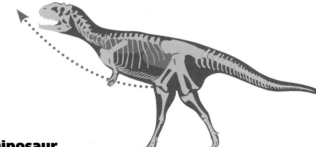

Dinosaur

Fossil clues show that Mesozoic dinosaurs had the same basic lung anatomy as modern birds, complete with air sacs, and it is reasonable to assume that dinosaurs had the same air tubes and other respiratory tissues as birds.

Teeth and beaks

Teeth are very important to our understanding of dinosaurs and similar extinct animals. This is partly because they often survive as fossils when all the other parts of an animal have vanished, including the bones. Many Mesozoic dinosaurs also had beaks, similar to those of birds. Their teeth and beaks can tell us a lot about what they ate, and how they gathered and processed their food.

DINOSAUR TEETH WERE CONSTANTLY **BEING RENEWED AS THEY WORE OUT.** EACH *DIPLODOCUS* TOOTH **LASTED JUST 35 DAYS BEFORE IT WAS REPLACED.**

MEAT-EATERS

Meat is easy to digest, but difficult and even dangerous to get hold of. This means that meat-eating dinosaurs did not need to chew their food much, if at all, but they did need effective weapons and tools for butchery. Most used a combination of teeth and claws to catch their prey, then got to work with sharp-bladed teeth that were adapted for slicing through tough hide and cutting meat off bones.

Tools for the job

Different types of prey or hunting styles demanded different types of teeth. Small prey could be scooped up and swallowed whole, so the main priority was getting a secure grip. Bigger prey needed taking apart, so the hunter needed teeth that could slice through skin and sinew. And the biggest prey of all had to be subdued with teeth that were specialized weapons.

Needle points
Fish-hunters such as *Baronyx* – a close relative of *Spinosaurus* (pages 102–103) – had sharp-pointed teeth suitable for piercing the slippery skin of a struggling prey and stopping it from wriggling free. Many fish-eating pterosaurs had even longer, needle-like teeth.

Butcher blades
The teeth of most meat-eating theropods such as *Allosaurus* were curved blades with sharp, serrated edges. They had sharp points, but their knife-like edges were their most important feature, used to take slashing bites from the bodies of prey.

Bite force

Most meat-eating dinosaurs needed sharp teeth for cutting their prey into bite-sized pieces. But their teeth were not always their main weapons, so they did not all need hugely strong jaws. The light, agile *Velociraptor* probably relied on its claws as much as its teeth for bringing down prey. The bigger *Allosaurus* probably had more muscle, but the real power belonged to *Tyrannosaurus rex*, which used its bite as a weapon to cripple powerful prey.

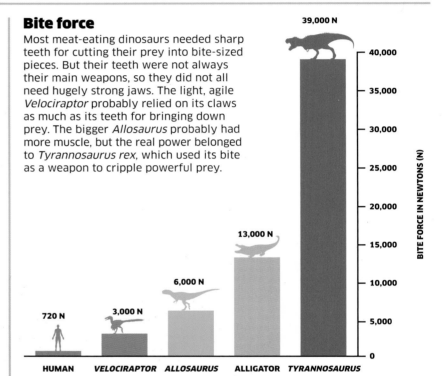

720 N	HUMAN
3,000 N	VELOCIRAPTOR
6,000 N	ALLOSAURUS
13,000 N	ALLIGATOR
39,000 N	TYRANNOSAURUS

BITE FORCE IN NEWTONS (N)

Bone crusher
The big, stout teeth of tyrannosaurs were much stronger than the slender blades of most theropods. They were adapted for biting through bone without snapping off, allowing *Tyrannosaurus rex* to inflict massive, bone-crushing, fatal bites.

PLANT-EATERS

Edible plants are usually easy to find, and don't need to be caught, killed, and torn apart. But plant material can be tough, woody, and difficult to digest. Chewing it thoroughly helps, so while many plant-eating dinosaurs had teeth and beaks adapted for simply harvesting food, a few of them developed some of the most specialized chewing teeth that have ever evolved.

Sharp-edged beaks

Many plant-eating dinosaurs had beaks for gathering their food. They included all the ornithischian dinosaurs, such as stegosaurs, ornithopods, and ceratopsians. Their beaks were made of tough keratin, like those of birds, and would have had sharp edges suitable for cutting through plant stems.

Iguanodon
This big ornithopod had an all-purpose beak for cropping a variety of foods, both from the ground and from trees.

Styracosaurus
Like other ceratopsians, *Styracosaurus* had a narrow, hooked beak like that of a parrot, for selecting the most nutritious foods.

Edmontosaurus
The broad, "duckbill" beak of this large hadrosaur was ideal for gathering a lot of plant food in a short time.

Corythosaurus
Although related to *Edmontosaurus*, this hadrosaur had a narrower beak, adapted for a more selective feeding habit.

Croppers and nibblers

The long-necked sauropods and their relatives did not have beaks. They collected leaves using teeth at front of their jaws. These were used for either stripping foliage from twigs or nipping through leaf stems. These dinosaurs did not have chewing teeth, but many beaked dinosaurs had simple leaf-shaped cheek teeth that helped them chew food.

Pencil-shaped
Diplodocus and its close relatives had front teeth like rows of worn-down pencils. They used their teeth to strip leaves from twigs, branches, and fronds.

Spoon-shaped
Many sauropods had slightly spoon-shaped teeth that were well adapted for seizing leaves by the mouthful.

Flattened crown

Leaf-shaped
This was the most common type of simple chewing tooth among plant-eaters. The bumpy edges helped shred leaves.

Long root

Grinders and slicers

The hadrosaurs and ceratopsians evolved amazingly efficient teeth that were used to reduce their food to an easily digested pulp. Hundreds of teeth were in use at once, and were continuously replaced as they wore down. Those of hadrosaurs formed broad grinding surfaces, while the teeth of ceratopsians had more of a fine-chopping action.

HADROSAUR TOOTH BATTERY

READY FOR ANYTHING

Many dinosaurs ate a wide variety of foods, picking and choosing between them to find the most nutritious, easily digested items. They would have eaten juicy roots, tender shoots, fruits, and even animals such as insects, lizards, and small mammals. Some of these omnivores had toothless beaks like those of birds, but others had different types of teeth in their jaws to cope with all the different foods they ate, just as we do. The most famous of these dinosaurs is *Heterodontosaurus*, but there were plenty of others.

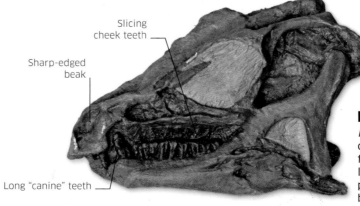

Slicing cheek teeth

Sharp-edged beak

Long "canine" teeth

Many types of teeth

Heterodontosaurus, a small, early ornithischian dinosaur, had short front teeth in its top jaw, blade-like cheek teeth, amazingly long, pointed "canine" teeth, and a beak. It was ready for anything.

Intelligence and senses

Dinosaurs are famous for having small brains compared to their often colossal size, so we assume that they had limited intelligence. But while this was true for many of the big plant-eaters, some of the hunters had bigger brains than most modern reptiles. This means that some, at least, could have been smarter than we usually think. Judging from the anatomy of their brains, many dinosaurs also had very keen senses – far more acute than our own.

DINOSAUR BRAINS

We can estimate a dinosaur's brain size by looking at the size and shape of the brain cavity in its fossil skull. This assumes that the brain fills this cavity, like the brain of a modern bird. But the brains of some reptiles do not fill the cavity, and we can't be sure which model to use. One thing is clear, though – the brains of some dinosaurs were very small indeed.

TYRANNOSAURUS REX
BRAIN CAST (23 CM/9 IN)

Brain cast
The brain cavity of a dinosaur's skull can fill with mud, which hardens to create a fossil cast that mimics the shape of the brain itself. This cast of a *Tyrannosaurus rex* brain reveals that its shape is quite different from a human brain, but similar to that of a bird.

BRAIN FUNCTIONS

Although the size of its brain is a rough measure of an animal's intelligence, the shape of its brain is important too. This is because different parts of the brain have different functions. Some are used for thinking, but other parts control the body, or process data gathered by the senses.

Human brain
The human brain has a huge cerebrum – the part used for thinking. This is what makes humans so intelligent. The optic lobes for vision are also relatively big, because we rely heavily on our eyes.

Dog brain
The cerebrum of a dog is relatively small compared with the rest of its brain. By contrast the brain stem and cerebellum, which process nerve signals and control the dog's movements, are relatively big.

***Citipati* brain**
Although small compared to the animal's head, *Citipati*'s brain had relatively large optic and olfactory lobes (which process scent). But its small cerebrum shows that this dinosaur was not very intelligent.

■ OPTIC LOBE ■ OLFACTORY LOBE ■ CEREBRUM
▨ CEREBELLUM ■ BRAIN STEM

HEARING

Medical scans of dinosaur brain cavities also reveal their inner ear bones. The scans show that these bones were very like the inner ear bones of modern animals, meaning that the dinosaurs could probably hear just as well. Indeed some seem to have been adapted for making loud calls, so they must have been able to hear well enough to pick up the calls and reply.

Call and response
Some hadrosaurs such as *Corythosaurus* had hollow crests that were probably used to add resonance to their calls, and make them carry further through dense forests.

DINOSAURS COMPARED

Scientists can use a measure called Encephalization Quotient to work out the likely intelligence of extinct dinosaurs compared to a modern animal such as a crocodile. The results show that long-necked sauropods were probably far less intelligent than crocodiles, but some theropod hunters could have been a lot smarter.

ALTHOUGH SOME DINOSAURS WERE **NOT AS STUPID AS WE** USED TO THINK, IT IS CLEAR THAT **EVEN THE CLEVEREST WERE NO SMARTER THAN A CHICKEN.**

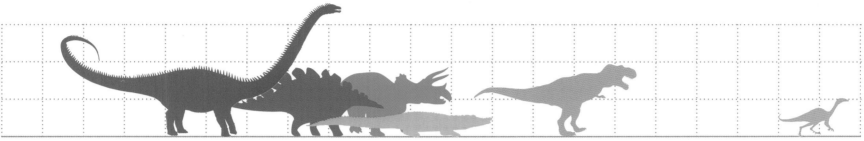

LEAST INTELLIGENT   **MOST INTELLIGENT**

Sauropods
The brains of these animals were tiny compared to their bodies, so they were not very intelligent.

Stegosaurs
The stegosaur *Kentrosaurus* is famous for having a brain no bigger than a plum.

Ceratopsians
The intelligence of ceratopsians such as *Triceratops* may have been similar to a crocodile's.

Crocodiles
Cleverer than you might expect, these hunters have sharp senses and very good memories.

Carnosaurs
Big hunters such as *Tyrannosaurus* would have needed to be quite smart to outwit their prey.

Troodontids
The most intelligent dinosaurs were small theropods such as *Troodon* and *Velociraptor*.

VISION

The big eye sockets of many dinosaurs show they had large, well-developed eyes, which were often linked to big optic lobes in their brains. Some, such as the tyrannosaurs, clearly had excellent sight, which was probably as good as that of eagles. These hunters needed good vision to find and target their prey – and their prey needed it to alert them to danger.

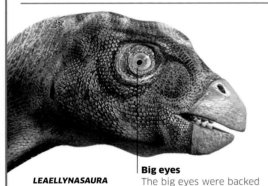

LEAELLYNASAURA

Big eyes
The big eyes were backed up by large optic lobes.

Seeing in the dark

One of the most intriguing dinosaurs is a small, Early Cretaceous plant-eater called *Leaellynasaura*. This animal lived in a region of Australia so near the South Pole that it suffered three months without sunlight each winter. *Leaellynasaura* had unusually large eyes, which were probably an adaptation for seeing in dim winter light. They would have helped it find food and keep a good look-out for its enemies.

Field of view

Nearly all plant-eaters had eyes set high on the sides of their heads. This gave them good all-round vision, so they could watch for any hint of danger. Hunters usually had eyes that faced more forward, so their fields of vision overlapped. This allowed the animals to see in depth – binocular vision – and judge distances when mounting attacks.

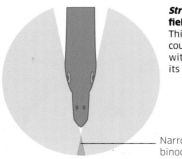

***Struthiomimus*'s field of vision**
This plant-eater could see all around without moving its head.

***Coelophysis*'s field of vision**
Good binocular vision for judging distances was important to *Coelophysis*.

Narrow field of binocular vision

Wide field of binocular vision

PREY ANIMAL

PREDATOR

SCENT

Tyrannosaurus's brain had large olfactory lobes – the parts that analysed scents. This indicates it had an acute sense of smell. Other scavengers and hunters would have shared this sensitivity. It allowed them to sniff out prey, and pick up the scent of blood that could lead them to an easy meal. Plant-eaters would not have needed such a good sense of smell, but it was useful for detecting danger.

TYRANNOSAURUS

Living together

Judging from their fossilized footprints, some dinosaurs travelled together in compact groups. Fossil hunters have also found vast "bonebeds" containing the bones of many dinosaurs of the same species, all apparently killed at the same time by some disaster. This kind of fossil evidence may mean that these dinosaurs lived in herds. We know that at least some dinosaurs formed very big breeding colonies, so it is likely that many lived together throughout the year, sometimes in huge numbers.

SOME MODERN BIRDS COME TOGETHER IN **COLONIES TO BREED,** THEN SPLIT UP WHEN THE NESTING SEASON ENDS. **DINOSAURS MAY HAVE BEHAVED** IN THE SAME WAY.

WORKING TOGETHER

It is possible that some predatory dinosaurs hunted in groups. This does not mean that they used clever hunting tactics, as wolves do; they were not smart enough. But the extra muscle would have helped them bring down larger prey than they could cope with alone.

In for the kill
On one site, the remains of several *Deinonychus*, lightweight hunters, were found with those of *Tenontosaurus*, a big plant-eater. The predators may have been a family group that joined forces to launch an attack.

HUNGRY HERDS

Many big plant-eating animals live in herds that wander across the landscape, eating what they can and moving on. It is likely that some large plant-eating dinosaurs did the same. It was safer, with many eyes watching for danger, and since food such as leaves are often easy to find, these dinosaurs did not compete with one another for food.

SAUROPELTA HERD

FOSSIL EVIDENCE

The evidence for some dinosaurs living and travelling in groups or herds is quite convincing. On several fossil sites, the bones of many animals have been found together, and it is almost certain that they all died simultaneously. Other sites preserve footprints of many dinosaurs, all travelling in the same direction at the same time, as you would expect of a herd in search of fresh food or water.

Footprint trackways

Parallel tracks of dinosaur footprints in Colorado, USA, were made by giant sauropods travelling along an ancient lake shore. These prints were all made at the same time, and since they show the animals moving in the same direction, they are convincing evidence that these dinosaurs were living in a herd.

Dinosaur graveyards

The bones of thousands of *Centrosaurus* have been excavated from this bonebed at Dinosaur Provincial Park in Alberta, Canada. It is likely that a vast herd of these ceratopsians was crossing a river when a sudden flash flood swept downstream and drowned the animals.

COLONIES AND PAIRS

The discovery of hundreds of dinosaur nests sited closely together on the ground proves that many dinosaurs came together to breed in colonies for safety. These would have been similar to the breeding colonies of many modern seabirds. But the nests of some other dinosaurs are isolated, and each was probably made by a male and female pair who sited it near the centre of a defended territory.

THE *MAIASAURA* BREEDING SITE **FOUND IN MONTANA** CONTAINED THE REMAINS OF AT LEAST 200 ADULT DINOSAURS, PLUS THEIR YOUNG, ALL LIVING TOGETHER IN **A TIGHTLY PACKED COLONY.**

Breeding colonies

Several dinosaur breeding colonies have been found. Some are very big, and were probably used year after year, like many seabird nesting sites. The most famous are those of the hadrosaur *Maiasaura*, found in Montana, USA, in the mid-1970s. The site had the remains of hundreds of nests, each roughly 7 m (23 ft) apart – less than the length of the adult dinosaurs. This clearly shows that *Maiasaura* had a well-organized social system.

Territorial pairs

By contrast with *Maiasaura*, a sociable plant-eater, many meat-eating theropods such as *Carnotaurus* may have defended areas of land against others who might compete with them for scarce prey. A pair would hold a joint territory, just like a pair of hawks in a modern woodland, and raise their young in a nest well away from others of their kind. Some plant-eaters may have done the same, if their food supply was worth defending.

Prey defence

Life in the wild is a battle for survival, especially between meat-eating predators and their prey. Over time the predators evolve more efficient ways of hunting, but prey animals respond by evolving more effective defences. During the Mesozoic this process created massive, heavily armed hunters like *Tyrannosaurus*. But it also led to prey animals, such as *Euoplocephalus*, developing thick armour and various defensive weapons. Many other dinosaurs relied on being able to run away or hide, or depended on their colossal size to discourage their enemies.

BODY ARMOUR

One solution to the problem of sharp-toothed predators is a thick skin. Early in the Jurassic some dinosaurs developed small, bony plates in their skin, and these evolved into the much thicker armour of the Cretaceous "tank dinosaurs". These dinosaurs included *Euoplocephalus* – which was also armed with a big tail club.

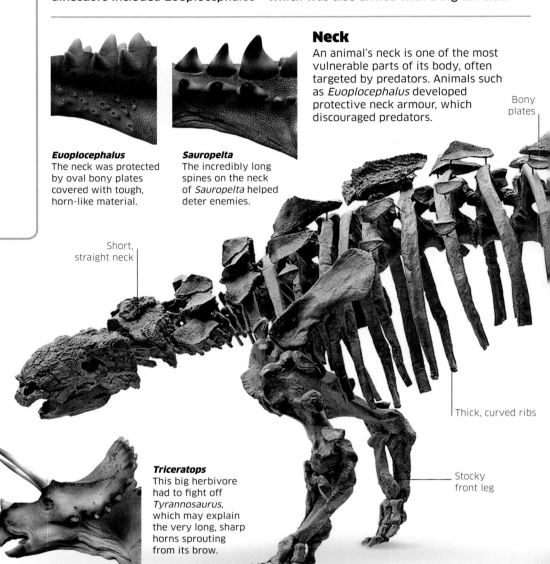

Euoplocephalus
The neck was protected by oval bony plates covered with tough, horn-like material.

Sauropelta
The incredibly long spines on the neck of *Sauropelta* helped deter enemies.

Neck

An animal's neck is one of the most vulnerable parts of its body, often targeted by predators. Animals such as *Euoplocephalus* developed protective neck armour, which discouraged predators.

Bony plates

Short, straight neck

Thick, curved ribs

Stocky front leg

Head

Few animals can survive serious head injuries, so it was natural that armoured dinosaurs developed tough defences for their heads. Some dinosaurs were also equipped with horns, which they may have used to defend themselves.

Euoplocephalus
The bony plates covering the head of *Euoplocephalus* were fused into an almost continuous shield of tooth-breaking armour.

Sauropelta
The thick skull of this spiny nodosaur was encased in a helmet of bony plates, forming an extra layer of protection for its brain.

Triceratops
This big herbivore had to fight off *Tyrannosaurus*, which may explain the very long, sharp horns sprouting from its brow.

AVOIDING TROUBLE

Fighting back is a last resort for most prey animals because it is much safer just to stay out of trouble. Dinosaurs must have been no exception. If they could hide, they would, and some small plant-eaters may have hidden in burrows. Others were probably well camouflaged. Many small, agile dinosaurs relied on their speed, and ran away from predators. At the other end of the size scale, the giant dinosaurs were just too big for any predator to take on by itself.

Size mattered

The colossal long-necked sauropods dwarfed even the biggest hunters, which could not hope to tackle them. Hungry predators, such as *Mapusaurus* (left and centre of this picture), might have been tempted to attack young *Cathartesaura* sauropods, but they risked being crushed underfoot by their prey's gigantic parents.

Back

Some Mesozoic predators clearly liked to attack by leaping on their prey's back. Over time many prey animals evolved stout armour on their backs and hips. In most cases, the armour was made up of bony studs embedded in the skin, but some dinosaurs had spikes or sharp-edged plates.

Euoplocephalus
The back of this massively built animal was covered with a flexible shield made up of small bony nodules dotted with big armour plates and short, sturdy spikes.

Kentrosaurus
The tall, sharp spikes on the lower back of this stegosaur were probably partly for show, but they would also have made life difficult for any attacking predator.

Tail

The tails of plant-eating dinosaurs were very effective weapons for driving off predators. Just swiping a long tail from side to side could be enough, but some tails were specially adapted for the job, with extra spikes, blades, or even a heavy bony club at the tip.

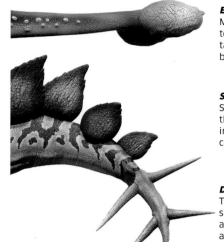

Euoplocephalus
Made of four bony plates fused together into a heavy lump, the tail club of this ankylosaur could break a hunter's leg.

Stegosaurus
Stegosaurs had sharp spikes at the ends of their tails. Driven into an enemy's body, they could inflict fatal injuries.

Diplodocus
The immensely long tail of this sauropod may have been used almost like a whip, to knock attackers off their feet.

Flexible tail section

Strong hind leg

Tail club

ALMOST EVERY PART **OF *EUOPLOCEPHALUS*** SEEMS TO HAVE BEEN **ARMOURED IN SOME WAY – EVEN ITS EYELIDS!**

Running away

Small, lightweight dinosaurs that stood on two legs, such as *Dryosaurus*, would have run away from trouble. Many would have been more agile than their enemies, and some were probably very fast. Smaller feathered dinosaurs could have run up trees, and this may have helped promote the evolution of flight.

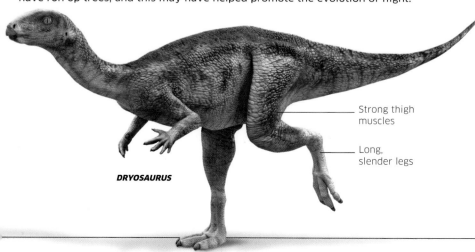

Strong thigh muscles

Long, slender legs

DRYOSAURUS

Camouflage

It is very likely that many small dinosaurs were camouflaged, which made them less visible to predators – especially if their enemies relied mainly on hunting by sight. *Hypsilophodon* may have blended into the dappled shade of its forest habitat with light and dark patterns on its skin.

HYPSILOPHODON

Showing off

Many modern animals have elaborate horns or other features that look like defensive weapons, but actually have a different function. These are often borne only by males who use them in contests with rivals over status, territory, and breeding partners. Often this is just a matter of showing off, so the most impressive male wins the day, though sometimes they clash in ritual combat. It is likely that the elaborate crests, spines, and frills of some dinosaurs had the same purpose – although they might have been partly defensive too.

HIGH PROFILE

A few dinosaurs had bony plates or spines projecting up from their backs. These included stegosaurs, with their dorsal plates and spikes, and animals such as *Ouranosaurus*, which had a tall "sail" on its back. The function of this "sail" is still not known, but it may have been partly for show.

Ouranosaurus
The tall structure on the back of this plant-eater was supported by bony extensions of its backbone.

Colourful crest
This spectacular pterosaur crest was made of lightweight soft tissue.

THE PTEROSAUR *NYCTOSAURUS* HAD A HUGE, ANTLER-LIKE, BONY CREST THAT WAS UP TO 90 CM (3 FT) LONG – TWICE AS LONG AS ITS BODY. NO MODERN ANIMAL HAS ANYTHING LIKE IT.

TUPANDACTYLUS

FLAMBOYANT CRESTS

The impressive crests on the heads of many dinosaurs clearly had no defensive function. They were almost certainly for display, either to rivals of the same sex or to potential mates. There is evidence that the crests of pterosaurs, such as *Tupandactylus*, were brightly coloured, increasing their visual impact.

Crested dinosaurs

Most of the crested dinosaurs that have been found so far are either duck-billed hadrosaurs or meat-eating theropods. As with crested pterosaurs, the crests were probably colourful to make them stand out. They may have been carried by both sexes, or just males.

Lambeosaurus
The bony crest of this hadrosaur was hollow, and may have enhanced the tone of its calls.

Corythosaurus
This hadrosaur had a smaller crest than *Lambeosaurus*, but its crest was probably just as colourful.

Cryolophosaurus
Some meat-eating theropods such as *Cryolophosaurus* had crests too, but they were generally quite small.

FEATHERY PLUMES

We now know that many small theropods such as *Velociraptor* (pages 108–109) had long feathers sprouting from their tails and arms. When they originally evolved, the feathers may have been suitable for protection and insulation, but this does not explain why some of the feathers were so long. However, feathers are ideally adapted for display, since they can be brightly coloured and also extravagantly long – as in many modern birds such as peacocks and birds of paradise.

Tail plumes

The detailed fossils of the small Jurassic theropod *Epidexipteryx* clearly show long, strap-like plumes extending from its tail. These had no practical value. They might have been a display feature, like the tail of a male peacock, used in courtship or to show off to rivals when competing for territory.

Fine feathers

The glorious plumes of this modern-day paradise flycatcher are purely for show. The males use them in competitive displays, and the winners – always the ones with the finest plumage – mate with the females. We can only guess if Mesozoic dinosaurs behaved in this manner – and maybe the females had fine feathers too.

SPINES AND FRILLS

Some dinosaurs had spectacularly long spines, and many ceratopsians had enormous bony frills extending from the backs of their skulls. These were far more elaborate than was necessary for defence. It is likely that they were at least partly for show, to impress mates and rivals – but they might also have discouraged enemies.

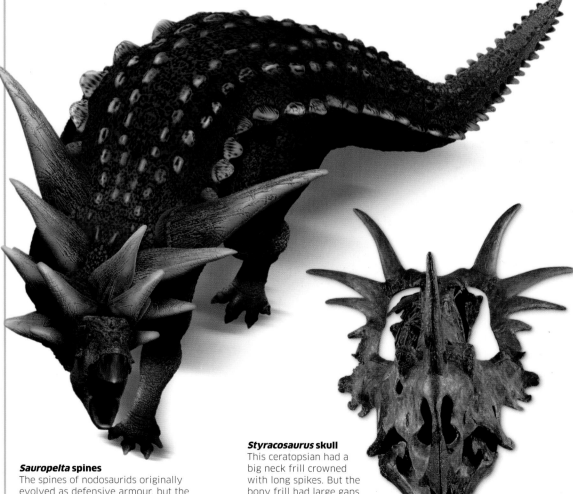

Sauropelta spines

The spines of nodosaurids originally evolved as defensive armour, but the extra-big neck spines of *Sauropelta* surely had another function: making the animal look more impressive.

Styracosaurus skull

This ceratopsian had a big neck frill crowned with long spikes. But the bony frill had large gaps in it, reducing its strength. This makes it likely that the frill was mainly for show.

INFLATABLE DISPLAY

Some dinosaurs seem to have had crests that were largely made of soft, fleshy tissue. The skull of *Muttaburrasaurus* had a bony structure on its snout that might have supported inflatable, brightly coloured nasal sacs. These may have made its calls more resonant, like the inflatable throat or cheek sacs of frogs.

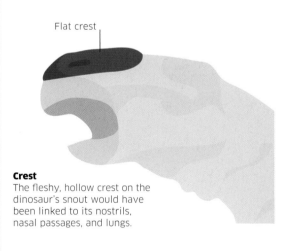

Flat crest

Crest

The fleshy, hollow crest on the dinosaur's snout would have been linked to its nostrils, nasal passages, and lungs.

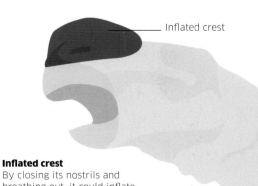

Inflated crest

Inflated crest

By closing its nostrils and breathing out, it could inflate the crest – which showed up more – and make its calls louder.

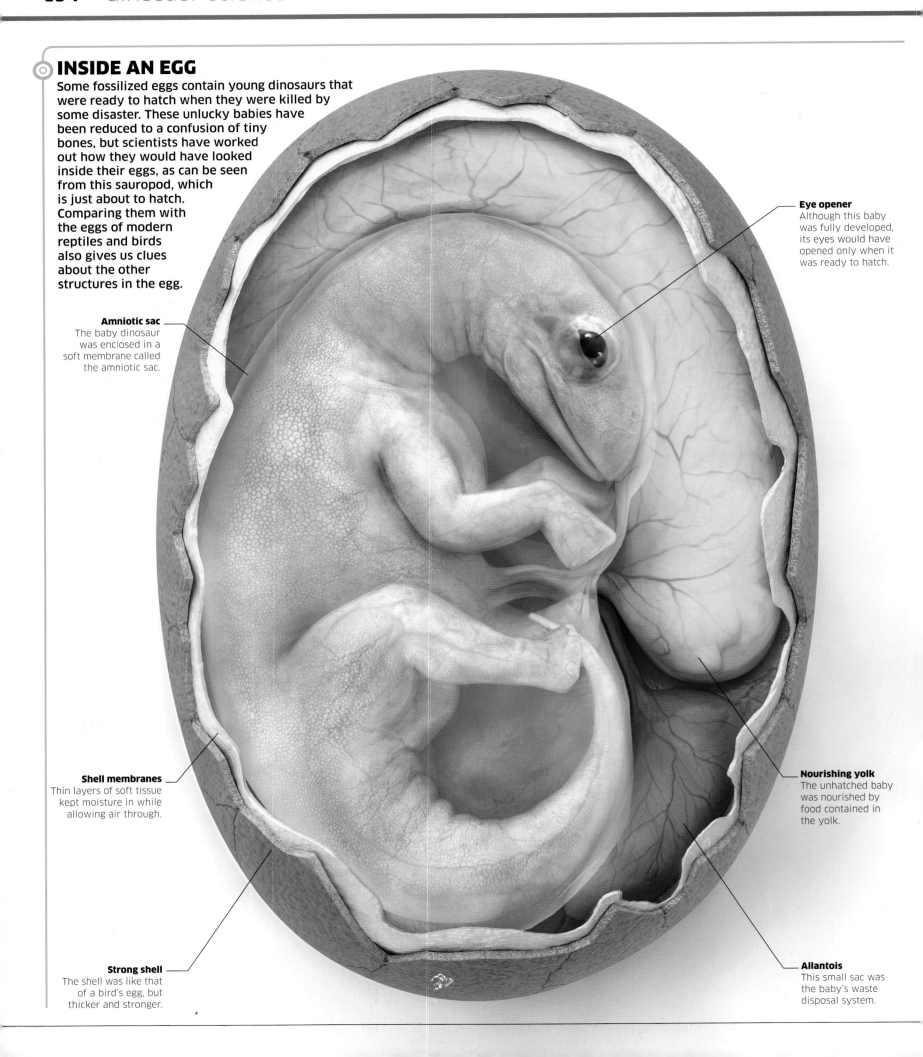

INSIDE AN EGG

Some fossilized eggs contain young dinosaurs that were ready to hatch when they were killed by some disaster. These unlucky babies have been reduced to a confusion of tiny bones, but scientists have worked out how they would have looked inside their eggs, as can be seen from this sauropod, which is just about to hatch. Comparing them with the eggs of modern reptiles and birds also gives us clues about the other structures in the egg.

Amniotic sac
The baby dinosaur was enclosed in a soft membrane called the amniotic sac.

Shell membranes
Thin layers of soft tissue kept moisture in while allowing air through.

Strong shell
The shell was like that of a bird's egg, but thicker and stronger.

Eye opener
Although this baby was fully developed, its eyes would have opened only when it was ready to hatch.

Nourishing yolk
The unhatched baby was nourished by food contained in the yolk.

Allantois
This small sac was the baby's waste disposal system.

Breeding

All dinosaurs laid eggs. They laid large clutches of eggs, which they either buried or incubated like birds, in nests built on the ground. Some dinosaurs probably left the eggs to hatch unaided, but we know that others stayed with their eggs until they hatched, and then reared the young by bringing them food. Either way, the sheer numbers of eggs laid by dinosaurs means that they could breed far more quickly than modern big mammals.

SOME ADULT DINOSAURS, **SUCH AS *MAIASAURA*,** SEEM TO HAVE LOOKED AFTER THEIR YOUNG FOR SEVERAL WEEKS OR MONTHS.

DINOSAUR EGGS

The eggs laid by dinosaurs had hard, chalky shells, much like modern birds' eggs. Some had bumpy shells while others were smooth, and it is possible that many had colours and patterns. They varied a lot in shape depending on the type of dinosaur. Some eggs were very elongated ovals, while others were almost perfectly round.

OVIRAPTOR EGG
18 CM (7 IN)

APATOSAURUS EGG
30 CM (1 FT)

PROTOCERATOPS EGG
16 CM (6.25 IN)

Small wonders

The most surprising thing about dinosaur eggs is that they were so small. Even the largest, such as those of *Apatosaurus*, were only the size of basketballs. That is tiny compared to a full-grown sauropod. The hatchlings must have been even smaller, which means that dinosaurs grew very fast.

CHICKEN EGG
5.7 CM (2.25 IN)

DINOSAUR NESTS

The biggest dinosaurs dug shallow pits for their eggs, then covered the pits with leaves and earth. As the leaves rotted, they generated heat that helped the eggs develop. Many of the smaller dinosaurs laid their eggs in nests that were like hollowed-out mounds, and then incubated the eggs using their own body heat, as chickens do.

Egg clutch

There could be 20 or more eggs in a single clutch. Some of the smaller feathered dinosaurs such as *Citipati* (pages 114–115) kept them warm by using their long-feathered arms to cover the eggs up and stop heat escaping.

Crocodile nest

Modern crocodiles use the same incubation system as the big dinosaurs – burying their eggs under mounds of warm, decaying leaves. They also guard their nests, and Mesozoic dinosaurs may have done the same.

GROWING UP

Some baby dinosaurs probably left the nest soon after hatching, but we know that others were fed by their parents. They grew up fast, changing in shape as well as size. The fossils of a few dinosaurs such as *Protoceratops* record each stage of growth.

Tiny neck frill

HATCHLING

Growing skull

JUVENILE

Developing neck frill

IMMATURE

Narrow beak

SUB-ADULT

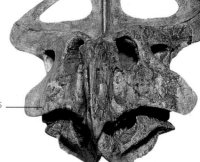

Strong neck frill

Cheek horns

ADULT

The great extinction

Just under 66 million years ago the Mesozoic Era ended in a mass extinction. It destroyed all the giant dinosaurs, the pterosaurs, most marine reptiles, and many other animals that we now know only from fossils. Yet lizards, crocodiles, birds, and mammals were among the creatures that survived. The extinction was probably caused by a colossal asteroid falling from space and crashing into Earth. But there were also massive volcanoes erupting in India at the time, and this may have added to the global climate chaos caused by the disaster.

IMPACT

We know that the mass extinction followed the impact of a huge asteroid on what is now the Yucatán peninsula in Mexico. At least 10 km (6 miles) across, the asteroid was instantly vaporized in a catastrophic explosion that was two million times as powerful as the biggest nuclear bomb ever detonated.

WORLD IN CHAOS

The disastrous events of 66 million years ago had a dramatic impact on all forms of life. The hardest hit were wiped out altogether, eliminating entire groups of animals. But even the survivors must have been reduced to a few lucky individuals clinging to life in a shattered, chaotic world.

CATASTROPHE

Scientists are still not certain whether the extinction was caused by the asteroid strike or by the devastating eruption of masses of lava and poisonous gases from gigantic supervolcanoes. Either or both could have radically changed the global climate, and ultimately resulted in the destruction of a large proportion of the planet's wildlife.

THE CRATER LEFT BY THE IMPACT OF THE ASTEROID ON MEXICO IS ONE OF THE BIGGEST ON EARTH – BUT IT IS INVISIBLE FROM THE GROUND.

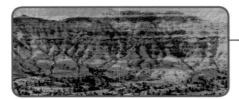

Supervolcanoes
Vast quantities of gas and molten lava flooded over half of India and cooled to form layers of basalt rock 2 km (1.2 miles) deep. The layered rocks are called the Deccan Traps.

Asteroid impact
The explosion caused by the asteroid strike formed a crater over 180 km (112 miles) wide, now buried deep underground. Debris from the impact would have filled the atmosphere.

Explosion debris
Dust mixed with a chemical haze would have blocked vital sunlight for at least a year.

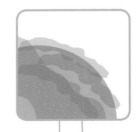

Global forest fires
Searingly hot molten rock ejected from the impact would have triggered huge wildfires across the world.

Victims

The most famous victims of the extinction were the giant dinosaurs. Some of the biggest and most famous were living at the time, including *Tyrannosaurus* and *Triceratops*. But the catastrophe also wiped out all the pterosaurs, most marine reptiles, and many other oceanic animals. At least 75 per cent of all animal and plant species on Earth vanished.

Survivors

While some types of animals disappeared, others somehow survived both the initial catastrophe and the years that followed, when plants struggled to grow and food was scarce. They included a variety of fish, reptiles, mammals, and invertebrates, as well as birds.

Sharks
Along with other fish, these survived in the oceans. They carried on evolving into the sleek hunters they are now.

Frogs
Freshwater animals seem to have been shielded from the worst effects, allowing many frogs to survive into the new era.

Crocodilians
Despite being archosaurs, closely related to the dinosaurs and pterosaurs, some crocodiles and alligators survived.

Turtles
Surprisingly, more than 80 per cent of turtle species alive in the Cretaceous still existed after the extinction event.

Snakes
Many lizards and snakes made it through the crisis, and became the ancestors of all the lizards and snakes alive today.

Mammals
All the main groups of mammals living at the time survived, eventually flourishing in the Cenozoic Era.

Insects and spiders
Small land invertebrates were badly hit, but many groups escaped extinction and eventually started to flourish again.

Shellfish
Many types of marine invertebrates such as the sea urchins survived. But others vanished, including the ammonites.

Volcanic cloud
Enormous clouds of gas and dusty volcanic ash shrouded the globe.

Acid rain
Chemicals in the volcanic ash mixed with water to cause deadly acid rain.

Blast and shock waves
The shock of the cataclysm must have destroyed all life near the impact zone.

Mega tsunami
There is evidence of huge tsunamis that swept across the Caribbean and Atlantic coasts.

Climate crisis
Whether it was colossal volcanoes, the impact of a massive asteroid, or a combination of the two, the effect was catastrophic climate change that chilled the Earth and wrecked the global ecosystem. The world took millions of years to recover.

Birds – dinosaur survivors

It is now clear that birds are theropod dinosaurs, with ancestors that were closely related to the ancestors of lightweight, feathered predators such as *Velociraptor* (pages 108–109). Clearly birds have many special features, but most of these evolved a very long time ago. By the end of the Mesozoic Era the air was already ringing to the calls of flying birds that looked very like those that live around us today. The mystery about birds is why they survived when all the other dinosaurs became extinct.

EVOLUTION

The earliest flying dinosaurs such as *Archaeopteryx* were very like the non-flying theropods that shared the same ancestors. By the Early Cretaceous a group called the enantiornithines had evolved, and looked like modern birds apart from a few odd details. The earliest true birds, or avians, appeared at the start of the Late Cretaceous, more than 90 million years ago.

Velociraptor
The ancestors of this feathered but non-flying hunter were related to those of the earliest flying dinosaurs, which is why they looked so alike.

DINOSAURS

FLYING DINOSAURS

The skeletons of the earliest birds were very like those of many non-flying dinosaurs, apart from longer arm bones that supported wings. Both also shared their feathers and highly efficient lungs. As birds evolved they developed modifications that helped increase wing strength without adding weight. These adaptations appeared during the Mesozoic, and were inherited by modern birds such as pigeons.

THE FIRST TRUE BIRDS EVOLVED LONG BEFORE MANY BIG, FAMOUS DINOSAURS SUCH AS *TYRANNOSAURUS REX*.

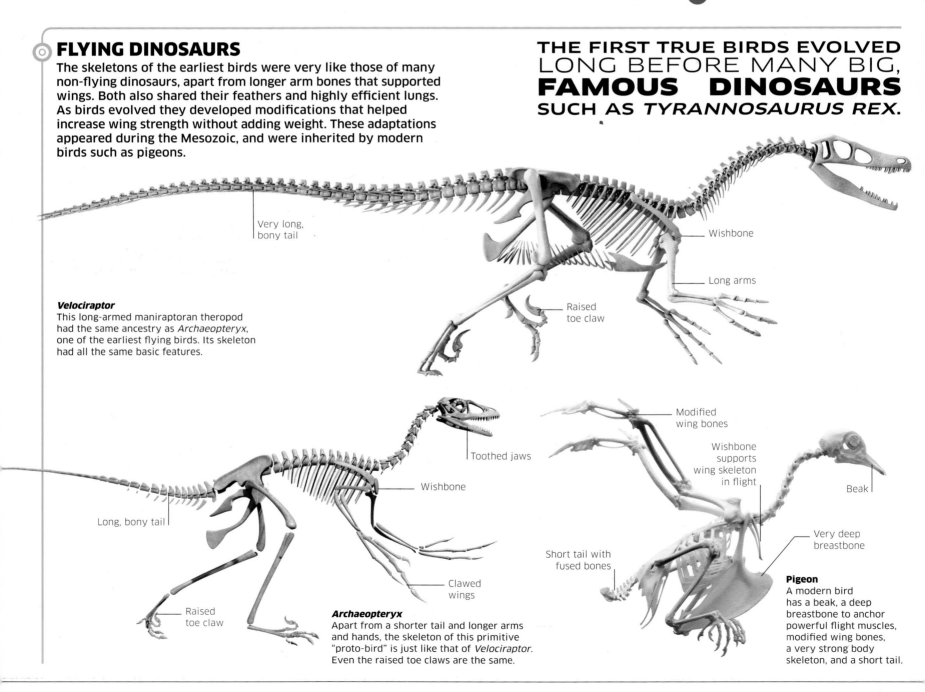

Very long, bony tail

Wishbone

Long arms

Raised toe claw

Velociraptor
This long-armed maniraptoran theropod had the same ancestry as *Archaeopteryx*, one of the earliest flying birds. Its skeleton had all the same basic features.

Long, bony tail

Toothed jaws

Wishbone

Modified wing bones

Wishbone supports wing skeleton in flight

Beak

Short tail with fused bones

Very deep breastbone

Clawed wings

Raised toe claw

Archaeopteryx
Apart from a shorter tail and longer arms and hands, the skeleton of this primitive "proto-bird" is just like that of *Velociraptor*. Even the raised toe claws are the same.

Pigeon
A modern bird has a beak, a deep breastbone to anchor powerful flight muscles, modified wing bones, a very strong body skeleton, and a short tail.

Archaeopteryx
Known as avalians, rather than true birds, the first dinosaurs to get airborne had long, bony tails and were not highly adapted for flight.

Confuciusornis
Later avalians had short, fused tail bones, but they still had wing claws and did not have deep breastbones anchoring big flight muscles.

Iberomesornis
The enantiornithines had evolved big breastbones and strong flight muscles. But some still had teeth, and a few had wing claws.

Modern birds
The avians, or true birds, have toothless beaks and other advanced features – but most of these evolved way back in the Mesozoic.

LIFE STUDIES

Since modern birds are now known to be living dinosaurs, studying their lives may tell us a lot about how the Mesozoic dinosaurs lived. Obviously birds are very different from their extinct ancestors, and their world is different too. But some features of their biology are the same, and some aspects of their behaviour could also turn out to be similar.

Hungry hunter
Sea eagles use their talons to seize and then hold down prey while ripping it apart. Small, sharp-clawed Mesozoic hunters may have used their claws in the same way.

Breeding colony
Fossil evidence shows that many Mesozoic dinosaurs nested close together in colonies. Seabirds such as these puffins do the same, and their social lives may be similar.

Parental care
Some young dinosaurs probably hatched as active chicks that found their own food. But the adults may have stood guard over them, just like this watchful mother hen.

NATURAL REVIVAL

Some modern flightless birds, such as ostriches, resemble certain dinosaurs, such as _Struthiomimus_, but their anatomy has features inherited from flying ancestors. This means that evolution has gone full circle, producing modern equivalents of the fast, lightweight theropods of the late Mesozoic.

Fast runner
This rhea may look like a Mesozoic survivor, but it is actually an example of evolution "reinventing" a successful type of animal.

DAZZLING DIVERSITY

There are more than 10,000 species of birds alive today, so it is clear that, far from being extinct, dinosaurs are flourishing in every corner of the globe. They have diversified into an incredible variety of creatures, including albatrosses, eagles, owls, hummingbirds, and penguins. They include some of the fastest, most beautiful, intelligent, and musical animals on the planet. And they are all dinosaurs.

Feathered glory
The dazzling plumage of the male peacock is just one example of the amazing adaptations that have been evolved by birds. The dinosaur story has not ended – it is still creating some of the most sensational animals on Earth.

Glossary

AMBER
Sticky resin that has oozed from a tree and become hardened over many millions of years.

AMMONITE
A marine mollusc with a coiled shell and octopus-like tentacles that was common in the Mesozoic Era.

AMPHIBIAN
A vertebrate animal that usually starts life in water as a tadpole, but turns into an air-breathing adult, such as a frog, that lives partly on land.

ANATOMY
The structure of an animal's body.

ANKYLOSAUR
One of the main types of ornithischian dinosaur, with a body that was covered with bony armour.

ANKYLOSAURID
A type of ankylosaur with a bony tail club for defence.

AQUATIC
Describes something that lives in water.

ARCHOSAUR
One of a group of animals that includes, or included, the dinosaurs, birds, pterosaurs, and crocodiles.

ARID
Describes a very dry climate or place.

ASTEROID
A large rocky object in orbit around the Sun – bigger than a meteor but smaller than a planet.

AZHDARCHID
A giant Late Cretaceous pterosaur.

BARREN
Without life.

BELEMNITE
An extinct mollusc (shellfish) with an internal reinforcing structure that often forms bullet-shaped fossils.

BINOCULAR VISION
Seeing a scene or object with two eyes, so an animal can see in depth, or 3-D.

BIPED
An animal that stands on two feet.

BONEBED
A massive deposit of fossil bones.

BREASTBONE
The bone in the middle of the chest, which is enlarged in birds.

BREEDING
Males and females coming together to produce eggs and/or young.

BRISTLE
A thick, flexible, springy, hair-like structure.

BROODING
Keeping young warm using feathered wings and body heat. Sometimes used to describe keeping eggs warm.

BROWSE
To feed on leaves gathered from trees or bushes.

CAMBRIAN
A period of the Paleozoic Era, lasting from 541 to 485 million years ago.

CAMOUFLAGE
Colours and patterns that make an animal hard to see.

CANINES
The long, pointed teeth of meat-eating mammals such as dogs, which are also present in some dinosaurs.

CANNIBAL
An animal that eats its own kind.

CARBONIFEROUS
A period of the Paleozoic Era that lasted from 359 million years ago to 298 million years ago.

CARNIVORE
An animal that eats meat.

CARNOSAUR
A type of large, powerful, meat-eating theropod that appeared in the Jurassic.

CELL
The smallest unit of a living thing. Animals and plants have many cells, but microscopic living things such as bacteria consist of just one cell.

CENOZOIC
Literally "new animal life", the era that followed the age of dinosaurs, from 66 million years ago to the present.

CERATOPSIAN
One of the horned dinosaurs, usually with horns on its face and a bony frill extending over its neck.

CLUBMOSS
A primitive plant with scale-like leaves and spores instead of seeds.

CONIFER
A plant – usually a tall tree such as a pine or spruce – that carries its seeds in scaly cones.

CONTINENT
A big landmass that is made of rocks that are different from the rocks of the ocean floors.

COPROLITES
Fossilized animal droppings, which often contain fragments of the animal's food.

COURTSHIP
Behaviour designed to encourage mating, often involving calling and displays of fine plumage.

CRANIUM
The domed top of the skull.

CRETACEOUS
The third period of the Mesozoic Era (the age of dinosaurs), which began 145 million years ago and ended 66 million years ago.

CROCODILIAN
A reptile that is or was closely related to modern crocodiles and alligators.

CYCAD
A tropical plant that bears its seeds in large cones, but has a crown of foliage, like a tree fern or palm.

CYNODONT
One of the extinct vertebrates that were the immediate ancestors of mammals.

DEINONYCHOSAUR
A small to medium-sized Cretaceous feathered theropod closely related to *Deinonychus* and *Velociraptor*.

DEVONIAN
A period of the Paleozoic Era that lasted from 419 million years ago to 358 million years ago.

DICYNODONT
One of a group of extinct vertebrates with two tusk-like teeth that were related to the ancestors of mammals.

DIET
The type of food that an animal eats.

DIGESTION
The breakdown of food into simpler substances that can be absorbed and used by an animal's body.

DIGESTIVE SYSTEM
An animal's stomach and intestines.

DISPLAY
In animals, a demonstration of fitness or strength, usually designed to intimidate a rival or impress a mate.

DORSAL
Describes something on or relating to an animal's back or upper side, such as a crest.

DROMAEOSAURID
A type of theropod dinosaur with long, clawed arms and a specialized "killer claw" on each foot – for example, *Velociraptor*.

DROUGHT
A long period without rain.

ECOSYSTEM
A community of living things that depend on one another in some way, and live in a particular place.

ENAMEL
The hard material that makes teeth resist wearing out.

ENVIRONMENT
The surroundings of a living thing.

EPOCH
A span of geological time that is part of a period – for example, the Middle Jurassic.

EQUATOR
An imaginary line drawn around Earth that is equally distant from both the North and South Pole.

ERA
A span of geological time that defines a phase of the history of life, such as the Paleozoic or Mesozoic.

EVOLUTION
The process by which living things change over time.

EVOLVE
To change over time.

EXCAVATE
To dig up, often using scientific methods when dealing with something such as a fossil.

EXTINCT
Having died out completely. An extinct species has no living individuals and is gone for good.

FERN
A primitive type of non-flowering plant with leafy fronds that grows in damp places, but has tall stems.

FLASH FLOOD
A flood that rises very quickly after a rainstorm, and may form a powerful torrent.

FLIPPERS
Limbs with broad paddle blades adapted for efficient swimming.

FLOODPLAIN
A flat area of land alongside a river, created from soft sediment that has been deposited by the water during seasonal floods.

FOSSIL
The remains or traces of any living thing that survive the normal processes of decay, and are often preserved by being turned to stone.

FOSSILIZATION
The process by which the remains of living things turn into fossils.

GASTROLITHS
Stones swallowed by some animals such as ostriches to help grind up food in the stomach.

GEOLOGICAL
To do with the science of rocks.

GEOLOGIST
A scientist who specializes in studying rocks.

GINKGO
One of a group of non-flowering plants that grows into a tall tree with more or less triangular leaves.

GRASSLANDS
Broad areas of land covered with grass, sometimes with scattered trees and bushes.

HADROSAUR
An advanced type of ornithopod dinosaur with a duck-like beak and batteries of chewing teeth.

HERBIVORE
An animal that eats leaves or grass.

HETERODONT
Having several different types of teeth for different functions, such as biting and chewing.

HORSETAIL
A primitive type of plant that produces spores instead of seeds, and has thread-like leaves that grow from the stem in rings or whorls.

ICHTHYOSAUR
One of a group of dolphin-like marine reptiles that was very common in the early Mesozoic Era.

IMMATURE
Not yet adult and therefore unable to breed.

IMPREGNABLE
Immune to attack.

INCISORS
Chisel-shaped front teeth that are specialized for nibbling or biting off food items.

INCUBATE
To keep eggs warm so they develop and hatch.

INFLATABLE
Able to be pumped up with air.

INSULATION
In animals, anything that helps stop heat escaping from the body, such as fat, fur, or feathers.

INTESTINE
The long, coiled tube that forms the main part of an animal's digestive system.

INVERTEBRATE
An animal without a vertebral column (backbone).

JURASSIC
The second of three periods making up the Mesozoic Era, from 201 to 145 million years ago.

KERATIN
A tough structural protein found in hair, feathers, scales, claws, and horns.

LAGOON
An area of shallow water that has been cut off from the sea.

LAVA
Rock that has erupted from a volcano in liquid, molten form.

LIGAMENT
A strong, slightly elastic, cord-like structure in the body that attaches bones to each other.

LIMESTONE
A rock made of calcite (lime), and often built up from the skeletons of microscopic marine life.

MACRONARIAN
One of a group of sauropod dinosaurs with large nasal openings in their skulls.

MAMMAL
One of a group of warm-blooded, often hairy vertebrates that feed their young on milk supplied by the mother.

MANIRAPTORAN
Literally "hand-grabber" – an advanced type of theropod dinosaur with powerful arms and claws, which gave rise to the birds.

MARGINOCEPHALIAN
One of the dinosaur group that includes the horned ceratopsians and boneheaded pachycephalosaurs.

MARINE
To do with the ocean or sea.

MARINE REPTILE
A reptile that lives in the sea, but also used to refer to the plesiosaurs, ichthyosaurs, and similar groups that became extinct at the end of the Mesozoic Era.

MARSUPIAL
A mammal such as a kangaroo that gives birth to very small live young and rears them in a pouch.

MASS EXTINCTION
A disaster that causes the disappearance of many types of life.

MATURE
Old enough to breed.

MEGAHERBIVORE
A large plant-eating mammal.

MEMBRANE
A thin, flexible, often elastic sheet of a material, such as skin.

MESOZOIC
Literally "middle animal life", the era known as the age of dinosaurs, from 252 to 66 million years ago.

MICROFOSSIL
A fossil that is too small to be studied without using a microscope. It may be a fossil of a microscopic form of life, or part of a larger form of life.

MICROSCOPIC
Something too small to be seen without a microscope.

MINERALS
Natural chemicals found in the rocks and soil.

MOLARS
Teeth at the back of the jaws that are specialized for chewing.

MONOTREME
One of a small group of mammals that lay eggs, such as the platypus.

MOSS
A primitive type of non-flowering plant that forms cushion-like growths in damp places.

NATURALIST
Someone who specializes in studying the natural world.

NECTAR
Sugary fluid produced by flowers to attract insects and other animals.

NEOGENE
The second period of the Cenozoic Era, lasting from 23 to 2 million years ago.

NODOSAURID
One of a family of ankylosaurs that did not have a heavy club on the end of its tail.

NOTHOSAUR
A type of marine reptile that lived in the Triassic Period.

NOTOCHORD
A stiff but flexible rod that forms part or all of the backbone of some vertebrate animals.

NUTRIENTS
Substances that living things need to build their tissues.

NUTRITIOUS
Rich in food value.

OMNIVORE
An animal that eats a wide variety of plant and animal foods, but is usually very selective.

OPPOSABLE THUMB
A thumb that can be used like a human thumb to pinch against the fingers for a tight grip.

OPTIC LOBES
Parts of the brain that process visual data.

ORDOVICIAN
A period of the Paleozoic Era that lasted from 485 million years ago to 443 million years ago.

ORGANISM
A living thing.

ORNITHISCHIAN
One of the two main divisions of dinosaurs.

ORNITHOMIMOSAUR
A bird-like theropod dinosaur, resembling an ostrich.

ORNITHOPOD
One of a group of plant-eating dinosaurs that mostly walked on their hind legs and were not armoured.

OSTEODERMS
Bony plates that form within the skin and often form the basis of defensive armour.

OVIRAPTORID
One of a family of theropod dinosaurs with beaks and feathered arms, named after *Oviraptor*.

PACHYCEPHALOSAUR
One of the very thick-skulled "boneheaded" ornithischian dinosaurs.

PALEOGENE
The first period of the Cenozoic Era. It began 66 million years ago and ended 23 million years ago.

PALEONTOLOGIST
A scientist who specializes in the study of fossils.

PALEOZOIC
Literally "ancient animal life" – the era that preceded the age of dinosaurs (the Mesozoic Era). It lasted from 541 to 252 million years ago.

PELVIC
To do with the pelvis, the skeletal structure that the upper leg bones are attached to at the hips.

PERCEPTION
Using the senses to detect objects and events.

PERIOD
A span of geological time that is part of an era – for example, the Jurassic Period is part of the Mesozoic Era.

PERMIAN
A period of the Paleozoic Era that lasted from 298 million years ago to 252 million years ago.

PHYTOSAUR
One of a group of extinct reptiles that resembled crocodiles and lived until the end of the Triassic Period.

PLACENTAL
Describes a mammal that gives birth to live young after a long period of development in the womb.

PLEISTOCENE
An epoch of the Cenozoic Era, from 2.6 million years ago to 12,000 years ago, during which there were a series of ice ages.

PLESIOSAUR
A marine reptile with four long flippers; many had very long necks.

PLIOSAUR
A type of plesiosaur, with a shorter neck, larger head and jaws, and a more predatory lifestyle.

PLUMES
Long or luxuriant feathers, which are usually decorative.

POLLINATING
Carrying pollen from one plant to another, as in bees.

POLYGAMOUS
Having more than one breeding partner.

PRECAMBRIAN
The vast span of geological time that preceded the Paleozoic Era.

PREDATOR
An animal that kills other animals for food.

PREMOLARS
Chewing teeth of mammals that lie in front of the molars.

PREY
An animal that is eaten by another animal.

PROSAUROPOD
One of a group of early long-necked, plant-eating dinosaurs, which lived in the Triassic before the sauropods.

PROTEIN
A complex substance that a living thing makes out of simpler nutrients, and uses to form its tissues.

PTEROSAUR
One of the flying reptiles that lived during the Mesozoic Era, with wings of stretched skin that were each supported by the bones of a single elongated finger.

QUADRUPED
An animal that stands on four feet.

QUATERNARY
The third period of the Cenozoic Era, from 2 million years ago to the present.

RAUISUCHIAN
One of a group of archosaur reptiles that were related to crocodilians, and became extinct at the end of the Triassic Period.

REPTILE
One of the group of animals that includes turtles, lizards, crocodiles, snakes, pterosaurs, and dinosaurs.

RESONANCE
A quality that increases the volume and richness of a sound.

RITUAL
In animals, an action used in display that other animals recognize, and often used in place of fighting.

SANDSTONE
A rock made of sand grains that have become cemented together.

SAURISCHIAN
One of the two main divisions of dinosaurs.

SAUROPOD
One of the group of long-necked, plant-eating dinosaurs that evolved from the prosauropods.

SAUROPODOMORPHS
All the long-necked, plant-eating, saurischian dinosaurs.

SCAVENGER
An animal that lives on the remains of dead animals and other scraps.

SCLEROTIC RING
A ring of bones that supports the eyeball in its socket.

SCUTE
A tough, often protective plate embedded in the skin, with a bony base and a covering of scaly keratin.

SEDIMENT
Solid particles, such as sand, silt, or mud, that have settled in layers.

SEDIMENTARY ROCKS
Rocks made of hardened sediments.

SERPENTINE
Like a snake.

SERRATED
Saw-toothed, like a bread knife.

SHEATH
A covering that protects or extends an elongated object.

SHELLFISH
Clams, oysters, crabs, and similar hard-shelled sea creatures.

SILURIAN
A period of the Paleozoic Era that lasted from 443 million years ago to 419 million years ago.

SNORKEL
A breathing tube used to gather air from above the water surface.

SNOUT
A long nose or muzzle.

SOARING
Circling or gliding for long distances on rising air currents.

SPECIES
A particular type of living thing that can breed with others of the same type.

SPHERICAL
Ball-shaped.

SPINE
Either a sharp spike, or the backbone of an animal.

STANCE
How an animal stands.

STATUS SYMBOLS
Things that advertise social importance.

STEGOSAUR
One of a group of armoured dinosaurs with large plates and spines on their backs.

STRATIGRAPHY
The science of working out the relative ages of rocks, and the fossils they contain, from a sequence of rock layers, or strata.

SUB-FOSSIL
The remains of any living thing that have survived the normal processes of decay, but have not been altered in any major way.

SUPERCONTINENT
A huge landmass made up of many continents that have joined together.

SUPERVOLCANO
A gigantic volcano that erupts colossal amounts of lava, volcanic ash, and gas. These catastrophic eruptions always have big impacts on the global climate.

SYNAPSID
One of a group of vertebrate animals that includes the mammals and their ancestors.

TENDON
A strong, slightly elastic, cord-like structure in the body that attaches muscles to bones.

TERRITORY
The part of an animal's habitat that it defends from rival animals, usually of its own kind.

TETRAPOD
A four-limbed vertebrate, or any vertebrate with four-limbed ancestors. All vertebrates except fish are tetrapods.

THEROPOD
One of the group of saurischian dinosaurs that are nearly all meat-eaters.

THYREOPHORAN
One of the group of dinosaurs that includes the stegosaurs and armoured ankylosaurs.

TITANOSAUR
One of a group of sauropods that evolved in the Cretaceous Period.

TOXIC
Poisonous.

TRIASSIC
The first period of the Mesozoic Era, from 252 to 201 million years ago.

TROODONTID
One of the small, agile theropod dinosaurs including and closely related to *Troodon*.

TROPICAL
A warm climate, or warm part of the world near the equator.

TSUNAMI
A vast ocean wave, or series of waves, created by a massive event such as an earthquake on the ocean floor, the explosion of a volcanic island, or an asteroid impact.

TUBERCLE
A small, rounded, bony structure, like a bony scale, or a small knob or cusp on an animal's tooth.

TYRANNOSAURID
One of the dinosaurs including and closely related to *Tyrannosaurus*.

VANE
A lightweight sheet of material that resists air pressure, like a wind vane.

VEGETATION
Plant material.

VERTEBRAE
The bones that make up the backbone of an animal such as a dinosaur, bird, or mammal.

VERTEBRATE
An animal with an internal skeleton and backbone.

Index

Acknowledgments

The publisher would like to thank the following people for their assistance in the preparation of this book: Carron Brown for the index; Victoria Pyke for proofreading; Simon Mumford for help with maps; Esha Banerjee and Ciara Heneghan for editorial assistance; Daniela Boraschi, Jim Green, and Tanvi Sahu for design assistance; John Searcy for Americanization; Jagtar Singh for color work; A. Badham for texturing assistance; Adam Benton for rendering assistance; Steve Crozier at Butterfly Creative Services for photoshop retouching.

Reviewer for the Smithsonian:
Second edition: Matthew T. Miller, Museum Specialist (Collections Volunteer Manager), Department of Paleobiology, National Museum of Natural History
First edition: Dr. Michael Brett-Surman, Museum Specialist for Fossil Dinosaurs, Reptiles, Amphibians, and Fish (retired), Department of Paleobiology, National Museum of Natural History

The publisher would like to thank the following for their kind permission to reproduce their photographs:

(Key: a-above; b-below/bottom; c-centre; f-far; l-left; r-right; t-top)

2 Dorling Kindersley: Andrew Kerr (cla). **3 Dorling Kindersley:** Andrew Kerr (bl). **4 Dorling Kindersley:** Peter Minister and Andrew Kerr (cla). **6 Dreamstime.com:** Csaba Vanyi (cr). **Getty Images:** Arthur Dorety / Stocktrek Images (cl). **8 Dorling Kindersley:** Jon Hughes (cl); Andrew Kerr (tc, cra, cr). **8-9 Dorling Kindersley:** Andrew Kerr (b). **9 Dorling Kindersley:** Jon Hughes (tc, ca/ Lepidodendron aculeatum); Andrew Kerr (tr, cr); Jon Hughes / Bedrock Studios (ca). **10 Dorling Kindersley:** Andrew Kerr (tr, ca/Rolfosteus, cra, cra/Carcharodontosaurus); Trustees of the National Museums Of Scotland (ca). **11 Dorling Kindersley:** Frank Denota (bl); Andrew Kerr (cb/ Argentinosaurus). **12-13 Dorling Kindersley:** Peter Minister and Andrew Kerr. **15 Dorling Kindersley:** Graham High (cr); Peter Minister (ca); Andrew Kerr (crb, br, cb). **16 Dorling Kindersley:** Masato Hattori (br); Jon Hughes (crb, crb/Ischyodus). **Dreamstime.com:** Csaba Vanyi (c). **17 Dorling Kindersley:** Jon Hughes (tc, tr, ftr). **Getty Images:** Arthur Dorety / Stocktrek Images (c); Ed Reschke / Stockbyte (tl). **Science Photo Library:** Mark Garlick (crb). **19-191 Dorling Kindersley:** Senckenberg Gesellshaft Fuer Naturforschugn Museum (c). **20-21 Plate Tectonic and Paleogeographic Maps by C. R. Scotese, © 2014, PALEOMAP Project (www.scotese.com)**. **20 123RF.com:** Kmitu (bc). **Dorling Kindersley:** Jon Hughes (br). **21 Dorling Kindersley:** Jon Hughes and Russell Gooday (cr); Natural History Museum, London (bc); Andrew Kerr (crb); Peter Minister (br). **22-23 Dorling Kindersley:** Peter Minister. **23 Dreamstime.com:** Ekays (br). **E. Ray Garton, Curator, Prehistoric Planet:** (bc). **24 Alamy Images:** AlphaAndOmega (tc). **26 Corbis:** Louie Psihoyos (tl). **27 Corbis:** Louie Psihoyos (cr). **Dorling Kindersley:** Instituto Fundacion Miguel Lillo, Argentina (bc). **Getty Images:** João Carlos Ebone / www.ebone.com.br (crb). **28 Dreamstime.com:** Hotshotsworldwide (bl). **SuperStock:** Fred Hirschmann / Science Faction (cla). **30-31 Getty Images:** Keiichi Hiki / E+ (Background). **32 Dorling Kindersley:** Natural History Museum, London (cb). **34 Corbis:** Jonathan Blair (cla). **Dorling Kindersley:** Natural History Museum, London (br). **36 Getty Images:** Patrick Aventurier / Gamma-Rapho (c). **37 Corbis:** Jon Sparks (br/Background). **38 Corbis:** Jim Brandenburg / Minden Pictures (crb). **Courtesy of WitmerLab at Ohio University / Lawrence M. Witmer, PhD:** (ca). **39 Corbis:** Louie Psihoyos (cla). **Dorling Kindersley:** State Museum of Nature, Stuttgart (bl). **42-43 Plate Tectonic and Paleogeographic Maps by C. R. Scotese, © 2014, PALEOMAP Project (www.scotese.com)**. **42 Dorling Kindersley:** Rough Guides (br). **Dreamstime.com:** Robyn Mackenzie (bc). **43 Dorling Kindersley:** Jon Hughes and Russell Gooday (br); Andrew Kerr (cra, crb). **45 Corbis:** David Watts / Visuals Unlimited (cr). **46 Dorling Kindersley:** Royal Tyrrell Museum of Palaeontology, Alberta, Canada (bc). **47 Dorling Kindersley:** Royal Tyrrell Museum of Palaeontology, Alberta, Canada (cra). **Getty Images:** Stanley Kaisa Breeden / Oxford Scientific (crb). **48 Dorling Kindersley:** Peter Minister (l). **49 Dorling Kindersley:** Peter Minister (cl); Natural History Museum, London (cr). **50-51 Dorling Kindersley:** Andrew Kerr. **50 Dorling Kindersley:** Andrew Kerr. **51 Alamy Images:** Photoshot Holdings Ltd (tl). **Dorling Kindersley:** Robert L. Braun (cr). **Getty Images:** Veronique Durruty / Gamma-Rapho (br). **52 Science Photo Library:** Natural History Museum, London (bc); Sinclair Stammers (cb). **53 Alamy Images:** Corbin17 (cb). **54-55 Dorling Kindersley:** Andrew Kerr (c). **54 Alamy Images:** Shaun Cunningham (crb). **55 Dorling Kindersley:** Andrew Kerr (c, tc). **56 Science Photo Library:** Natural History Museum, London (tr). **57 Dorling Kindersley:** Natural History Museum, London (bl). **58 Corbis:** Imaginechina (cl). **Dreamstime.com:** Konstanttin (bl). **59 Corbis:** Joe McDonald (crb). **Maria McNamara / Mike Benton, University of Bristol:** (br). **62 Corbis:** Jonathan Blair (cra); Tom Vezo / Minden Pictures (cl). **Prof. Dr. Eberhard "Dino" Frey:** Volker Griener, State Museum of Natural History Karlsruhe (bc). **64-65 Dorling Kindersley:** Andrew Kerr. **65 Museum für Naturkunde Berlin:** (bc). **66 Dorling Kindersley:** Senckenberg Gesellshaft Fuer Naturforschugn Museum (bl). **67 Dorling Kindersley:** Senckenberg Gesellshaft Fuer Naturforschugn Museum (cr). **68 Corbis:** Naturfoto Honal (tl). **69 Corbis:** Naturfoto Honal (bc). **Dreamstime.com:** Rck953 (crb). **70 Dorling Kindersley:** Senckenberg Gesellshaft Fuer Naturforschugn Museum (tl). **72 123RF.com:** Dave Willman (br). **Dorling Kindersley:** Natural History Museum, London (cl). **74 Corbis:** Sandy Felsenthal (cl). **Dreamstime.com:** Amy Harris (br). **Reuters:** Reinhard Krause (cra). **76 Science Photo Library:** Herve Conge, ISM (bc). **78 Dorling Kindersley:** Rough Guides (c/Background). **Getty Images:** P. Jaccod / De Agostini (cl/Background). **80-81 Plate Tectonic and Paleogeographic Maps by C. R. Scotese, © 2014, PALEOMAP Project (www.scotese.com)**. **80 Corbis:** Darrell Gulin (bc). **Getty Images:** Christian Ricci / De Agostini (br). **81 Dorling Kindersley:** Jon Hughes and Russell Gooday (br); Andrew Kerr (cr, crb). **Getty Images:** Prehistoric / The Bridgeman Art Library (cra). **82 Dorling Kindersley:** Natural History Museum, London (bl, tl). **83 Science Photo Library:** Paul D Stewart (c). **84 National Geographic Stock:** (br). **85 Dreamstime.com:** Veronika Druk (br). **TopFoto.co.uk:** National Pictures (cr). **87 Dreamstime.com:** Callan Chesser (bl). **John P Adamek / Fossilmall.com**. **TopFoto.co.uk:** (br). **88 Dorling Kindersley:** Natural History Museum, London (br). **89 Corbis:** Gerry Ellis / Minden Pictures (cr). **Science Photo Library:** Natural History Museum, London (ca). **90 Alamy Images:** Dallas and John Heaton / Travel Pictures (bl). **91 Dreamstime.com:** Dule964 (cr). **Getty Images:** Mcb Bank Bhalwal / Flickr Open (tl); O. Louis Mazzatenta / National Geographic (br). **93 Dorling Kindersley:** Senckenberg Gesellshaft Fuer Naturforschugn Museum (bc, br). **94-95 Dorling Kindersley:** Andrew Kerr. **94 Getty Images:** Morales / Age Fotostock (tc). **95 Dorling Kindersley:** Swedish Museum of Natural History, Stockholm (cra). **Science Photo Library:** Peter Menzel (bc). **97 Jürgen Christian Harf/http://www.pterosaurier.de/:** (ca). **Corbis:** Danny Ellinger / Foto Natura / Minden Pictures (crb). **Dreamstime.com:** Jocrebbin (cr). **98 Dorling Kindersley:** Natural History Museum, London (tr). **Getty Images:** Arthur Dorety / Stocktrek Images (tl). **99 Corbis:** Mitsuaki Iwago / Minden Pictures (tc). **100-101 Getty Images:** P. Jaccod / De Agostini (Background). **102 Corbis:** Franck Robichon / Epa (bl). **Dorling Kindersley:** Andrew Kerr (bc). **104-105 Dorling Kindersley:** Andrew Kerr. **104 Dorling Kindersley:** Museo Paleontologico Egidio Feruglio (bc). **105 Corbis:** Oliver Berg / Epa (bl). **Photoshot:** Picture Alliance (cra). **107 Corbis:** Ken Lucas / Visuals Unlimited (tc, cla). **108 Photoshot:** (tl). **109 Corbis:** Walter Geiersperger (bl); Louie Psihoyos (cr). **111 Dorling Kindersley:** Natural History Museum, London (bl). **Image courtesy of Biodiversity Heritage Library. http://www.biodiversitylibrary.org:** The life of a fossil hunter, by Charles H. Sternberg; with an introduction by Henry Fairfield Osborn (tc). **112 Dreamstime.com:** Igor Stramyk (bc). **David Hone:** (c). **www.taylormadefossils.com:** (tr). **113 Dorling Kindersley:** Royal Tyrrell Museum of Palaeontology, Alberta, Canada (bl). **115 Corbis:** Louie Psihoyos (br). **Dreamstime.com:** Boaz Yunior Wibowo (tc). **116 Dr. Octávio Mateus**. **117 Dreamstime.com:** Liumangtiger (br). **Getty Images:** O. Louis Mazzatenta / National Geographic (cr). **118 Photoshot:** NHPA (tl). **118-119 Dorling Kindersley:** Andrew Kerr. **119 Dorling Kindersley:** Andrew Kerr (b). **The Natural History Museum, London:** (tl). **120-103 Dorling Kindersley:** Andrew Kerr. **122-123 Dorling Kindersley:** Andrew Kerr. **124 Dorling Kindersley:** Senckenberg Gesellshaft Fuer Naturforschugn Museum (tc). **125 Dorling Kindersley:** Senckenberg Gesellshaft Fuer Naturforschugn Museum (cr). **127 Alamy Images:** Corbin17 (ca). **128 Corbis:** Louie Psihoyos (cr). **E. Ray Garton, Curator, Prehistoric Planet:** (bl). **Getty Images:** Tim Boyle / Getty Images News (br). **130 Photoshot:** (bl). **131 Alamy Images:** Kevin Schafer (tr). **The Bridgeman Art Library:** French School, (18th century) / Bibliotheque Nationale, Paris, France / Archives Charmet (bl). **132 Dorling Kindersley:** Oxford Museum of Natural History (tr, bl). **Mary Evans Picture Library:** Natural History Museum (cla). **135 Corbis:** Darrell Gulin (bc); Layne Kennedy (br). **Dorling Kindersley:** Oxford Museum of Natural History (tl, cb). **138 Dreamstime.com:** Corey A. Ford (br). **139 Dorling Kindersley:** Natural History Museum, London (bc). **140 Dorling Kindersley:** Senckenberg Gesellshaft Fuer Naturforschugn Museum. **141 Dorling Kindersley:** Senckenberg Gesellshaft Fuer Naturforschugn Museum (tl). **US Geological Survey:** (tr). **144-145 Plate Tectonic and Paleogeographic Maps by C. R. Scotese, © 2014, PALEOMAP Project (www.scotese.com)**. **144 Dreamstime.com:** Michal Bednarek (bc). **Getty Images:** Kim G. Skytte / Flickr (br). **145 Dorling Kindersley:** Jon Hughes and Russell Gooday (cr); Oxford Museum of Natural History (br); Andrew Kerr (cra). **147 Getty Images:** Danita Delimont / Gallo Images (tl). **148 Dreamstime.com:** Isselee (tl). **149 Dreamstime.com:** Mikelane45 (br). **Richtr Jan:** (crb). **152-153 Dorling Kindersley:** Andrew Kerr. **152 Dorling Kindersley:** Jon Hughes (clb); Andrew Kerr (bl). **153 Alamy Images:** Paul John Fearn (cra). **156-157 Alamy Images:** Jack Goldfarb / Vibe Images (Background). **158 Corbis:** Bettmann (bc). **Getty Images:** Life On White / Photodisc (bc/Wild boar). **159 The Natural History Museum, London:** (cra). **161 Corbis:** DLILLC (bc). **162 Alamy Images:** Natural History Museum, London (bl). **Dorling Kindersley:** Natural History Museum, London (c). **165 Corbis:** Ted Soqui (br). **Dorling Kindersley:** Natural History Museum, London (clb). **166-167 Dorling Kindersley:** Andrew Kerr. **166 Corbis:** Aristide Economopoulos / Star Ledger (clb). **Dorling Kindersley:** Natural History Museum, London (tc). **168 Getty Images:** Roderick Chen / All Canada Photos (cl). **Science Photo Library:** Mark Garlick (cr). **171 Corbis:** James L. Amos (tr); Tom Bean (ftr). **Dorling Kindersley:** Natural History Museum, London (tl). **172 Corbis:** Bettmann (br). **Dorling Kindersley:** Natural History Museum, London (cl, bl, bc). **Dreamstime.com:** Georgios Kollidas (tr). **Getty Images:** English School / The Bridgeman Art Library (cr). **173 Alamy Images:** World History Archive / Image Asset Management Ltd. (tl); The Natural History Museum, London (tr). **Corbis:** Louie Psihoyos (c). **Science Photo Library:** Paul D Stewart (tc/William Buckland, Gideon Mantell). **176-177 Corbis:** Louie Psihoyos. **176 Alamy Images:** Rosanne Tackaberry (bl). **Dorling Kindersley:** Rough Guides (bc). **177 Dorling Kindersley:** Natural History Museum, London (bl). **Getty Images:** Ken Lucas / Visuals Unlimited (br). **Science Photo Library:** Natural History Museum, London (cr). **178 Getty Images:** Roderick Chen / All Canada Photos (tr). **Science Photo Library:** Paul D Stewart (bl). **178-179 Corbis:** Louie Psihoyos (b). **179 Getty Images:** STR / AFP (tl); Patrick Aventurier / Gamma-Rapho (tc/Wrapping in plaster); Jean-Marc Giboux / Hulton Archive (tr). **iStockphoto.com:** drduey (tc). **180 Alamy Images:** Chris Mattison (bc). **Dorling Kindersley:** Natural History Museum, London (cra). **Dreamstime.com:** Gazzah1 (clb). **Getty Images:** Ralph Lee Hopkins / National Geographic (cr). **181 BigDino:** (b). **Corbis:** Brian Cahn / ZUMA Press (cr). **Press Association Images:** AP (cra). **Science Photo Library:** Pascal Goetgheluck (cla); Smithsonian Institute (cl). **182-183 Getty Images:** Leonello Calvetti / Stocktrek Images. **182 Dorling Kindersley:** Robert L. Braun (bl). **183 Getty Images:** Visuals Unlimited, Inc. / Dr. Wolf Fahrenbach (tr). **184 Dorling Kindersley:** Natural History Museum, London (cl); Staatliches Museum fur Naturkunde Stuttgart (bl); Senckenberg Gesellshaft Fuer Naturforschugn Museum (br). **185 Alamy Images:** Natural History Museum, London (cb). **Dorling Kindersley:** Roby Braun- modelmaker (cra); Royal Tyrrell Museum of Palaeontology, Alberta, Canada (bc). **186 Dorling Kindersley:** Andrew Kerr (br). **187 Dorling Kindersley:** Jon Hughes and Russell Gooday (cl). **188 Alamy Images:** Eric Nathan (b/Background). **Corbis:** Nick Rains (cra). **Dorling Kindersley:** Andrew Kerr (br); Peter Minister (b). **189 Corbis:** Louie Psihoyos (tr). **Getty Images:** Stephen J Krasemann / All Canada Photos (ca). **Photoshot:** Andrea Ferrari / NHPA (bl). **190-191 Dorling Kindersley:** Senckenberg Gesellshaft Fuer Naturforschugn Museum (c). **190 Corbis:** Sergey Krasovskiy / Stocktrek Images (br). **Dorling Kindersley:** Andrew Kerr (tc). **191 Corbis:** Radius Images (br/Background); Kevin Schafer (br). **Dorling Kindersley:** Jon Hughes and Russell Gooday (bl). **192 Corbis:** Nobumichi Tamura / Stocktrek Images (ca). **Sergey Krasovskiy:** (tc). **193 Dorling Kindersley:** American Museum of Natural History (bc); Peter Minister (cl). **Getty Images:** Mcb Bank Bhalwal / Flickr Open (tr). **195 Corbis:** Louie Psihoyos (cra). **Dorling Kindersley:** Courtesy of The American Museum of Natural History / Lynton Gardiner (br); Natural History Museum, London (cb). **Getty Images:** Bob Elsdale / The Image Bank (cra/Crocodile nest). **196-197 Corbis:** Mark Garlick / Science Photo Library. **196 Alamy Images:** Ss Images (cb). **Science Photo Library:** Mark Garlick (cl); D. Van Ravenswaay (bc). **197 Getty Images:** G Brad Lewis / Science Faction (br). **198 Dorling Kindersley:** Francisco Gasco (tr). **Turbo Squid:** leo3Dmodels (bl). **199 Dorling Kindersley:** National Birds of Prey Centre, Gloucestershire (cla). **Dreamstime.com:** Elena Elisseeva (ca); Omidiii (cra). **Fotolia:** Anekoho (br).

All other images © Dorling Kindersley

For further information see:
www.dkimages.com